FROM CRADLES TO ARMS:
WOMEN AND SOCIETY

SOPHIA Z KOVACHEVICH

Gotham Books

30 N Gould St.
Ste. 20820, Sheridan, WY 82801
https://gothambooksinc.com/

Phone: 1 (307) 464-7800

© 2024 *Sophia Z Kovachevich*. All rights reserved.

No part of this book may be reproduced, stored in a retrieval system, or transmitted by any means without the written permission of the author.

Published by Gotham Books (April 18, 2024)

ISBN: 979-8-88775-622-6 (P)
ISBN: 979-8-88775-623-3 (E)

Because of the dynamic nature of the Internet, any web addresses or links contained in this book may have changed since publication and may no longer be valid.

The views expressed in this work are solely those of the author and do not necessarily reflect the views of the publisher, and the publisher hereby disclaims any responsibility for them.

Books by the Same Author:

Betrayal – A Political Documentary of Our Times (Published under the Pseudonym Ashley Smith)

The Sands of Time A Book of Poems Vol 1

The Chalice A Book of Poems Vol 2

Growing Up A Collection of Children's Stories and Pet Stories

Conflagration Documentary of a World in Turmoil

A Book of Plays

Wake Up Dead A Collection of Short Stories

The Raped Earth

Exporting Democracy - Death or Slavery

Nostalgia New Expanded Edition: a book of poems Vol 3

A Matter of Honour

Directly from the author

CD format only: Available from author only

From Across the Waters: A Book of Recipes Appetizers to Desserts

Study Book Macro Skills –A Teacher's Guide and a Self Help Book for Post-Intermediate ESL learners

Study Book Micro Skills –A Teacher's Guide and a Self Help Book for Post-Intermediate ESL learners

Contents

Introduction 1

Part I

Prehistoric times 6
    Palaeolithic Age 6
    Neolithic Age 12
Role of women in Ancient societies 16
    Patterns of Goddess Worship 18
    Goddess worship around the world 26
    India 26
    Ancient Near-East 27
    Rome 30
    Greece 31
    China and Japan 32
    Contemporary goddess worship patterns 34
    Ancient Goddesses - Mother Earth and her Acolytes 40
Goddesses: Primordial earth goddesses 47
    Middle -East and Asia 49
    Egypt and Africa 57
    New Zealand & Australia 60
    Europe 61
    Native Americans (pre-colonisation) 78

Part II

Matriarchy 83
    Prehistory 84
    Palaeolithic and Neolithic Ages 88
    Bronze Age 89
    Iron Age to the Middle Ages 91
    20-21st centuries 91
Patriarchy 98
    Conclusion 113

Part III

- Women and religion 122
  - In the Middle-Ages 122
  - Difference in Western and Eastern Europe in the status of women 131
  - The Bandraoi or Bandruí (female druids) 133
  - Sparta 137
  - Athens and other states 141
  - Minoan Crete 147
  - Roman Empire 150
  - Rome: 155
  - Celts 156
- Women and religion in pre monotheism 157
  - Monotheism: changing role of women 159
  - Judaism 160
  - Modern Judaism 167
  - Christianity 169
  - Islam 180
  - Women and Religion in Modern Times 185
  - Modern Feminist Movements 208
  - Some Modern Female heads of states 215

Part IV

- Powerful women in history 221
- Some International women who wielded power 234
- Ancient warrior Queens: women and war 252
- Women warriors in Ancient Times 254
- Famous Warrior Women groups 256
- Some other recorded warrior women 319
  - Warrior women around the World 323
  - Europe 325
  - Warrior Women of Asia 328
  - North Asia 331
  - West Asia including Yemen 332

Central Asia 339
South Asia 342
South East Asia 347
East Asia 349
China 350
Africa 357
Native American Warrior Women 369
Comparison of Asian and European women in the same historical Timeline 376
Women Then and Now 381
Conclusion 394

BIBLIOGRAPHY 398

Web 398
By authors 403

Foreword

Women are the backbone of life and existence. They give birth, nurture and teach the basic moral precepts of life to their offspring. They protect guard and guide all their children through the most difficult and formative years of their lives. They give comfort and succour to their spouses, their families, putting all others before their own comfort and needs. So, yes women are the backbone of society. They are mothers, carers, comforters, protectors and warriors of the home, hearth and motherland. *Sophia Z Kovachevich*

"Although women military leaders are rare throughout history, they are far from unheard of. Joan d' Arc and Boudica are two of the more famous examples; there are many more. **Military history**

Note: they have not been rare but they have never had the media coverage that male military leaders have had and still have.

The material world is all feminine. The feminine energy makes the non-manifest, manifest. So even men, are of the feminine energy. We have to relinquish our ideas of gender in the conventional sense. This has nothing to do with gender, it has to do with energy. So feminine energy is what creates and allows anything which is non-manifest, like an idea, to come into form, into being, to be born. All that we experience in the world around us, absolutely everything (is feminine energy). The only way that anything exists is through the feminine force." *Zeena Schreck*

"I am a warrior in the time of women warriors; the longing for justice is the sword I carry." *Sonia Johnson*

Acknowledgements

I would like to acknowledge all the webpages and modern technology for their great help. For a disabled person like myself, it is help that I cannot acknowledge enough. I am housebound and modern technology – computers are my lifeline to sanity. They enable me to research and access information as and when needed. I also wish to extend my thanks and appreciation to the libraries. What would we do without them!!!

Also, I would like to acknowledge all the writers, authors, historians, archaeologists, poets, bards, storytellers who have made it possible for me to access information.

A big thanks to libraries again for the use of books in my research, Amazon to order books and book stores for me being able to buy books I needed.

Dedication

To those before me who were brave enough to light the way for us, generations later and most of all, to all womanhood for their dedication to giving, nurturing, supporting and most of all creating new life. Women have stood the test of time and endured a harsh male world for centuries yet here we are again. The truth is the world needs both men and women. The brashness of men cannot and does not show their strength – it underlines their weakness and fear of female strength and endurance. Women are the mainstay of generations. This book is for all womanhood. Viva la féminité!!! Viva la mujer! Long live Woman!!

Introduction

Throughout written post-organised religion, men have been the primary focus as contributors to written history. Therefore, most early written histories are based around males, their roles in society, their prowess in war and male leadership. When women have been written about, it has generally been condescending and biased. Strong powerful women were not really wanted around. They were a threat to male dominance and authority. Until recently, historians have largely ignored the women who helped build the great societies of the world. In ancient oral cultures, this was not the case. Women and their contributions were esteemed and celebrated. These cultures kept their history alive through story-telling, legends and myths, through their bards, storytellers, druids, priestesses and those responsible for keeping their cultures and traditions alive.

The most ancient traditions of societal power lay in the hands of women. The gods to be worshipped were all females. The world came into existence from a woman as did creation. And women dominated the scene for millions of years. Women ruled, went to war and were a force to contend with. In many ancient societies, **God was a woman.**

The prevalence of patriarchy in the modern world was a deliberate, planned stratification of society into gender roles. It was not accidental at all. Perhaps the first seeds were sown as settled life and agriculture began. Women began to be relegated to a lesser status. This was completed and came to full fruition with organised religion as power of the goddess was whittled away and slowly stripped to land in the hands of gods and men in most organised societies especially in The Middle East – Mesopotamia, Judea (Moses) and then Europe.

I will first look at the three theories of male dominance as presented by Amanda Penn (2019) based on the Book by Yuval Noah Harari 1st published (in Hebrew, 2011). **The first theory** is that men are naturally stronger, so they forced women to submit to them. Looking at ancient history, we see, women were just as strong and warlike as men. So their physical prowess (male or female) had to be developed, it did not come to them naturally. And in agricultural societies, it was not because of their physical strength but the protection of children in case of attacks/raids that, I think, became the primary reason for women to take a back seat. In time women stopped training and became weaker as men became physically stronger and more dominant.

Theory two is about the aggressive, war-mongering nature of men and their desire to seize and conquer. As men became more powerful, they controlled the armies and so controlled the land through power. Some studies show that men are more aggressive by nature than women. I'm not so sure about this as history has recorded many very aggressive women not just warrior women but women who wielded power behind the scenes as in Rome and elsewhere — recorded in this book later. Moreover, conquest and then assimilation requires more than physical prowess. It requires the iron hands in the velvet gloves; it requires diplomacy, tact, cooperation and the ability to have more than one perspective. Both men and women have these qualities. I think men dominated because they took power and manipulated it to reduce female input until it was and is difficult to really change the imbalance. Power corrupts and it has corrupted the male psyche to this day. In many ways men are weaker than women. Modern women, no matter how equal they appear to be, do not have the physical power and freedom of ancient feminine societies before organised religion especially the Abrahamic religions, to which most of us belong, took over. We have been helpless to stop male encroachment into all aspects of our lives and to regulate our lives as they have chosen to do. There is **some** redress the 21st century now. But we still have a long way to go to attain parity — equality in every way.

The third and last theory is that males had to become competitive and aggressive as a reproductive strategy. So, the males competed with each other for progeny. Females on the other hand, did not need to compete to produce and raise children. They could choose the most seemingly productive male. The problem lay in the need for food, shelter and protection during pregnancy and initial care of the child. Men supplied that as society had become more and more patriarchal with the development of male-dominated religious organisations in society. All the important priests by this time were males. Female power was greatly feared and so females were disempowered especially by the priests and prophets, using any ammunition in their arsenal to target women. One became the monthly moon cycle and another was pregnancy. Women came to be regarded as unclean during those times and so unable to worship in the temples or associate with the men who were deemed clean as they did not go through the same processes. But if women did not get pregnant, there would be NO humanity and then what would be the reason to fight and strive? Whatever, it became a thoroughly male-dominated society. The females had become dependants. And the more dependent they became, the worse their condition became till they were a short step above enslavement.

I believe we changed from a matriarchal to a patriarchal society for a number of reasons, the most important one being **men abrogating power to become prophets and speak in god's voice** and in places women were no longer allowed to enter and essentially forbidden to do so. This was unheard of. Women were probably stunned and so succumbed. This was their greatest mistake. Now we are still fighting for equality. We are thrown crumbs to appease us but in actuality, there **is no equality between men and women even now.** Women in similar positions do not earn the same pay; very few are leaders of their nations, rape cases are all oriented to help the men who carry out the abuse of women, sex trafficking is flourishing more than ever; women, especially young girls, are kidnapped and forced to become sex slaves, abused and mistreated; women rarely, if ever, head the topmost positions of power socially, politically, religiously, militarily or in any other way.

This power imbalance is a hotly debated and discussed topic in the present atmosphere. If we really consider, it is pointedly imbalanced. Only one gender, the male, benefits from our present patriarchal systems. Males got to spend their lives, though to a lesser extent now, within their familiar living groups. Women did not. They had to change their environment once they married. Many still claim it is because males are physically stronger, and possess male testosterones so, power imbalance is produced. It has been disproven by the existence of olden warrior women societies. It should be redressed and is perhaps now in the process of being so.

This book is for women, about women and the achievements of women throughout civilisation. For too long women have been voiceless or their voices muffled, their achievements nullified. It is time to take our rightful place on the canvas of life. Without women there would be no life!!

Part I

Prehistoric times

In prehistoric times, both the Palaeolithic and Neolithic periods from 40,000 to 5,000 years ago, all worship was devoted to the female entity, whether it was in Europe, in Asia, Africa or anywhere else. And this worship continued for millennia. Long before the main monotheistic religions came into existence, human development and belief systems all venerated the creator as a female. Merlin Stone (2012, pp. 55; *When God Was a Woman*) corroborates this theory and says that female worship can be traced back right to the Neolithic and Palaeolithic ages, not only in Asia and the Middle East but also in every part of Europe. The centre of worship was the Great Goddess. In the Near-East we see the *development of the religion of the female deity in this area was intertwined with the earliest beginnings of religion so far discovered anywhere on earth.* She was "*creator and law-maker of the universe, prophetess, provider of human destinies, inventor, healer, hunter and valiant leader in battle*" (Ibid). She was unquestionably the supreme deity to rule over all.

Palaeolithic Age

During the Upper Palaeolithic period, society was matrilineal. Women held the supreme status in the household. This was because as Merlin Stone (1976) says: "*the concept of the creator of all human life may have been formulated by the clan's image of the woman who had been their most ancient, primal ancestor."* In other words, she was the divine Ancestress, the mother and the giver of life. All rites and rituals centred around the woman. Figurines of pregnant women have been found in many places in Europe, Near East, Middle East, India... some dating back to 25,000 BC all pointing to female worship only. McChoppin, (2015 pp. 45) bears this out. Female worship was widespread and extremely powerful. Statuettes have been uncovered in Canaan (Palestine / Israel), Anatolia (Turkey), and other places. In Egypt they have been found dating back to Neolithic times (4000 BC). Some of the earliest archaeological finds of Palaeolithic ages are sculptured images and cave paintings of many upper Palaeolithic sites in not only northern Asia but also in Europe, like France, Spain, Italy, Germany, Austria, Ukraine, and Siberia. The images are carved in bone, stone, antler and mammoth tusks, and the female figurines vastly outnumber male ones. They have been identified as a part of elaborate and pervasive goddess worship. They are called Venuses, in modern times, after the Roman goddess. Interpretation of these artefacts is not uniform.

Sylvia Brown (*Mother God*, 2004, pp. 1-15) gives us a detailed history of the feminine spirit that flourished in Palaeolithic times. Some peoples who worshipped the great feminine were: The Inuit who worshipped **Sedna**, Ocean Mother and goddess of the sea; **Ishtar,** goddess of love and war, worshipped by the Babylonians and Assyrians; **Teleoinan** the mother of all gods, patroness of midwives and childbirth was worshipped by the Aztecs; **Isis** goddess of children and magic, among other qualities, was worshipped in Egypt; **Anat** the goddess of fertility and **Astarte** the mother Goddess, regarded to be the planet Venus was worshipped by the Phoenicians. Every culture had its own goddess. These goddesses were very powerful. They were never an afterthought as Eve was to be. A strange phenomenon that is particularly visible here is that when women are strong and powerful, misogyny often ensues and so it happened as time passed. By 15,000 BC the power of goddesses had been effectively reduced and they were rendered powerless in many places. Patrilineal custom was brought to Europe by Indo-European invaders, assert some scholars. Whatever the reason goddess worship was suppressed in Europe and that made for bleak times ahead. Lynn Rogers says (2004, pp. 57) *25,000 years of bountiful creativity (of the Goddess) were obliterated.* Creation myths were rewritten, symbols of goddess worship were denigrated, destroyed and *the ancient belief in the Goddess as the Ground of Being, The Universe from which they All emerge was overturned* (Ibid*).*

With the evolvement of the Abrahamic religions and monotheism in the Middle East, the new religions began to cement their control of an exclusively male dominated world: God, King, Priest, Father in place of Goddess, Queen, Priestess, Mother. It placed too much power in male hands over females including the power of life and death. Stone (2012 pp 16) in her book talks about the erasure of female deities and believes that in time Goddess worship became a victim of the following centuries when her power was totally eroded while men lauded over everything. Female deities became: *victims of centuries of continual persecution and suppression by the advocates of the newer religions which held male deities as supreme"* (Stone 1976). And to make the situation even more unwholesome this denigration of women led to their loss of status around the world in every sphere.

But not all religions subscribed to this path. Many olden religions, older by far than the Abrahamic religions, did not relegate the female deity to subservient positions. Bess (*The Path of the Mother*, 2000), in the Chapter: *The enduring presence of the divine feminine in Hinduism*: points out that Hindus have never stopped Mother Worship. She writes: *The Mother, who has been obscured in the shadow of Western religions for thousands of years, is considered to be the sum total of the energy in the universe.* The female power abounds in Hinduism from the power of *Durga*, the fearless goddess who conquers her enemies riding a tiger, to *Saraswati* the protector of knowledge and encompassing *Shakti* the divine force, the Great Mother responsible for all creation in the universe who is *"known to be the activity in all things, the great power that creates and destroys the primordial essence, the womb from which all things proceed and into which all things return (Ibid).*

Buddhism too celebrates the feminine principle through the Bodhisattva Guan Yin whose name signifies *"the one who hears and sees the cries of the world."* Her beauty, grace and boundless compassion for the suffering of humanity encompasses all of humanity. *Her greatest significance is as the outpourings or embodiment of the divine feminine* (Palmer, 2009, pp. 53).

The feminine deities continued losing power and importance over the centuries. In 27 BC Gaius Julius Caesar Octavianus was conferred the title of Augustus Caesar, the first Roman Emperor. He gave the goddess Cybele the title of Supreme Mother of Rome, but by 500 AD all goddess temples in Rome and Byzantine were shut down by the Christian emperors and the polytheistic "pagan" goddesses were banished forever, their temples destroyed, their reputations maligned.

And in place of the goddesses we have the story of Adam and Eve, the forming of Eve as an afterthought to keep Adam company; their expulsion from Eden for which Eve is blamed <u>though Adam, the first created, had the free will to refuse the apple</u>, and so from the place of goddess, women were demoted to the place of having been responsible for sin and fall of man, the source of weakness and sin, to be treated as *'incapable of distinguishing right from wrong'*. The Old Testament does not even have a word for Goddess and *in the Bible* writes Stone, (1976), *the Goddess is referred to as Elohim, in the masculine gender, to be translated as God. But the Koran of the Mohammedans was quite clear.* In it, she says: *Allah will not tolerate idolatry... the pagans pray to females.* However, the Koran does put the **mother** in a very high position: *"heaven lies beneath* the *feet* of your *mother"*. (hadith).

Some believe goddess worship disappeared **as a natural phenomenon** but many historians and theologians point out that **patriarchy destroyed the rule of goddesses** by painting it as a gross, pagan religion. Yet, goddess worship was much more humane and equal in most ways than what came later.

Another theory for the start of overthrowing the goddesses is the following which I believe is more feasible: People started living in clans of about 20-30. Men first began gaining power from this point. Not much, not enough to worry anyone. Women were treated equally as men. Both hunted together, cared for their young and so on. They worshipped Mother Earth the provider of all — sustenance, shelter, water, life itself. Figurines unearthed of these times show many statuettes of pregnant women leading to the assumption that they worshipped the female goddess for fertility. Other figurines found were also of women whether it was that of Mut, Maut, Mout — all worshipped in ancient times and believed to be that associated with the primal deity signifying the primordial waters that the world and all born into it, needed to survive. Every ancient religion believed the world was created from water. Religion began most probably during the Upper Palaeolithic times. All members participated equally, unlike later times with the introduction of shamans, medicine men, priests and priestesses. Cave paintings and images suggest belief in the supernatural also began around this time.

People at this time were hunter-gatherers and used ancestor worship to try and exert control over the clan members. Elitism may have started at this time through this. Female figurines abound suggesting that they attempted to ensure success in the hunt, fertility in the land and in the clan through this. Female figures depicting the earth goddess like Gaia the earth mother or goddesses as rulers and mothers of all and producers of sustenance were also uncovered. The earliest known Palaeolithic shamans (30,000 years ago) **were all females** (Tedlock, Barbara, 2005). The abundance of female figures representing the mother goddess led to the theory that religion in Palaeolithic and later Neolithic societies were led by women. Adherents to this theory, among others, are archaeologist Marija Gimbutas (1991 pp. 227-275) and feminist scholar Merlin Stone (1978, pp. 265). James Harrod, Research Director, (Center for Research on the Origins of Art and Religion, Cultural Evolution Department), says they were representations of mainly female but also a few male shamanistic rituals.

Neolithic Age

The term Neolithic was first used in 1865 by Sir John Lubbock. It is taken from the Greek term *lithos* meaning stone and *Neo* meaning new.

This began when the nomadic, hunter-gatherer way of life changed quite drastically to the more settled one of farming, domesticating animals and a sedentary life in settled areas. Village life began. This was due to climatic change. This was the third and last stage of Stone Age life. It began around 12,000 years ago in the Levant — the vast region of the Eastern Mediterranean and all its surrounding islands with the Natufian people of Syria and Palestine. This culture was unusual because they were semi-sedentary even before agriculture began. Farming communities soon spread to North Mesopotamia, North Africa and Asia Minor.

Goddess worship from Palaeolithic times continued into the Neolithic period. Agriculture had begun and the goddess symbolism was transformed to fit the new times and new social organisations. Use of stone tools and domestication of animals and plants began in Europe, North Africa, the Middle East and other parts of Asia. Female images have been found representing the continuity of tradition from Mesolithic and Upper Palaeolithic times. But Neolithic symbolism was, now, strongly linked to the moon derived from much earlier roots. The goddesses are connected to the supply of wild animals, but now due to agriculture, were added the domesticated animals like the dog, the bull, the male (billy) goat and so on. The goddess of vegetation is also represented. There are also male images. They are not yet subordinate to the females, but it is the females that are worshipped for life, the harvest and livelihood.

Neolithic culture spread everywhere to Europe, Asia, Middle East, Mesoamerica and Peru. Different crafts began appearing at this period like pottery and weaving, building shelters from tree branches and twigs and basket making. A temple region from this period was discovered in Turkey. It had seven stone circles with limestone pillars having carved birds, animals, and insects. Pottery was found in many places including in Ubaid and Halafian and in Mesopotamia, Syria and Turkey.

Stone tools like sharpened stones, hand axes and similar tools were used by Palaeolithic people. They were transformed into arrows, bows and harpoons. In the Neolithic period they were improved upon and the first polished stone tools appeared in Japan. Tools in jade, jadeite, basalt, greenstone and similar materials began to be used now. Stone tools also included axes, adzes etc.

Neolithic people were animists. They believed in all aspects of the natural world — animals, trees forests and rivers. They believed all living creatures had self-consciousness and souls that could help or harm you, according to your deeds. Self-consciousness also began around this time. There were many religious rites related to climate and crop. The first temples appeared. Funerary rites also evolved at this time.

Religion became more structured and centralised. Ancestor-worship both individual and that of the group was practised. The stone circles in Britain appeared, the most famous being Stonehenge. The Chalcolithic religion, (a Proto-Indo-European mythology) of the people who first spoke Proto-Indo-European languages began at this time.

The Neolithic era focused on the importance of fertility in nature and the home. They worshipped the Mother Goddess of fertility of the earth. She represented the cycle of birth and death also in the seasons – sowing, planting, harvesting and the cold barren months. She was the mistress of nature, procreation, protector of animals and crops. She was generally portrayed in the form of a small clay statue of a woman giving birth.

There were many religions during this era but in all, the Mother Goddess or the Great Goddess was the most important. Other important goddesses were the Bird and Snake Goddess, and the Pregnant Vegetation Goddess. **No male gods were likewise represented.**

In Neolithic times all the figures were of nude women representing the goddesses of fertility, abundance, sustenance and so on. The female was the giver of life and so highly valued. And once temples started being constructed, again women held a high position in the rituals.

Venus figures were also discovered from the Neolithic period. In the Aurignacian (in Eurasia,) deposits, they dated back 30,000 to 40,000 years ago (Palaeolithic times). These were artefacts made of stone and bone, paintings and engravings. But they seem to be more numerous around 25,000 years go. One of the earliest figures found, was in the Dordogne region of France, dating back to 32,000 years ago. From around the same time, Neanderthal ceremonial burial artefacts were also found. The pregnant female figures were carved of reindeer antlers marked by decorative notches, the symbolism still undetermined, though theories abound.

Neolithic figurines are of different forms – some are thin and geometric representing snake and bird goddesses who represented the cosmic symbols of regeneration of life (water and air). Some figurines are faceless, unclothed and corpulent. Still others are obviously pregnant with exaggerated breasts and buttocks. The most famous of these is the one of Venus of Willendorf (Austria) believed to be a mother-goddess figure of the Upper Palaeolithic age. It is faceless painted in red ochre, about 3/8 inches high and not obviously pregnant. Goddess worship was widespread in the Upper Palaeolithic age.

Role of women in Ancient societies

In ancient societies the role of women differed considerably from post organised religion in societies. In ancient societies there was no great distinction between the sexes except all worship was directed to the mother earth — the giver and provider of sustenance. Most of the earliest figurines that archaeologists have dug up, are only of women whether it was Mut, Maut, Mout worshipped in ancient Egypt as the primal deity who was associated with the primordial waters that the world was created from. In other cultures too, the same belief held. The sacred female images that have been unearthed are not only of nude woman but also of a wide range of forms from the aniconic representations of reproductive organs in the abstract to the ones decorated in their queenly finery. These images/figurines are linked to all aspects of life, be it birth, initiation, marriage, reproduction or death. Goddess worship was continuous in spite of the ebb and flow of fortune during critical periods.

In Neolithic times the figurines are all of nude women — fertility goddesses or images for fertility. They represented life, fertility, abundance, food from the land and so on. The female was the giver of life. Later in temples too, they were an essential part of the temple ritual.

In prehistoric times — Palaeolithic and Neolithic periods 40,000 to 5,000 years ago, divinities were female. In Europe the Great Goddess was the centre of worship. In the Near East, in the Jordan Valley by the Dead Sea shore, were found crude female figures of clay. Female figurines were also found in central Anatolia, the Tigris-Euphrates basin, (in alabaster), in Mesopotamia (clay figurines), in Bactria, the Zagros Mountains and other places. They all point to religious customs of female worship.

Goddess worship has had a central role in the development, organisation and transition of societies into civilisations in India, ancient Near East, Greece, Rome, China and Japan most prominently. These were complex agricultural societies where female deities have been closely linked to the fertility of crops, sovereignty of rule, protection of urban ceremonial centres and the waging of war. Though there were wars, there were very few mass killings. Those discovered were all in Europe. In Britain there was one around 5,500 years ago. Two others were Neolithic mass grave found in Germany and Austria between 7000 to 6800 years ago. There were about 30 to 100 bodies in total.

Patterns of Goddess Worship

A number of themes of goddess worship were common around the ancient world. Some of these were as nurturers, protectors, virgins (purity) for resolution of problems, fertility – human or crop; healers, mediators between humanity and the heavens, and the source of all life.

Purity, virginity, perfect piety — in some places the goddess represented this: as **Kannagi,** Tamil goddess of chastity and motherhood and sacred power, in Nepal and India, the tradition *Kumār pūjā* celebration, practised until recently, in the Near East the worship of **Innana, Ishtar** and **Anat**, signifying purity and fertility simultaneously. Leach (1966, pp. 42) says the Virgin Mary belongs somewhat to this theme. She is pure, pious, and intercedes on behalf of humans.

Motherhood: is the widest dimension of goddess worship. She is the source, the bearer, the provider, the nurturer, the beginning of all life. The female nurturing power goes back to the beginning of time. In some societies it is signified by the mother's milk. E.g. in Sri Lanka they practise a ritual in the Sinala community in which the mother's milk brings health and well-being. The milk symbolises the goddess and underpins the matrilineal link between mother's blood, her health and the well-being of the community (Weeramunda, A. J. in Preston, 1982, pp. 251-262). This theme was recapitulated in Roman, Greek and Coptic miracles and that of the Virgin Mary and her milk and her tears bled to cure and heal.

Wifehood: Goddesses are often also wives but in no way are their powers diminished. E.G. Innana, the supreme goddess of ancient Sumer, was queen of heaven and earth foremost of all though she was the wife of Dumuzi, the shepherd king, his role was less important. The Sumerian New Year always ended with the sacred marriage of Innana to the reigning king. This was to signify the continuing fertility of the land and the womb with the king's progeny. Hera, the wife of Zeus in much later times too, was no less powerful than her husband, as were many other goddess-wives. The list is long.

Earth Goddess: Not only goddesses represented the earth, but sometimes male gods, like the Egyptian male god Geb did so too. Female Egyptian goddesses like Nut represented the Sky. Bleeker, CJ (in Olson 1983, pp. 31) believed that Egyptian goddesses were not intrinsically earth deities. Another, is Japan's Shinto goddess Amaterasu who is the sun, not earth, goddess. In my opinion godly representation was much more fluid in ancient times. But in general, earth goddesses were regarded as female for the ability to create, produce, to regenerate and give birth. They were also associated with the cycle of the moon, various natural phenomena and especially the sea. Even today many references are made to the sea as a woman for her moods, her mystery, her power, her unpredictability and the deep attraction that the sea has for us — after all it is water which is the first home all living creatures know.

Protection: Goddesses had a tripartite role — queen, protector and emblem; nurturer, fertility and healer. E.G the

Chinese goddess **Guanyin** is *wife, bodhisattva* and *celestial bureaucrat.* There is also the **Virgin of Gaudalupe**, who is simultaneously an emblem of the integrative, protective and sacred female image. **Bethen of Bavaria** called Berchta in South Germany personifies the land and patroness of mothers, **Hulda** in Northern Germany, **the Matronae** in the Rhine area belonging to both the Germanic people and the Celts often pictured as a three-hooded druidic triad of deities. The Bavarian Triple goddess Bethen personifying the sun, moon and earth (heaven, earth and underworld) is rooted in **pre-Christian** religion. They always wear white, red, and black, signifying according to Austrian author Georg Rohrecker: ***white** for becoming, waxing, sunrise;* ***red** – fertility being in full blood;* ***black** – waning, going down, homeward, nightfall.* They also symbolise the three stages of the fertility cycle in women: white maidenhood / purity; red (blood) child-bearing years; black barren, old age. Taken further still it symbolises the land and it agricultural cycle of the growth, harvest and finally bare fields till the next cycle. Human life for all ancient people depended on the cycle of crops and the harvest and so in a way the triad signified life itself, the becoming, (birth), the being, (productive years) and the vanishing or the end of the cycle, (death).

The images of sacred female are still assumed to have protective qualities. In Mexico during the war of Independence they carried an image of the **Virgin of Remedios** into battle. **Mazu**, the Daoist goddess protects fishermen and sailors in the dangerous Taiwanese Straits; In Spain, Our **Lady of Macarena** protects bullfighters; In Japan

Amaterasu is the supreme national deity; the **Black Madonna** of former of Częstochowa, in Southern Poland, is considered queen of Poland and her image is worn as a badge by the Solidarity Movement members. She is an important focus for pilgrims and was revered by Polish Catholic Pope John Paul II.

Fertility: is a very important aspect of life. If there is no birth, there is no life. Without females, goddesses or women there is no new generation to replace the old and dying. Ancient cultures were aware of this and so valued birth and life and the bringers of new life. As society became "advanced" they started devaluing those that produced life and life itself. In ancient times the fecundity of the earth was extremely valuable. **Mother** earth produced the crops, the fruits, the vegetables, the grass the animals fed on; **women** produced children to carry on, care for them, hunt for them as they grew older. Such was the respected cycle of life. So they believed. An example is ancient Neolithic city of Çatal Hüyük, in Southern Anatolia that offers evidence of the goddess of the hunt and the abundance of crops, Meelart (1961-62).

Marshack A (1972, pp. 355) thinks that female animal figures found in the Neolithic period exhibit the Neolithic goddesses' affinity to animals that were already there in the Upper Palaeolithic era in the red ochre-stained animal horns. Even now goddesses are associated with plenty (crops, food). E.G. The Eskimo goddess **Sedna**, if angered by the behaviour of the people withholds the bounty of the sea. Hultkrantz, the American Indian prof. of religion, believes the idea of the mother goddess as the mistress of animals began around 2000 BCE by the cultivation of maize, squash, gourd and other crops. In Europe it was with the cultivation of fields of corn by peasants that the same idea came into existence. The fertility of the earth has always been intertwined with goddess worship in every part of the ancient world, Europe, Asia, Africa – everywhere. And even now, barren women turn to the goddesses for help to such an extent that goddess worship became a source for the sustainability of human life. Women who could bear many children were regarded as especially loved by the goddesses most specially among the labouring class where labour enhanced wealth, the more hands who worked the fields, the wealthier they were likely to become.

Healer: Goddesses are regarded as healers, though their wrath can also cause great harm. Throughout the world, in times of sickness people turn to a divine power for cures. It happened in ancient times and even happens today; people visit the shrine of saints for cures for health. In India for example the Anger of the goddess **Sitala** can cause smallpox and only interceding with her can bring about a cure. So they both greatly fear her and greatly adore her.

Perhaps the reason why people turned to goddesses rather than the male gods was because of the feminine aspect of caring, comforting, nurturing that females are generally endowed with. Females are the primary source of life, the first carers, they comfort in pain and travail; they minister to wounds both physical and otherwise. They stand at birth between life and death. We do not really know why it is, that all turned to the goddess in pain, travail and sickness. But this seems a good reason why. We can only surmise. Even in later periods when the goddesses were made subservient to the gods, people still turned to the goddesses for succour, not the gods. It almost seemed as if the female sacred imagery represented the bringing together of disparate elements and so a better chance of recovery. They provide the ongoing spiritual sustenance whereas the male gods are for the more physical aspects of life like war. They can destroy, kill, give martial victory or death but they cannot heal or succour or give life.

Female deities are widely represented in home rituals, in roadside shrines, in pilgrimage sites around the world among non-Christian cultures and, of course, female saints in churches and in their shrines. Mary, Mother of Jesus is always an especially revered person in Roman Catholicism. Bhardwaj (1973) says Hindu goddess shrines are visited not just for healing but also for small favours all the time whereas the god shrines are for a sight of the god, mainly because goddesses are more accessible, kinder, more nurturing. Their goddess helps them to embrace both the male and female principle because the gods and goddesses are not adversaries but complement each other.

Anger, Violence: The still practised ancient religions like Hinduism features this dichotomy, this ambivalence, very clearly, much more so than the ancient European religions which have more or less died out though traces remain in some rites and rituals. It is most clearly visible in Hinduism.

Some major female deities give and take life just as easily. Their compassion but more generally, wrath, is very easily aroused. One exception where compassion is concerned is the Balinese goddess Rangda. She is linked to the terrible aspect of divine power. Her name means widow, which she is and is constantly battling with her arch-enemy Barong, the dragon. This is depicted in the famous trance dance of Bali that tourists flock from all over the world to see even today. Rangda, unlike her Indian counterpart is associated with evil and death, whereas Kali is more nurturing. Though Kali is angered very easily, she grants boons too, to all who win her respect. Kali always has a necklace of demon skulls that she wears around her neck, as her chief role is to battle and destroy demons. Both Rangda and Kali are closely associated with death and graveyards. Mackenzie-Brown, (in Olson, 1983 pp. 110-123) says that Kali's intoxication with blood is not an indication of evil – she, after all, is the "mother of all." She is kind and cruel, she gives birth and takes life. She evokes great fear and total devotion, much like the same devotion evoked in other world religions by, Artemis the Huntress goddess in ancient Greece; Ishtar in the Middle East, Isis in Egypt who both evoked the dark side of cosmic forces as well as the nurturing and compassionate aspects and the Aztec goddess Mictēcacihuātl, associated with death.

One theme of this ambivalence is that of the *vagina dentate* (practised by North American Indian Tribes) where the womb of the earth goddess is the death trap too — a devouring mouth with teeth. In her anger the goddess can take away the life she has so freely given. She is thus the procreator and the slayer. But this is not punishment for wrong doing always. Sometimes it is necessary to remove the old or infirm to make way for the strong; to give death in order to continue the proper social and religious order in life. The entry into the *vagina dentate,* is in a way, the initiation ceremony through a dangerous passage before entry into a new life, a new birth. This act of being devoured by the earth is an idea found in many other cultures too, like among the American Indians, Australian Aborigines, Hinduism, in parts of Africa and in Polynesia.

Generally, one assumes blood sacrifice was for the male gods but that is not the case. It has also been a part of goddess worship around the world. Blood sacrifice whether human or animal or fowl was present in most ancient religions and is still practised today in some cultures like the ones stated above. This blood sacrifice is considered to be a bond between the goddess and humans especially on the fulfilment of some wish or desire as a means of giving thanks and venerating the deity. And even though blood sacrifice has been outlawed, it still continues, often surreptitiously. More often however, fruits, vegetable and money are now offered at shrines.

Enthroned Mother Goddess. Çatalhöyük and Lepenski Vir in Serbia as well as in many other places.

Goddess worship around the world

India

Goddess worship was the most elaborate here. Terra-cotta figurines of the goddess dating back to 2500 to 1500 BC have been found here along with abstract tone rings representing prototypes of the later god Shiva and his female consort. Goddesses functioned apart from gods there and their importance really became a major focus from 600 BC in their literature, like in the *Upanishad*. It emerged in Hinduism and Buddhism around the 7th century and was strongest in Eastern India where it still exists.

But goddess worship was never completely separate from their devotion to male gods. Goddess worship has been unbroken since Neolithic times. Goddesses are sought out to increase fertility, cure diseases, bring good fortune, enhance crop productivity and destroy demons. The only goddesses that stand alone are Kali and Candi (Chandi similar to Durga) who are very ferocious aspects for worship.

Ancient Near-East

Goddess worship displayed a very elaborate and subtle nuance in this region. There were several different civilisations here and they borrowed heavily from each other. Some were prominent in Egypt like **Nut,** goddess of the sky and consort of the earth god, **Geb**; **Neith,** patroness of victorious weapons and the art of weaving; **Isis**, goddess of wisdom; and **Hathor**, another sky goddess who assumed various forms. Some of these goddesses were deeply entwined in the development and continuity of divine kingship. The name *Isis*, linguistically means *"chair"* or *"throne."* The throne of the pharaoh was the *"mother of the king."* The pharaohs believed themselves to be the sons of Isis. In due course of time, Isis became the universal, benevolent goddess of the harvest and, her cult spread to Greece and the Roman Empire.

By 300 BC her cult had become a mystery religion promising salvation and rebirth.

Another ancient Near Eastern tradition of goddess worship came from the Mesopotamian civilization located on the Tigris and Euphrates Rivers. It was the worship of the goddess **Inanna,** queen of heaven and earth, goddess of love, and deeply involved in the rise of Sumeria. Although she was one of many goddesses of ancient Sumer, Inanna outlasted and overshadowed them all. She was also known as **Ishtar** and later worshiped by different Semitic peoples, and with the West Semitic as **Astarte.** These goddesses along with The Canaanite goddesses, **Asherah** and **Anat** (wrathful, warlike deities) were worshipped by the ancient Hebrews. King Solomon praised the pillars representing **Asgerah (Asherah)** and his son erected an image of her in the temple in Jerusalem. These deities did not really disappear but changed with monotheism in spite of the effort to wipe them out. Raphael Patai (1967) said that these goddesses assumed different disguises in later Judaism some being seen as a **cherubim** (depicted with a man in close embrace); or **Astarte the wife of Yahweh,** the only God having two aspects male and female; and in the form of **Shekhinah** (God's presence personified on earth) in which form she argues in defence of mankind. She is also sometimes personified as Wisdom, at other times as the Holy Spirit. She played an important role in qabbalistic thought especially in the 13th century Zohar (aspects of the Torah and scriptural interpretations on Jewish mysticism) which stressed **Shekinah's divinity.** She was also **Matronit** (divine Matron). She was seen as the intermediary between God and the scattered people of Israel among the Jews from the 15th to the 18th centuries. Patai (1967) believes that **Shekhinah and God are one**, filtered down to the Jewish masses, and this led to the belief she was a goddess. However, this **was incompatible to the rabbis'** way of thinking and **so she was removed and purged from Jewish religious tradition**. Exactly when this purge took place is uncertain – centuries ago or in more recent times? Many feminists believe this was act of suppression of women. The reason is still only surmise. Another theory posited, which I believe, is quite valid is that theologically, monotheism cannot allow competition or rather that all *extraneous* deities must be removed. There is only place for the one monotheistic god called, Yahweh, God, Christ or Allah. If we consider, no monotheistic religion has any female deity as an important centrepiece. Is it because they fear the female? This needs to be researched much further before we make any further judgements.

Unlike other Egyptian and Indian goddesses, Inanna was an ancient goddess from the Neolithic and even possibly the Palaeolithic times and played a vital religious role in their societies. She was an amalgam of Sumerian and Akkadian religious and political beliefs, extending back to at least 3000 BC. She was connected to crop fertility, the emergence of sedentary patterns of social organisation, and the development of the first urban centres. Her status was the same as that of the sky god An, the highest Sumerian god. She was responsible for victory in war and urban welfare of the people which was mostly allotted to male deities.

In Mesopotamia, populated by various peoples like Sumerians, Akkadians, Amorites, Kassites, and Arameans, goddesses were deities like **Inanna** (goddess of love, war and sexuality), **Nidaba** (goddess of the grain, **Ninhursaga** (goddess of Birthing) and so on. **Male gods, like Marduk came into prominence only much, much later.**

In Egypt: **Tefnut** was the goddess of many things including law, justice, fertility, water and rain. She was primarily venerated for making Egypt fertile. There was **Nut** who gave birth to Ra, the sun. She was the protector and nourisher. And **Maat**, who kept all in balance among all the other gods and goddesses.

Rome

Rome inherited a great many of the Greek deities when it conquered Greece. In fact, most Roman gods and goddesses are counterparts of their Greek versions. Then in 204 BC Rome officially adopted the Anatolian goddess **Cybele (later called Magna Mater or Great Mother)** and later that year, her image was carried through the city by the Roman matrons and a temple dedicated to her as a Roman goddess. No Roman man was allowed to be a priest of Cybele (but foreign eunuchs were allowed to be in her temple) as Roman men were barred from the priesthood until the reign of Claudius (41-54 CE). It was believed Cybele drove her Consort and son, Attis, to self-castrated death but his mother's following violent mourning caused him to be reborn. Every spring ritual included the carrying of a pine tree (representing Attis' death) to her temple and there his rebirth was celebrated in violent mourning and the bathing of Cybele's statue.

Greece

The theme of rebirth is found most specifically in the Eleusinian mystery cult associated with the earth goddess, **Demeter** where instead of the rebirth of a male deity, **a female deity is reborn. Persephone,** Demeter's daughter is resurrected after Hades abducts her to the underworld. Most pre-Olympian goddesses were connected with the earth, vegetation, fertility and so on. The best example would be **Gaia**, earth mother and chthonic mother of the gods. She was associated with the Delphic Oracle before it became exclusively Apollo's forte. Her rituals included animal sacrifices, offerings of grain and fruit, and ecstatic possession and trance. Many later Greek goddesses emerged from pre-Hellenic earth goddess Gaia. The famous twelve deities of Olympus included goddesses like Hera, Athena, Aphrodite, Hestia, Artemis, and Demeter conforming to their original spheres of influence. But their original chthonic aspects were diminished and they became subordinated in the Olympian hierarchy ruled by Zeus. These goddesses were no longer linked to the organic generative forces of life and death. Instead, they became highly compartmentalised in their new roles in the new male-dominated Olympian pantheon. **This compartmentalization demarcates a transformation in the role of goddess worship in the development of Greek civilisation.**

China and Japan

The Vajrayāna tradition of *Tantric Buddhism* mainly practised in Tibet and Mongolia is widely associated with goddess worship. Male and female though opposites are complimentary manifestations of divine power. The two are generally closely interlinked. There are exceptions as some female deities retain complete autonomy like **Tara**, a female *bodhisattva*, the universal protectress. In Chinese *Pure land Buddhism*, **Guanyin,** goddess of mercy, is also a *bodhisattva*, principal teacher, a saviour who gives enlightenment to her students and takes them to the western paradise of O-mi-tʻo-fo's Pure Land. She is still widely worshipped throughout China and in Japanese Buddhism.

In Japan, goddess worship was present not only in Buddhism but also in Shintoism that propitiates both male and female deities. To the Shintō, the world was created by a couple: **the god Izanagi and the goddess Izanami**. They had the sun goddess, **Amaterasu** and her brother **Susanoo-no Mikoto**, God of storms, and other nature deities. **Amaterasu eventually became the cult deity of the Japanese Royal family,** retaining both her Shintō function as sun goddess and a new role as Shining Buddha of Heaven. In fact, until this century, the emperor was regarded as a descendant of Amaterasu and responsible for world peace and all major pilgrimages to her site in Ise.

In the Neolithic age the cult of fertility was very important and figurines of goddesses were modelled and planted in cultivated fields. Religious concepts during this period, the cults and the rituals — carried out by both men and women trained in the art began around 8000-3000 BCE. Women played an important role in the growth and harvest and their maternal power. **Earth the Mother** was worshipped in almost all ancient cultures. Very elaborate terracotta figurines of the mother goddess were made and worshipped. Though male gods were also worshipped but were of less importance.

Since ancient times, goddess worship has played a central role in the worldwide transition from small-scale social organization to the emergence of civilizations in many places like India, the ancient Near East, Greece, Rome, China, and Japan. In these agricultural societies female deities were variously linked to the fertility of crops, the sovereignty of kingship, the protection of urban ceremonial centres, and the waging of war.

And not just in the East but also in Europe. Goddess worship began long before the male gods took over. Contemporary Celtic women in Europe were in a better and stronger position than the Greek or Roman women. Ancient Egyptian women were, in perhaps the best position of all. Egyptian women had a rare status for women of that time. They could own property, go to court legally same as men, sometimes hold high positions like **Nebet** did to become Vizier, second only to the pharaoh in the Sixth Dynasty (Henry G Fisher, 2000). Societies like in Egypt preferred **kingship to be traced for purity's sake through the female lines.** For example, the son of the first concubine could only inherit the throne by marrying his half-sister, if there was one or the Queen's daughter in order to inherit the throne. But a king in his own right could choose his queen as long as his choice met with the conditions expected and verified of royal lineage.

It is a fact that goddess worship played a major part in the development of civilisations. In places they were the main factor for urbanisation and kingship. Elsewhere they were consorts of male gods, heading mystery cults and early shamanistic religion. They formed a bridge between the Neolithic and Palaeolithic times. They waged wars, collected taxes, were responsible for the organisation of social life and so on. **Every ancient civilisation was deeply associated with goddess worship.** That cannot be denied. The *Great Goddess*, the *Great Mother* may have been called by different names but she connected all of the civilisations — Neolithic, Palaeolithic and all other civilisations until the advent of our Abrahamic, monotheistic, female-demeaning religions.

Contemporary Goddess Worship Patterns

The sacred female image is still worshipped in some form today, without having the same power in many societies except for Islam, Judaism and in some Protestant denominations. Even in heavily iconoclastic cultures, there are hints of goddess worship. E.g. Joanna Hubbs (in Preston, 1982, pp. 123–144) *traces images of a divine feminine in contemporary Russian folk art, film, and literature, noting strong national themes that continued to thrive in the Soviet era.*

Goddess worship is very well represented in Hinduism, Buddhism and Shintoism in Asia. In Europe too Catholics have numerous shrines devoted to the Virgin Mary. Of these some are associated with older pagan goddesses while others celebrate Marianism that started flourishing from the 19th and 20th centuries. In North America, in predominantly Protestant areas, sacred females are venerated in Catholic enclaves like the shrine devoted to **Saint Anne de Beaupré** in Quebec, Canada. In the US itself about a quarter million pilgrims visit the Shrine of the North American Martyrs (in Auriesville, New York), devoted to the Jesuit martyrs as well as the American Indian *Kateri Tekakwitha, "Lily of the Mohawks,"* a candidate for canonization. Åke Hultkrantz (in Olson, 1983, pp. 202-16) points out that there is an **extensive pattern of goddess worship among American Indians** despite the widespread misconception that these religions are mostly oriented around male deities. Native American goddesses are often earth mothers linked to the cultivation of corn. Goddess worship played an important role in ancient **Aztec, Maya, and Inca** civilizations, traces of which continue to thrive in descendant Mesoamerican populations. The goddess *Tonantsi* is still a vibrant focus of worship among the Nahuatl of Mexico (remnants of the great Toltec and Aztec civilizations). Goddess worship, here, expresses a typical syncretic pattern. Images of Tonantsi are displayed on altars alongside Christian sacred images, like the statue of Joseph, who is considered by the Nahuatl to be a son of the goddess.

Goddess worship is also evident in Latin America and the Caribbean, specifically with the transformation of the local Indian goddesses into Marian images. This syncretic expression is best expressed in the Roman Catholic pilgrimage icon in Guadalupe of the dark-skinned Virgin Mary whose site now is on the site of the ancient Aztec goddess *Tonantsi*.

In many African Tribal religions, even today, goddesses play a prominent part. McCall, Daniel F. (in Preston, 1982, pp. 304–322) shows how Neolithic goddesses from Southwest Asia to West Africa became syncretized with local deities and were soon absorbed and became an integral part of **Akan, Yoruba and Igbo** religious traditions.

Goddess worship was extremely important in antiquity and has still managed to survive in spite of attacks by monotheism on it. Goddesses played an integral role in prehistoric culture and throughout the development of agriculture and the beginning of urban life in civilisations. It is found in some watered-down form in many religions today and strongly in some very ancient religions that still practise it. Culture and tradition in the modern world, besides religious beliefs have weakened the position of women in general, not only goddess worship. For example, Hinduism still practises goddess worship but women in that society no longer have a voice. They are generally regarded as the possessions of the husband and fathers with hardly any rights.

However, goddesses still continue to be a fertile source of religious experience in the contemporary world. Goddesses are multivalent, sacred images that can only really be understood within the historical and cultural contexts.

Books written about this period also portray the same idea of mother worship. Ancient women were child-bearers, hearth keepers, comfort givers, seeresses, priestesses and warriors. With the passage of time, things changed and women became relegated to a very subordinate position. In modern times there is some improvement to their position. In most Protestant denominations women are allowed to be ordained like in the Anglican, Lutheran, Hussite, Methodist, Moravian Churches (since 1973 as well as the Anabaptist (since 1958) and the Presbyterian Church (since 1930 and as ministers since 1956). Other Christian churches like the Roman Catholic Church, Orthodox Church and some Protestant Churches still do not allow female ordination or overt religious participation in Church services.

In modern history only a few names of women from ancient times have come down giving us the impression that their lot was much worse than the position of women today. We also mostly hear of women who wielded power behind the scene. I beg to disagree. Many women were very powerful in their own right and even went to war, mustering armies and leading them, determining policies, treaties etc. In many societies they were trained in warfare from childhood. Many were active Queens, deciding policies, running the country, commanding the warrior, men and women. But women make men nervous. So they are not talked or written about. They are often a footnote. Here we shall look at some of them.

Modern history has not dealt with women fairly nor recorded their achievements correctly. Without women there would have been no civilisation. Women not only bear children but they are the first and primary teachers and role models. Olden society was aware of the importance of women and paid due homage. The first societies were matriarchal where men were equally welcome contributors. But olden cultures were aware that if there were no women, there would be no life nor civilisation, so worship of the mother goddess was all important. The earth that feeds us has always been regarded as a female entity — not a male one. Modern man, I think, fears the influence of women beginning with organised religion. Olden religions all honoured womankind but the modern religions advocated that women were weak, unworthy, impure and not fit for any high position. They were to be emasculated, relegated to lower second-class citizens. Men were the final arbitrators, the final judges, the rulers and women's roles were to serve them and put their needs, wants desires, as their (women's) reasons to live. We forget without Mary there would have been no Jesus and Joseph has never regarded as an important part of the Jesus story. Yet Christianity, Judaism and Islam today have reduced women to minor supporting role. In spite of how far women's suffragette has come, women are still not regarded as equal to men. When women become leaders of a state, all sort of whispers are spread to bring them down as happened with Margaret Thatcher. Men are **never** judged as harshly as women. They are allowed to be immoral and corrupt and cruel and still their sins are forgiven. If any woman were to do the same things, the judgement passed on them would make all woman-kind cringe. Yet women are generally better at what they do than men and they are much better at multi-tasking. Yes, there are many very bad women in the world, immoral, cruel but they are not in the same sort of power position as men with similar tendencies.

There is more rape and sex traffic of women, girls and children and women in bondage today than ever before in the history of the world. And worst of all, often in rape cases we are told: *women like it, women want it and* simply sweep male guilt under the rugs. In the past couple of years, men would again (like in Hammurabi's time) be the decision makers of what should happen with women's bodies and childbearing. If this is not stupid and crass, I do not know what is! I say to men first bear the children, go through childbirth, spend sleepless nights, be used when you don't desire it, then sit with women and discuss what is the best way about it. Till then do not assume to pass judgement on matters that are none of your concern. In our so-called democratic world of equality, let men then judge about how men should deal with their needs and women with theirs. Don't just spout democracy. Practice it! It is not democracy for one section of society to control the other.

In ancient times women were treated much better. They were equal to, men able to participate in every aspect of life. At the very start, women were held in very high esteem and position. They represented Mother Earth. They were the life givers and on them depended the continuance of humanity – as it still does today. Even gay couple need a surrogate woman to bear their child. Women were warriors, hunters, commanders of armies into battle, priestesses, oracle-speakers, equal, if not better than men in everything. In some societies the inheritance of the throne, power, property passed through the female line, not the male line. Women not only kept the hearth fire burning, ministered to all the needs of the family but participated in the running of the clan, tribe or whatever. They could choose their partners and leave them as they wished. **They could not be raped or forced. That was taboo. In our <u>modern</u>, <u>democratic</u>, <u>advanced</u> world rape is a very common occurrence.**

Wife beating is common enough not to raise eyebrows. Women (much earlier) could not be traded, bought and sold like horseflesh. Now sex trafficking is a very lucrative business, popular among many men around the world. And some women, who betray womanhood for wealth and power, help the men to entrap and abuse women and girls like in the Epstein case (with the help of Ghislaine Maxwell, 2019) in very recent times.

The time has come for us to re-evaluate history through the ages and see where humanity took a wrong turn. And correct it. **Men and women are partners, equals and that is the way it should be.**

Ancient Goddesses - Mother Earth and her Acolytes

Since earliest times women have played a powerful role in society. Goddesses were the *first deities to be worshipped and venerated since the beginning of time. Many people* believe that about 7,000 years before Abraham served as a prophet of

Yahweh, and about 30,000 years ago, based on the findings of Palaeolithic female figurines, cave paintings and other artefacts, female deities began to be worshipped in all regions of Europe, Asia, Middle East and Africa. This increased about 25,000 years ago as figurines have been dug up from many areas from the Neolithic period. In Egypt goddess figures were dug up from 4000 BC. So goddess worship is an old, old ritual, in fact the oldest, to our knowledge. We have found representations of the Supreme Being – the female creator of life in Sumer, Ethiopia, Libya, India, Elam, Babylon, Anatolia, Canaan, Ireland, Mesopotamia, and even ancient Judah and Palestine. Lynn Rogers (2016) commented *the deifications of the Goddess in the ancient world were variations on a theme*, with representations of the same supreme female creator. Robert Graves, the mythologist said that there could be no doubt at all that she was *immortal, changeless, and omnipotent.* **God was a Goddess**.

In different societies they went by different names and served different needs. For example, the very first was the *Great Mother* of Neolithic times who became *Maat* (Egypt), *Gaia*, (Greece & Europe), Terra Mater (Roman), Pachamama (Andes), Prithvi – the Vast One, (India), Kokyangwuti, (Hopi) and Spider Grandmother, (Native American) who with Tawa (sun god) created the earth and its creatures, to name only some.

Goddesses can be found in every religious tradition in the world, whether in the ancient cultures of Egypt, Greece Mesopotamia, the Americas or religions like Hinduism,

Buddhism, paganism or any other one. It decreased first with settled societies and then ceased with the advent of Abrahamic religions and modern religions. But there is a wave to revive female worship in modern times.

Every goddess has her own unique qualities, and is associated with specific rituals. They embody characteristics of mothers, warriors, magicians, lovers, wise women and so on. Following are some well-known and celebrated ones from around the world.

In the groundbreaking book *When God Was a Woman*, (1976), historian Merlin Stone traces goddess worship back to Paleolithic and Neolithic times. In the Near and Middle East evidence was found that *"development of the religion of the female deity in this area was intertwined with the earliest beginnings of religion so far discovered anywhere on earth."* The goddess was therefore unquestionably the supreme deity who ruled over all. She was the *"creator and law-maker of the universe, prophetess, provider of human destinies, inventor, healer, hunter and valiant leader in battle."* She was the mother, the one who creates, gives life.

During the Upper Palaeolithic age, society was matrilineal and the head of the household was a female. Stone images are mostly of pregnant women as the primal ancestor who gave life (very different from modern female portrayal of women as sex objects). Such figurines were discovered across Europe, Middle East, Asia and India dating back to 25,000 BC when female worship is thought to have been very widespread. And it was not just there. Goddess worship extended all over the ancient world. According to Sylvia Brown (2004) in America the Inuit worshipped **Sedna** the sea goddess, the Aztecs worshipped **Teleoinan**, the mother of gods, The Babylonians and Assyrians worshipped **Ishtar**, goddess of love and war; the Egyptians had **Isis** goddess of children and magic; in Sumer the main goddess was **Inanna**, goddess of love and war; the Phoenicians had two equally important female goddesses they worshipped: **Anat**, the fertility goddess and **Astarte** the Mother goddess, These goddess were procreators, givers of life, birth was in their domain. They were the valiant ones the wise ones, the counsellors, the bearers of culture and tradition. They were All-Important.

But as women rose to power and prominence, misogyny also began from around 1500 BC or perhaps around the time of patriarchy more probably at the start of the Bronze Age around 3,000 to 5,000 years ago with the advent of monotheism, the one male god and the replacement of pantheism and matriarchal religions. Goddess worship started diminishing and male gods started coming into prominence, dominating religions and patrilineal customs started taking over. Goddess civilisations were being overturned, creation myths rewritten, goddess symbols denigrated and *"the ancient belief in the Goddess as the Ground of Being, The Universe from which The All emerged, was overturned."* (Lynn Rogers, 2016)

Beginning with Judaism then Christianity followed by Islam, appeared in the Middle East and Europe. These were monotheistic, exclusively male religions: God, King, Priest,

Father. Women were reduced to very subordinate positions, their voices silenced, their rights taken away, even murder being sanctioned in some instances. Merlin Stone (1976) writes how female deities were eliminated and goddess worship became the victims of *centuries of continual persecution and suppression by the advocates of the newer religions which held male deities as supreme.*

As the major monotheistic religions became stronger and took hold of the world, the feminine deities faded away or were pushed away, hidden, covered. In 27 BC Augustus Caesar gave the goddess Cybele the title of Supreme Mother of Rome. But by 500 AD all temples to female goddesses were shut down and all *'pagan'* religions driven out from Christian Rome and the Byzantine Empires, as the rulers and ruling powers were staunch, **patriarchal** Christians.

Some religions particularly in Asia and Africa did not follow the trend of disempowering the female deities. Savitri, Bess, L (2006) in her book underlines that mother worship never ceased in Hinduism. *"The Mother, who has been obscured in the shadow of Western religions for thousands of years,"* she writes, *"is considered to be the sum total of the energy in the universe."* From Durga, the fearless goddess to Saraswati, the guardian of knowledge and encompassing all the others, to Shakti, *The Great Mother*, they continued to be venerated. Shakti, Bess explains, *is known to be the activity in all things, the great power that creates and destroys, the primordial essence, the womb from which all come, and to which all return.*

Buddhism too celebrates the feminie principle through the Bodhisattva Guan Yin, who according to their belief is *"the one who hears and sees the cries of the world,"* through grace and boundless compassion for the sufferings of humanity. This is done through the embodiment of Yin, the divine feminine.

Today all those old religions, celebrated for thousands of years are more or less sidelined, perhaps even lost. They have come down to the story of Adam and Eve with Eve being guilty for their expulsion from Eden. Adam is supposed to have been innocent. Eve tempted him and so they lost Paradise. Was Adam that weak, and that incapable of judging right from wrong, incapable of thinking for himself? Was he not created first supposedly in god's image?

Patriarchal cultures followed by the three main monotheistic religions saw to the loss of status of all women, not just the goddess. Female power was shackled, their voices silenced, their views discarded. They were reduced to possessions, like cattle and generally treated as such. And as these cultures conquered indigenous peoples, they repeated the pattern until women had nowhere to go and no one to turn to. When they exerted their views, or rights, they were treated as pariahs or as disgraced women or as witches and killed or burned or drowned. History is replete with examples of this – brave and innocent Joan d Arc burned three times in one day by fearful men of the Church, John Knox and his all-consuming fear and hatred of women, the Spanish Inquisition, the burning of witches in England from 15th to 18th centuries for the tiniest infraction or complaint often false against one.

The witch hunts of Cromwell's' time, the Salem witch trials in the USA and the list goes on. And not just in England and USA but all over Europe. These are shocking, shameful episodes in the male history of governance. Men fear and have always feared women power!!

To conclude here, archaeological evidence suggests that God was considered to be a woman, for the first 200,000 years of civilisation, in spite of patriarchy attempting to destroy all evidence of that. Today women are attempting to reassert themselves, but they have a very long and hard way to go before they are **really** equal with men. At the moment they are thrown scraps to keep them quiet. Take for example rape. When a woman is raped, **she, not he, is guilty**. If she complains she is forced to relive that humiliation over and over again, often in public, and in the end, she is told she was asking for it. The male perpetrator is not subjected to humiliation in the same way. Why is he exempt when he is the real guilty party? **How much lower can we get when the innocent are guilty and the guilty are allowed to strut about as if they have done a heroic deed!** Ancient civilisations at least treated all equally. Men were not treated simply as egg donors but as individuals. Women had a say in all such relationships and allowed men to have theirs – not like today in many countries. And women could choose who they wanted to mate with, when and where.

Goddesses: Primordial earth goddesses

The earth goddesses were often connected to the chthonic deities of the underworld. The oldest probably being **Ki** and **Ninhursag (mother goddess of the mountains, Sumerian fertility goddess)** who were Mesopotamian earth goddesses. Mesopotamia is considered one of the oldest civilisation and to be the birthplace of civilisation. However, the Indus Valley Civilisation predates it by 2,500 years. In the present times the oldest continuous civilisation is that of China (over 4,000 years of recorded history) stretching from the eastern seaboard to Afghanistan, Tajikistan, Kyrgyzstan, and Kazakhstan in the west. Civilisation originated in Asia and Africa and Andean America before coming to Europe.

Some of the most important primordial earth goddesses of the world were:

Gaia was the Greek goddess of the Earth. She was born from Chaos and is known as the goddess of the Earth and the first guardian of the oracle in Greek Mythology. She, with Cronos gave birth to the Titans. And later came the Olympians. So she was the most important character in Greek Mythology as nothing would have existed without her. She was the primordial deity succeeded by all others at the dawn of creation. Gaia later came to be called Demeter (earth), Persephone, (underworld), and Rhea (mother of all gods) her threefold nature in her triple entity.

Mut, also known as **Maut and Mout** (Mother), was a mother goddess of ancient Egypt. She was considered a primal deity, associated with the primordial waters from which everything was born through *parthenogenesis* (spontaneous development of an embryo from an unfertilized egg cell). Mut had many different aspects and attributes that changed and evolved a lot over thousands of years of ancient Egyptian culture. She should not be confused with Ma'at who had a different role.

Ma'at another ancient Egyptian deity signified concepts of perfect order and balance, truth, harmony, law, morality, and justice. Since chaos lurked at the heart of civilisation, all were expected to defend Ma'at to hold chaos at bay. After death the soul was judged in the hall of Ma'at and a balanced life weighed against a feather gained eternal life or not.

Earth goddesses are often associated with the underworld (Chthonicin) deities. Some Earth goddesses of ancient times were:

- **Ki** and **Ninshurag** were Mesopotamian goddesses of the earth later known as Ishtar.
- Ancient Roman religion and myth, **Tellus Mater** or Terra Mater ("Mother Earth") later came to be called Ceres, Ops, Proserpina (underworld)
- Indic mythology (Hinduism) she is ***Prithvi***, Goddess of the Land - The Mother Earth
- Chinese folk religion - **Houtu (Di Mu)**
- Phrygian (Anatolian) **Cybele,** mother of gods
- Slavic - **Mat Zemlya** Mother earth
- Andean (Inca, **Aymara) - Pachamama**
- Native American - **Spider Grandmother**
- Mongolian and Turkic - **Umay (Eje)**

- Old Norse religion - **Sif and Jörð**
- Lithuanian mythology - **Žemyna**
- Māori - **Papatūānuku**
- Latvian mythology - **Zemes māte** and **Māra**
- Vietnamese folk religion - **Mẫu Địa** and so on

Many goddesses took on a triple entity like ***Morrigan,*** (Irish), Gaia (Greek), ***Norns:*** (Norse), **S*hakti*** (Indian), ***Hecate*** (Greek), ***Diana*** (Roman), Matronae (Rhine area) belonging to both the Germanic people and Celts often pictured as a three-hooded druidic triad of deities and Bethen (Bavarian) Triple goddess and others. Still others always appeared as a group like the Greek: ***Moirai, Charites, Erinyes, Furies,*** Norse: ***the Valkyries.***

In **Neo-paganism** the goddess took the triple forms of the Maiden, the Mother, and the Crone, (similar to Bethen) each of which symbolizes both a separate stage in the female life cycle and phases of the Moon, which is said to rule one of the realms of heaven, earth, and underworld. In other words: youth, prime and old age. Her masculine consort in modern Wicca religious practice is the *Horned God*.

Middle-East and Asia

Inanna (the Enduring Goddess) was the most worshipped deity in Sumeria. Inanna is from the ancient Akkadian culture. She is among the oldest deities whose names are recorded in ancient Sumer. In Sumeria, Inanna is called the Queen of Heaven and is also the goddess of sexual love and procreation.

Later she was amalgamated with the Eastern Semitic Goddess, Ishtar. **Ishtar** is identified as a later form of Inanna.

Inanna is also associated with the Phoenician/Canaanite goddess **Astarte,** the goddess of love, sex, war, and hunting. Astarte was skilled in war and politics and is often depicted with lions to represent her courage and prowess. She is usually associated with the Canaanite storm god, Baal but seems to have been much more popular. Offerings to Inanna were made in the form of special cakes, wine, grains and meat. Inanna was also worshipped by the Akkadians, Assyrians (Inanna), Hittites (Sauska, Shaushka, Sausga, Anzili, goddess of fertility, war & healing), the Greeks (Aphrodite), and others.

Tiamat: This Babylonian goddess is an ancient figure. She appears in the creation epic, the *Enuma Elish*, in which she forms the world with her consort, Apsu and gives birth to all the gods. The gods kill Apsu and Tiamat raises a demon army to fight them. She loses the battle and Marduk, the new king of the gods, splits her corpse to create the seas and the sky.

In other stories, Tiamat is a primordial goddess of the ocean. She represents chaos as well as creation. She also takes the form of a giant sea dragon to fight her warring children.

Ishtar was the goddess of sex, power, fertility, love and war in ancient Mesopotamia. She is also closely related to familial love, romantic love and loving bonds within the community. Her sex appeal was so great that when she descended into the underworld, all sexual activity ceased on earth. Some myths claim that Ishtar entered the land of the dead to rescue her lover, Tammuz. It is very similar to the

Greek tale of Orpheus and Eurydice. She is the first deity that we have written proof of as she features in the *Epic of Gilgamesh*. Ishtar is in Akkadian, but she is also known as Inanna in Sumerian.

Izanami-no-Mikoto was the Japanese goddess of, creation and destruction, birth and death. She bore many children to her husband, Izanagi. Her name means *'She who invites.'* She died in childbirth and descended into the Yomi (underworld). Her husband entered the shadowy lands of the dead but he couldn't persuade her to return with him as she had eaten the food of the underworld. It is very similar to the tale of Persephone and Hades in Greek mythology.

It differs in the conclusion. Izanagi couldn't accept her answer and made a torch out of a hair comb. Seeing Izanami by firelight, his once-beautiful wife was now a rotting corpse. Izanagi fled but his wife pursued him. He sealed the Yomi shut with a giant boulder, locking Izanami in the underworld forever.

Shakti: is one of the most powerful Hindu goddesses. In Sanskrit, she represents pure, divine, female power and is often referred to as the Great Divine Mother. In art, she is portrayed as having many arms denoting power and force over mankind. Shakti means energy, power. She is the creatrix — deeply connected to her own feminine source and her creative power. She is dynamic, responsible for creation, maintenance and destruction of the universe and all in it. She is the Mahadevi or great goddess; all other goddesses are aspects of her, like Kali, Parvati and Durga. She has over a hundred names to express different aspects of herself. She is also called Addi Shakti, the Earth Mother. Durga is her form as the warrior goddess, standing for both good and evil, and Parvati is her gentler earthly form.

In Hindu tradition, women are thought to be vessels of Shakti and thus possess powers of creation and destruction. Shakti worship is a key element of Tantra Yoga, a form of meditation that developed in the 5th century CE in Hinduism.

The three most popular manifestations of Shakti are the following:

- **Parvati:** she is the daughter of the mountains and the goddess of love, devotion, marriage, fertility, children, beauty, strength and power. This is most similar to Shakti herself. She has two arms, the right holding a blue lotus. She is the calm aspect of Shakti, the light in the darkness with the procreative powers of Shiva, the god of war. She has three children with him Ganesha, Kartieya, and Ashokasundari. Her love and devotion to her family is so strong, she forces Shiva to find a head for their son Ganesh when he loses his. Shiva finally finds him an elephant head so he becomes a human god with an elephant head.
- **Durga:** is the next aspect of Shakti. In Sanskrit it means: *She who is incomprehensible or difficult to reach."* Durga is the warrior goddess, the protector of mankind and destroyer of evil. She is depicted wearing a red sari — a type of Indian clothing and always riding her vahana — some kind of vehicle used by Indian gods or on a tiger or lion. The former signifies unlimited power that she possesses, which

she uses for good and to destroy evil. Her main function is to preserve moral order and righteousness by destroying negative aspects of human nature such as selfishness, jealousy, prejudice, hatred, anger, and ego.

- **Kali:** is another aspect in which she often appears as a dark or angry goddess with blue skin, a necklace of skulls, demon heads as earrings and a knife. Her tongue is red with the blood of those she has devoured. She is generally depicted with four arms. In one hand she holds a scimitar, in another a demon head by its hair, the third is open, offering blessings and the fourth has a trident or spear. She is typically shown standing with her consort, Shiva. In her, wrath emerges through anger to destroy evil forces. There are many tales about this. In one tale, two demons attack the goddess Durga and can't be defeated by any of the gods. Kali emerges from Durga's wrath through the Third eye, turning blue in the process and defeats the demons. In another story, she fights an ancient demon, Raktabija. Each drop of his blood gives birth to a clone when it touches the ground. During the battle, Kali cuts Raktabija and drinks his blood. She even eats his clones. She has an insatiable lust for demon or evil blood. The aggressive effect of his blood turns the goddess into a destroyer. But in spite of her terrifying reputation, she is the Goddess of eternity watching over all temporal changes in her people and facilitating those who promote their inner growth. Kali is the ultimate protector against evil.

Many Indians believe she will continue to exist after the end of the universe.

Guanyin, Guan Yin or **Kuan Yin:** in Chinese mythology and in Buddhism, she is the goddess of mercy and the physical embodiment of compassion. She is an all-seeing, all-hearing being who is called upon by worshipers in times of uncertainty, despair, and fear. She is the Buddhist bodhisattva and in East Asia is the equivalent of Avalokiteśvara and has been adopted by other Eastern religions, including Chinese Folk religion. She was called *goddess of mercy* by Jesuit missionaries to China. Guan Yin is the shortened form of the original name *Guanshiyin* which means *the one who perceives the sounds* (cries & weeping) *of the world.* She is the goddess dedicated to alleviating the suffering of mankind. Offerings made to her are usually in the form of sweet cakes, lotus incense, fresh fruit or flowers, particularly when a person hopes to invoke her blessing or to conceive children. Her attainment of Buddhahood is celebrated on the sixth lunar month.

Due to her symbolization of compassion, in East Asia, Guanyin is associated with vegetarianism. Buddhist cuisine is generally decorated with her image and she appears in most Buddhist vegetarian pamphlets and magazines. Some Buddhists believe that when one of their adherents dies, they are placed by Guanyin in the heart of a lotus, and sent to the Western pure land of Sukhāvatī. Guanyin is often referred to as the "most widely beloved Buddhist Divinity with miraculous powers to assist all those who pray to her." Several large temples in East Asia are dedicated to Guanyin.

Mazu – Buddhist Mazu is a Chinese Buddhist goddess of the sea. She is the patron of sailors and seafarers including, fishermen and comes to the aid of those who call to her. She was born Lin Moniang or Lin Mo in 960 in a village on Mizhou Island. A lot of refugees from Northern China had fled there in the 10th century. Her cult is a hybrid of Chinese and local culture. The earliest record of this cult is from 1150, about two centuries later inscriptions were found which say *"she could foretell a man's good and ill luck"* and, *"after her death, the people erected a temple for her on her home island"*.

From a young age Mazu was a shamaness and guided ships safely to harbour. She was also known as a healer who cured the sick and had the power to predict the weather and even quell storms at sea. Her worship spread throughout China's coastal regions and to overseas Chinese communities throughout Southeast Asia. It also spread through mainland China. She was thought to roam the seas, protecting her believers through miraculous interventions. She is now generally regarded by her believers as a powerful and benevolent Queen of Heaven. Mazu worship is popular in Taiwan as large numbers of early immigrants to Taiwan were the Min people. Her festival is a major event in the country, with the largest celebrations around her temples at Dajia and Beigang.

Tara: personifies compassion and offers salvation from the suffering of rebirth and death. She is believed to have been born of empathy for the suffering world and is regularly invoked for protection, guidance, and deliverance from difficult situations. She belongs to both Buddhism and Hinduism. In Buddhism she is a *bodhisattva* (*"essence of enlightenment"*) in *Mahayana Buddhism,* and as a Buddha and the mother of buddhas in *Esoteric Buddhism,* particularly Vajrayana or Tibetan Buddhism.

The first textual evidence about her is from the 5th century but she is much older than that. She is mentioned in the Rigveda (1500-1000 BC) and was known throughout the Vedic period (1500-5000 BC). In Buddhism Tara is not only a deity but also a Bodhisattva (enlightened person) and is depicted either as the White Tara (goddess of health and prosperity) or as the Green Tara (goddess of fertility and protection). As a mother and goddess figure she also figures in the Buddhist schools of many cultures. To the West she is known as Guanyin, the Chinese goddess of compassion. She is still one of the most powerful goddesses in Esoteric Buddhism and is still widely worshipped in both Buddhism and Hinduism today.

Princess Liễu Hạnh was and still is one of The Four Immortals in Vietnamese folk religion, and also a leading figure in the mother goddess cult in which she governs the celestial realm. This cult began in Nam Định Province, but was prohibited during the first years of the North Vietnamese Communist regime. It has begun again by women since the 1980s. She is the goddess of female emancipation and power. Princess Liễu Hạnh was the daughter of the Jade Emperor, one of the four immortals, and a central figure in Taoism and other East Asian religions.

Egypt and Africa

Sekhmet (*Powerful One*) is one of the most powerful Egyptian deities. Her main centre of worship was in Memphis. This lioness-headed goddess also represented *The Destroyer*. However, in spite of being such a destructive figure, her priests were skilled doctors and healers and so she was also worshipped as their patroness. She sent the plagues but also cured the affected ones.

Sekhmet was fearsome. In a legend, Ra angry with mankind for disobeying his laws, sent Sekhmet to punish them. Her rampage decimated mankind until Ra called a halt. But she refused to stop as she was consumed by blood lust. So Ra mixed beer with pomegranate juice and poured this 'blood' in front of her. Sekhmet got drunk on it and promptly fell asleep. Her blood lust disappeared when she woke up 3 days later and things continued normally. It was best never to arouse her wrath.

Isis (Egyptian) was one of the most powerful deities in the Egyptian pantheon. She was the goddess of nature and magic, the Ancient Egyptian goddess of children and the dead. With her brother Osiris, Isis gave birth to the falcon god Horus. Her name meant "throne" and she was often depicted with the hieroglyphic sign of the throne or a solar disk and cow's horns on her head. Her magical abilities were believed to be so great they could heal the sick and bring back the dead. Primarily, she was in the role of the mother, mourner, and healer. But she also had the ability to create and destroy with mere words.

In her role as mother of the god Horus, Isis was viewed as a powerful protector and a role model for mothers. To keep her son from being harmed, Isis hid Horus in the marshland of the Nile, where she protected him from the poisonous snakes, scorpions, crocodiles and wild animals. As he grew up, he learned to ward off danger and became strong enough to fight Seth and claim his rightful inheritance, the throne of Egypt.

The annual floods of the river Nile are tied to her. Ancient Egyptians believed that her tears flowed heavily in memory of her brother, co-king and husband Osiris. Seth, her other brother, was envious and wanted the throne. He killed, dismembered and scattered Osiris' body parts. Isis, with the help of her younger sister Nephthys, Seth's wife, collected, then pieced and put them back together and they had the falcon-headed god Horus born to them. The tears of Isis caused the annual Nile floods. The floods were preceded by the appearance of the star Sept (Sirius) in the sky. This legend is known even today as the yearly celebration of *The Night of the Drop.*

Isis was the most widely worshipped goddess in the first millennium BC. She was also later incorporated into Graeco-Roman worship. She had a large religious following in Nubia also. Her prominence ended with the advent and rise of Christianity.

Bast / Bastet / Basthet were different names for this cat goddess of Ancient Egypt. Her worship was very strong since the second Dynasty (2890 BC). Originally, she was the lioness goddess. Bast and Sekmet characterised two aspects of the same goddess, Sekmet the fiercer role and Bast the gentler cat role. She was the goddess of warfare. She was a fierce protector said to possess the Utchat, the all-seeing eye of Horus. She also symbolised sensual pleasure, fertility, and health. Bast was also associated with perfume. The hieroglyph for her name is the same as that of the base jar, used to hold expensive perfumes. For that reason, people left her offerings of perfumes and scented oils. She was a goddess by day, and transformed into a cat at night to fend off serpents that sought to attack her father Ra. Her symbols were lioness, cat, ointment jar, sistrum (ancient Egyptian musical instrument) and solar disk.

Mami Wata or La Sirene who is a water spirit venerated throughout West, Central, and Southern Africa and in the African diaspora in the Americas. She embodies the spirit of water. As a water deity, she sometimes appears as a mermaid. Much like the ocean, she can be volatile and dangerous, as well as protective and nurturing. (Sometimes this deity is represented as a male).

Mami Wata often absorbs the characteristics unique to a particular region or culture into herself to fit better. Her colours are always red for blood, violence and death, and white to symbolise spirituality. In the mermaid form she is always represented naked, to celebrate beauty and the female body. Mami Wata has remained respected and celebrated since before African contact with Europe. She is still celebrated today. She is one of the most powerful goddesses in the African religion of Voudun – not Voodoo. As a goddess, she is both loved and feared for her duality. She is an immortal spirit that personifies polar opposites – beauty and ugliness, peace and danger, natural force and healing, wealth and destruction, health and disease, and good and evil and like those old mermaid deities, she is extremely powerful, dangerous, pleasant, sexual and able to destroy anything in her path. She brings good financial fortune and also governs water sprites known as *mami watas* and *papi watas*.

Yemaya: In Ancient Nigeria, she was the goddess of the river among the Yoruba Orisha people. But, when Africans were taken as slaves to the Americas, she became the goddess of the ocean and continued in their stories. She was also the goddess of motherhood and the patron of women. She was associated with the moon and is still said to exert a powerful influence on women. She is portrayed as a mermaid and also represents the great earth or Mother Earth. It is believed that when you hold a seashell to your ear and hear the sound, it is Yemaya speaking to you.

New Zealand & Australia

Papatūānuku (New Zealand) is the Earth Mother in the Māori world. She represents the land. Mountain ranges represent the curves of her body. According to the Māori story of creation Papatūānuku and the sky father, Ranginui, bore many children. But their parents' tight embrace was crushing them. So they pushed Papatūānuku and Ranginui apart so they could see the stars. Different iwi (tribes) have different stories. In some, the gods made humans directly from the earth.

Warrazum/Warrajam or Grandmother Rainbow Serpent (Australia): is considered the most powerful of all Aboriginal Ancestral Beings. Creation emerged from her belly. She belongs to the Dreamtime. Rock art featuring her dates back to at least 6,000 years making it one of the oldest continuous religious beliefs in the world.

Europe

Hecate presides over crossroads, entrances, witchcraft and sorcery in ancient Greek mythology. She is connected to the moon in all its phases.

There are many stories to explain her appearance in the Greek pantheon. In some tales, she was the only one to aid Zeus in his fight against the Titans. In others, she is an import from other cultures. Eventually, her followers associated her with the supernatural. Homeowners placed protective shrines to her at their doors to hold the wandering dead at bay. She appears as a three-formed goddess. She ruled the triple kingdoms of earth, sky, and sea. Modern Wiccan practices associate her with the 'crone' period of a woman's life. She is the goddess of boundaries, crossroads, witchcraft, the Moon, necromancy, and ghosts.

The Morrigan The shape-shifting Celtic Goddess presided over war, fate, and death. As a patroness of revenge, magic, and witches, she also ruled rivers, lakes and other freshwater bodies. She was a war goddess and took the form of a raven or crow. She flew over battlefields to spur on the troops. Her name means many things, including *the Phantom*. She is a member of the trio of sister goddesses called the Morrigna along with **Badb** and **Macha**, who, unlike her, serve as fertility goddesses.

The Morrigan is a prominent figure in Irish mythology and is primarily associated with war/ battle, conflict, fate and death. She is a gifted shape shifter and is known to favour changing into the crow or raven. She also takes the shape of a wolf as she did in her battle with the Irish hero Cú Chulainn. The Morrigan was one of the Tuatha De Danann, who were the folk of the Goddess Danu Enzy of battle; and finally, as the bringer of death. She has the ability to foretell victory, doom and death; to turn the tide of battle as she chooses; and can shape shift at will. Some tales call her the *Washer at the Ford.* She washes the clothes of men who will die in battle, choosing who will die and who will live. The survivors always leave the battlefield until dawn to allow the Morrigan to claim the heads of the dead. She is similar to the **Norse Valkyries,** who also decide the fate of the warriors in battle. And both choose who lives and who dies. Both are very strong deities.

She is a part of the Celtic languages and cultures of Ireland, Scotland, Wales, Cornwall, the Isle of Man, and Brittany.

The Valkyries: are armour-clad, warrior-maidens closely associated with the Norse god Odin whose main job is to choose the most valorous among the fallen in wars who may be given another chance to fight again. Literally translated it means *chooser of the slain*. Skuld, the Norn was one of them and her job was to cut the thread of life of human beings. The Valkyries flew over battlefields and cut the thread of those who were chosen to be slain and gave victory to those Odin had chosen to be victorious. Later they led the slain to Asgard where they were divided between Freyja's Hall Folkvangr and Odin's Hall Valhalla. These were privileged to fight all day and be resurrected for feasting at night. They are core to Norse narratives of Valhalla, the great hall of the Norse gods and at Ragnarok (*Doom of the Gods*- Old Norse or end of the world,) the gods of Aesir meet the powers of Hel led by Loki in the final confrontation. It is also called the *Twilight of the gods*. Valkyries means *Choosers of the slain*. They hover over battles and choose the fallen warriors who will fight again to go to Valhalla to join the bands of the *einhrjar* and fight again to the death during Ragnarok (the final confrontation). They (the Valkyries), represent the concept of fate.

Frigg is the official wife of Odin, king of gods and mother of Balder. She is a goddess of Aesir. Her name means *Beloved*. In Norse mythology, she is *associated* with fertility, marriage, prophecy, clairvoyance, and motherhood as well as being the primary goddess of wisdom, strategy, war and queens. She is the highest-ranking Aesir goddess in Norse mythology and dwells in Asgard. Her home is called *Fensalir* meaning halls of the marshland or wetland (Fen Halls in Old Norse). She was worshipped as a sky goddess and is believed to be responsible for weaving the clouds. The legends depict Frigg as a *völva* – a type of Viking magical practitioner. She reworks the web of fate to alter the course of destiny. Frigg also possesses the power to shapeshift into a falcon.

Her spirit animal is a *great-horned owl* which symbolizes courage, beauty, and strength. Frigg also has falcon feathers which she uses to shapeshift into a falcon. Her religious practices involve springs, bogs, or swamps in Norse paganism. In Icelandic sagas she tried to save her son's life and failed and so is often depicted as a weeping, loving mother. Some stress her loose morals. Frigg was often associated with Venus, the Roman goddess of love, beauty and fertility.

Freyja or Freya (Old Norse "Lady"), was the most powerful and renowned of the Norse Asgardian goddesses. She was the goddess of beauty, love, fertility, magic, war and death. She was also the most beautiful of all the goddesses. Besides being the foremost Norse goddesses, she was also queen of Valkyries. She was a practitioner of magic with an aptitude for manipulating reality to suit her desires. She learnt magic in her youth, which she later taught to Odin. She could also prophesy. Freya was also associated with the dead, as she presided over Folkvang, (Fólkvangr) the afterlife realm (not Hel or Valhalla but in-between the two – perhaps purgatory), whose inhabitants she selected from among slain warriors. As goddess of war, after the battle, the slain is divided between her and Odin. In this capacity she was believed to help guide the recently deceased to the afterlife. Those wishing to invoke her help to do magic or attract love, leave offerings of mead, honey, meat and more.

Her father was Njörd, the sea god. And her mother is assumed to have been Nerthus. Her twin brother was Freyr. They ruled from Vanir. Freya had been a leader of the Vanir gods during the Aesir-Vanir War and eventually agreed to marry Odin in order to bring peace between the two sides. She thus became an honorary member of the Aesir gods.

Aesir or Æsir (Old Norse) gods were the principal pantheon in Norse religion. They included Odin, Frigg, Höðr, Thor, and Baldr. The second Norse pantheon was the **Vanir**. In Norse mythology, these two waged war against each other which ended only when Freya from the Vanir finally agreed to marry Odin, ruler of the Aesir and they became a unified pantheon. She later gave birth to their son, Thor, who would eventually become the God of Thunder. When Freya weeps for Odin, she weeps tears of gold. She was regarded as the kindest of all the goddesses.

Pigs and the golden boar were sacred to her, and she rode a boar with golden bristles. When Freyja goes anywhere, she travels in a chariot pulled by cats. She had three kinds of animal companions: two cats which pulled her chariot, a golden boar named Hildisvini, and a mare, called night-mare. Her symbols include the Brisingamen necklace, boars, and a magical feathered cloak.

Freya was a goddess of the full moon too. She was a goddess from the Vanir group of gods, who had powerful connection with the Earth and practiced magic. Freya was also a protection goddess as she looked after the dead.

Unlike the other Norse gods, her death was never mentioned and so worship of the goddess continued long after the gods and their religion fell and were replaced.

Freya and Frigg are often confused. They had many things in common but were not the same goddess.

- Frigg was Odin's official wife. Odin married Freya later to bring about peace between the two pantheons.
- Frigg means Beloved while Freya means Lady.
- Frigg belonged to the Aesir, Freya to the Vanir. Odin also Aesir, united the two groups of gods by marrying Freya.
- Odin was simply called Od in reference to Freya, but he was called Odin by Frigg.
- Friday (Frigg's Day) Old English Frīgedæg was named in honour of both Frigg and Freya.
- Both developed from an earlier fertility deity.
- Both were associated with weaving, combining the aspects of love goddess and domestic goddess.
- In Sweden and some parts of Germany, the asterism of Orion's Belt was known as Frigg's Distaff or Freya's Staff.
- Both Frigg and Freya were married to Odin and Frigg's son Baldur by Odin and Freya's son Thor by Odin were half-brothers.
- Both were associated with Venus, the Roman goddess of love, beauty and fertility.

- Both were highly revered in Norse mythology and especially worshipped by Vikings.

The Norns: In Germanic lore they were the weavers of fate (ørlög). There were three women: Urdhr, Verdhandi, and Skuld who were responsible for the weaving of fate. The first Urdhr, was time *"that which was"* or the past; Verdhandi was time *"that which is becoming"* or the present and Skuld was time *"which should become"* or the future. The Norns were kept busy all year, all time around. They are mentioned in many places like the Eddic poems: *Voluspa, Helgi Hundingsbani* and in *Njal's Saga*. Human fates were in their hands. They were associated with destiny, knowledge and what was to come. The Norns, like all women, were mystical beings and responsible for many spiritual duties.

Ēostre was a West Germanic spring goddess. The name comes from Old English *Ēastre Ostara / Oestre*. This goddess of dawn, spring-time and fertility was very popular with the pagan Anglo-Saxon brigade who worshipped her long before Christianity. *Ēostre* is often depicted with a hare, or rabbit, alongside her. There are myths about her but the first mention of her is by the monk Bede with regard to a pagan festival Eosturmonath in a book in 750 AD. Theories have connected Ēostre with records of Germanic Easter customs, including hares and eggs, have been proposed but none can vouch for their veracity. However, hares and eggs, are symbols of our Christian Easter to celebrate rebirth and renewal.

Nerthus: or Mother Earth was first recorded by Tacitus in 98. She was probably Freya's mother and her father's sister. There is confusion between the names Nerthus and Njord as etymologically they are the same. Her cult was widespread especially by the sea-living folks, in northern Germany and the islands of Denmark. Her temple was tended by a priest and her chariot was kept there. Her priest rode with her when she went in her chariot. It was the time for all weapons and all thoughts of battle to be shelved momentarily. Before she returned to her temple, slaves bathed her and her chariot in a sacred lake. Later, the slaves were all killed and their bodies sunk in the lake as a sacrifice. Some believe that this accounts for the large number of bogs in those areas.

Nemesis: was the Hellenic goddess of Divine retribution, of implacable justice and of revenge. She was the goddess who would show her wrath to any human being who committed hubris, i.e. arrogance before the gods. She was considered a remorseless goddess. She acted as a form of cosmic justice by punishing the evildoer as well as the undeserving. Every case was judged within its context before judgement was passed. She represented balance and could promise happiness or bring misery in equal measure. Nemesis is always even-handed. Nemesis was widely used in the Greek tragedies and various other literary works, being the deity that would give what was due to the protagonist.

As an avenging goddess she had the measuring rod (tally stick), a sword, a scourge, and she rode in a chariot drawn by griffins. In Ancient Greek religion, she was called

Rhamnousia or **Rhamnusia.** She was often called "Goddess of Rhamnous," an isolated place in Attica, where a temple was attributed to her. Some believe she was the daughter of the primordial god Oceanus. But Hesiod claimed that she was a child of Erebus and Nyx. In some traditions, Nemesis, not the mortal Queen Leda, is the mother of Helen of Troy.

She was a much honoured and placated goddess. Her sanctuary was in an isolated place in Attica. She is portrayed as a winged goddess wielding a whip or a dagger. Her favourite animal is the goose.

Minerva: was the Roman equivalent to Greek Athena, or rather the Etruscan counterpart of Greek Athena. Originally as an Italian goddess she was closely associated with handicrafts under the name Menrva (**meminisse**) meaning *to remember.* She was widely worshipped across all of Italy, and later the Roman Empire. Her temple, the Delubrum Minervae was founded around 50 BC. The church of Santa Maria Sopra Minerva now stands there. From there she passed into Roman mythology incorporating many of Athena's characteristics and deeds. A version of Minerva claims deeds that are the same as for Athena. According to Ovid (in Metamorphoses 4. 794–803), she turned the beautiful Medusa into a hideous gorgon, helped the Greek heroes in their quests and battles, her confrontation with the Lydian human, Archane led to her turning Archane into a spider; her turning of Aglauros to stone for envying her and other myths, showing direct borrowing from Greek Mythology, in existence earlier when Rome conquered Greece (146 BC). Like Athena, she was the goddess of wisdom, justice, law, victory and the sponsor of strategy, arts and trade. She did not support violence. She only fought defensive wars. She was one of the deities in the Capitoline Triad along with Juno and Jupiter. She was also one of the most important Roman goddesses and was much revered throughout the Empire from the 2nd century BC. Minerva is the equivalent of Athena in Greek mythology, Briganti in Celtic mythology and Minerva in Etruscan myths. Like Athena, she was a virgin goddess.

Her birth was similar to Athena's and equally strange. Jupiter, her father swallowed her when she was born as she was supposed to overthrow him. But soon after, he started suffering from excruciating headaches. The god Vulcan used a hammer to split Jupiter's head open and Minerva, fully armoured and grown stepped out. The headaches stopped.

She is said to have invented the flute but because blowing detracted from her beauty, she threw the flute away until it was found by a satyr who made beautiful music on it.

Bellona: The Roman Goddess of War, Conquest and Peace was considered one of the greatest goddesses in the history of ancient Roman mythology. She was originally an ancient Sabine goddess of war identified with **Nerio,** the consort of Mars, and later with the Greek war goddess **Enyo.** Her temple in Rome was dedicated in 296 BC. It had extraterritorial status. Bellona was derived from Latin meaning "war" or "warfare". She had many temples scattered throughout the Empire. But the place where war decisions were made was in her temple outside Rome. Her bloodlust and battle madness made her a great favourite with the soldiers but not so much among the farmers, tillers and others. Besides her priests and those strongly dedicated to her cult, she was worshipped in secret to appease her for her volatile nature. The day dedicated to her was called the day of blood (*dies sanguinis*). Her priests were called *Bellonarii*. They cut their own arms or legs as blood sacrifice to her.

She rode to battle in armour - shield, helmet, sword or spear, driving a four-horse chariot. Her symbols were the helmet and torch. In battle **she was always accompanied by Discordia, Strife, and the Furies** and they terrified her enemies. The belief in her bloodlust and madness in battle was widely accepted. Ammianus Marcellinus, Roman soldier and historian, wrote that the Scordici people believed in the violent worship of Bellona. They were brutal and they worshipped both Mars and Bellona with savagery. They even offered human sacrifices and drank blood from the skulls of their victims. In the military cult of Bellona, she was associated with Virtus, valour personified, manliness and travelled with the imperial legions to other countries. Her temples were recorded in France, Germany, Britain, and North Africa.

Athena: Athena was the Greek goddess of wisdom, knowledge, counsel, crafts, excellence and a friend to warriors. She was also the patron and protector of various cities across Greece, especially Athens, which was named for her. The Parthenon on the Acropolis was dedicated to her. She was often called upon to protect and help in matters of war and governance. She was the patroness of crafts, and skilled peacetime pursuits, especially weaving and spinning. She personified wisdom and righteousness. Athena represented the intellectual and civilized aspect of war. She was the divine form of the heroic, martial ideal and personified excellence in close combat, victory, glory and the virtues of justice and skill. She was most probably a pre-Hellenic Minoan goddess later incorporated into the more martial Greeks but still retaining the domestic side to her along with the warlike side. Her aid was synonymous with military prowess. She personified excellence in close combat, victory and glory. **She was always attended by fear, strife, assault, defence and death.** She was a major protagonist and helped Greek heroes, like Hercules, Perseus, Odysseus, Achilles and the other Achaeans including Helen's husband Menelaus (from Pandarus' arrow) and Diomedes from a spear throw, among many other Greeks, in Homer's *The Iliad* and *The Odyssey* to victory and honour and fame. She was the guardians for the welfare of kings giving them wise counsel, prudent actions, restraint and practical insights.

Athena inspired the Greek sculptor Phidias to make three sculpture masterpieces about her; and the great playwright Aeschylus, to write his famous tragedy *Eumenides*. Her major symbols include owls, olive trees, snakes, and the Gorgoneion. In art, she was depicted wearing a helmet and holding a spear. As one of the only three virgin goddesses, Athena is poised and courageous but also a lover of arts and literature. The other two virgin goddesses were Artemis and Hestia. They had children but did not bear them in the usual way.

Athena sprang fully grown and fully armoured from the head of her father, Zeus, the king of the gods of Olympus. Her mother was Metis, Zeus's first wife or first love, daughter of Cronus. Zeus fearing the birth of the child as it was foretold his child would rule Olympus and tricking Metis, he swallowed her when she was pregnant and soon after started having excruciating headaches. Finally, the god Hephaestus god of fire, blacksmith and metal works, and Zeus' son used his hammer and split open Zeus' head. Out sprang grey-eyed Athena, beautiful and fully armoured — shield, helmet and spear. She became Zeus' favourite child. There were never any scandals attached to her name.

Even though she was a virgin goddess, Athena had demigod children, who were born from her own thoughts combined with the thoughts of mortal men she loved. These children were "gifts" to the men she favoured. This meeting of minds was, for her, the purest kind of love. Only once she had a child by accidentally mixing her divine essence with Hephaestus when she used a handkerchief to wipe the tears off of her skirt. As a result, the handkerchief turned into a human.

A lot of Roman gods parallel the earlier Greek gods of Olympus. The Roman Goddess Minerva is based on Athena and they helped the same heroes — Hercules, Odysseus, Perseus for the same tasks and in the same way.

Hestia is another virgin goddess. She is the goddess of hearth and family. She never wanted to marry and when she was much sought after by both Apollo and Poseidon, she rejected them and went to Zeus. In order to avoid a fate similar to her mother, Rhea's, Hestia swore to Zeus that she would never marry. Instead, she would care for every family member and all the humans who needed a hearth. Zeus admired his sister and cared for her, so he blessed her oath of virginity and bestowed on her the honour of presiding over all sacrifices. Her symbols were the hearth and the fire.

Artemis: was the third virgin goddess. She was goddess of the hunt and the moon. She didn't want marriage or children because she was very affected while helping her mother, Leto, give birth to her twin brothers. She was born first. Artemis saw the pain and the length of time it took her mother to have the twins and swore to be a virgin goddess. Like Athena and Hesta, there was never any scandal about her either. She, instead, formed a group of female hunters who shared her views. Zeus loved and admired his daughter, so he blessed her oath of virginity like he did with his sister.

Artemis was the goddess of the hunt, the wilderness, wild animals, nature, vegetation, childbirth, care of children, chastity and midwifery. Animals most dear to her were the deer, serpent, dog, boar, goat, bear, quail, buzzard and guinea fowl. Her symbols were the bow and arrows, crescent moon, animal pelts, spears, knives, torch, lyre, and amaranth. Her trees were the cypress, walnut and palm. Her mount was a golden chariot pulled by four golden-horned deer.

Her wrath was formidable. One example was when Actaeon, the hunter saw her bathing naked and tried to rape her. She turned him into a stag and then he was devoured by his own hunting dogs. She did not really hate men. Her hunting companion was Orion and there were many versions about his death. One was that Apollo challenged her to shoot at a dot in the ocean. She did so. It was Orion. Another version was that Orion boasted he could kill any living animal. This upset Gaia and she sent a scorpion which stung and killed him. Artemis wept and begged her father to do something. Zeus put him in the constellation as Orion.

Hel is a goddess in Old Norse Mythology. She ruled Niflheim, the realm of mist and cold. Anyone who died of sickness or old age went to her hall. She was also queen of the realm of the dead, a region of the same name, where she received a portion of the dead. Hel is attested in the Poetic Edda, compiled in the 13th century from earlier traditional sources. She was the daughter of Loki and the giantess Angrboda. She was alive from the waist up and dead from the waist down. Most tales portray her as indifferent to the struggles of the gods.

Hel had a central role in the tale of Baldur. Loki caused his death through trickery and Baldur, the beloved god journeyed to the land of the dead. Hermod (Hermóðr, Old Norse) son of Odin and brother to Baldr, often the messenger of the gods, travelled to the underworld to bargain with Hel for Baldur's release. It was an important mission since Baldur's death was a herald of Ragnarok – the Norse apocalypse. Hel agreed on condition every living creature in the cosmos wept for him. All agreed except Loki who took on the form of a giantess and refused to weep. So Baldur was condemned to remain with

Hel. Davidson (1998, 2002, pp. 179) compared Hel to the Celtic goddesses Badb and the Morrígan and she concluded that: *"here we have the fierce destructive side of death, with a strong emphasis on its physical horrors, so perhaps we should not assume that the gruesome figure of Hel is wholly Snorri's literary invention."*

It was believed that during Ragnarok (the Norse apocalypse) she led an army of the dead into battle. Snorri wrote the *Gylfaginning*, Norse legends in 13th century and mentioned about Hel (hell). The concept of hell did not exist in pre 10th century mythologies. It was first written down by Snorri as a place where evil people go. Christian historians made her (Hel) into an evil, demonic character partly beautiful and partly a demon. In fact, she was not like that at all. Snorri's version talks about when Baldur died and went to Hel's Hall. He was welcomed warmly and feted and feasted. Pagans did not see death in the same light as later Christians did. Hel was a very powerful goddess.

Brigid, or Brid, was one of the foremost deities of the Irish Celtic pantheon. Among the Tuatha De Dannan, she was one of the most popular and well-loved goddesses. She was one of the few pagan figures who not only was not lost with the advent of Christianity into Ireland, but was incorporated into the Christian saints as a Catholic saint. She inspired veneration well beyond the shores of Ireland.

Historians believe that she was a personal goddess and the people found many attributes to worship her for. She was the goddess of spring, the dawn, and fertility, music, art, the goddess of poets, of knowledge. She was the protector of livestock, and the young. She inspired wisdom, craftsmanship and song. There were many wells named for her and coins were always dropped in them as offerings especially for healing. She protected mothers and children, in part because she was unable to protect her own son, Ruadan when he was wounded in battle and died in her arms. She keened for him so loudly and long that it is believed that is the time from which keening for the dead became an Irish tradition. It also led to her becoming the goddess of life and death in spite of primarily being goddess of fertility and light. She influenced many rituals at death. Because of her many aspects she has also been identified as a triple goddess like the Morrigan who, too, appears in three forms. Brigid was the goddess of spring but she had two other sisters, one a smith and one a healer. All were named Brigid. She was celebrated on the pagan holiday of Imbolc, which falls in February in the Northern Hemisphere. From a protective goddess to a patron saint, Brigid is one of the most enduring and influential figures in Celtic mythology! Her fame and importance endures till today.

Eos is the Greek goddess of the dawn, a patron of new beginnings. She is the sister of Helios, the sun god, and Selene, the moon goddess. She is frequently depicted with wings and is said to dispense the morning dew on the earth. Eos is also believed to have an insatiable lust for love and adventure. Her symbol is saffron, cloak, roses, and her tiara. Her animals are the cicada and horse. Her colours are red, white, pink and gold. Her mount is a chariot drawn by two horses. In Roman mythology she is Aurora; in Etruscan she is Thesan; in Slavic she is Zorya or Zora.

Native Americans (Pre-Colonisation)

Spider Woman is one of the most important deities in the traditional Navajo religion. Unlike the Hopi Spider Grandmother, the Navajo Spider Woman did not create humans, but she is their constant helper and benefactor. For example, when monsters threatened humans, she sent *Child-Born-of-Water* and *Monster-Slayer* to find the Sun God, who taught them how to destroy the monsters. Spider Woman made her home on Spider Rock in Arizona in the Grand Canyon. In one legend, a rival tribe chased a Navajo youth into her canyon. She dropped a silken cord down into the valley and pulled him up to her home. He waited with her until the enemy left. When he reached home, he told his tribe of his narrow escape.

Navajo spider woman legends were told by the Hopi people. Navajo spider woman was said to first weave the universe and then she taught Navajo (Diní) to spread the "Beauty Way" and create beauty in their own lives, teaching them about balance within the body, mind and soul. The Elders told creation stories that they were told about having Four worlds and after having passed through dark three now they are in the fourth or Glittering world. Here as the Earth people Diné, they must do everything possible to maintain the balance between Mother Earth and man. As a helper and benefactor to mankind, she taught humans how to weave and farm. She protected the innocent and fought to restore balance.

Their four worlds were:

- First, The Dark World where the first man and woman came into existence too dark for comfort or happiness. So they moved to the next world
- The Blue World inhabited by a few First inhabitants and mammals. But the First inhabitants offended the Swallow Chief, Táshchózhi. and were asked to leave
- They left and arrived at the Yellow World with the four sacred mountains but a great flood had destroyed them and so the First Man and Woman were forced to leave
- They arrived to the Glittering world and here they found true death, the changing seasons, the moon and stars.

Pachamama: is the Mother Earth goddess of the Andean people. In Inca mythology, she is the Earth Mother who presides over planting and harvesting and so embodies nourishment and abundance. She encompasses all of creation, similar to the Greek goddess, Gaia. She embodies the mountains and causes earthquakes. She is also an ever-present and independent deity who has her own creative power to sustain life on this earth. Her shrines are hallowed rocks, or the boles of legendary trees, and to artists she is seen as an adult female, bearing harvests of potatoes and coca leaves. She is associated with rituals for fertility, protection and healthy crops. Those who venerate her typically leave offerings of food, tobacco, alcohol and coca leaves. Priests sacrifice offerings of llamas, cuy (guinea pigs), children (The Capacocha Ritual) and elaborate, miniature, burned garments to her.

The four cosmological Quechua principles: Water, Earth, Sun, and Moon-all claim Pachamama as their prime origin. She is the mother of *Inti* the sun god, and *Mama Killa* the moon goddess. As Andean cultures formed modern nations, the figure of Pachamama was still believed to be benevolent, generous with her gifts, and she became a local name for *Mother Nature*. In the 21st century, many indigenous peoples in South America base environmental concerns in these ancient beliefs, saying that problems arise when people take too much from nature because they are taking too much from Pachamama. She is widely celebrated even today.

Ixchel or Chel: the Mayan goddess was nicknamed *"the aged jaguar goddess of midwifery and medicine in ancient Mayan culture."* Some say she corresponds, to Toci Yoalticitl *"Our Grandmother the Nocturnal Physician,"* an Aztec earth goddess inhabiting the sweat bath, and is related to another Aztec goddess invoked at birth. But this is questionable. She was the goddess of war, childbirth, rain, goddess of the moon, fertility, physical love and weaving. Her opposing aspects were those of a sensual young woman and an old crone. Her shrines now are in Cozumel and Isla Mujeres, Mexico.

Pele was and is still also known as Pelehonuamea, *"She who shapes the sacred land."* She is one of the daughters of Haumea (the Earth goddess) and Kane Milohai (creator of the sky, earth and heavens). She came to Hawaii after being exiled from Tahiti by her father because of her violent temper. She is the Hawaiian goddess of fire and volcanoes, both destroying and creating land. Her creative and destructive powers allowed her to form the volcanoes that would eventually create the Hawaiian Islands. Legend has it that she resides in one of the most active volcanoes in the world – the summit of Kīlauea, within Halema'uma'u crater in Hawaii which erupts due to her passionate and volatile temper. In folklore, Pele travels throughout the islands, appearing to mankind as a beautiful young woman, or as an old woman, sometimes accompanied by a white dog. She is the most visible of all ancient Hawaiian gods and goddesses today. Lava is sacred to this goddess and should not be removed without permission. It can cause her to lose her temper and unleash havoc.

White Buffalo Calf Woman or **White Buffalo Maiden** is a sacred woman of supernatural origin, central to the Native American tribes. She was a Lakota woman and taught the children to love and care for wild animals; she taught them all people of the earth came from the same beginnings and many other things.

Once during a famine, the Lakota chief sent two scouts to hunt for food. They came upon a beautiful girl. One hunter thought she looked magical but the other rushed and embraced her. He turned into a pile of bones. Then she beckoned the other and he fearfully approached. She gave him the "Seven Sacred Rites" to protect Mother Earth and the *čhaŋnúŋpa*, the sacred *ceremonial pipe* which would make them rise again during the time of famine. Since then, she has been the primary goddess there.

Itzpapalotl/Ītzpāpālōt: In Aztec mythology, she was a fearsome skeletal warrior goddess who ruled over the paradise world of *Tamoanchan*, where victims of infant mortality went and the place where humans were created. She was also called *Obsidian Butterfly*, or *"Clawed Butterfly,"* as she was sometimes depicted with bat wings. She also appeared as a clear or eagle butterfly. Her wings were obsidian or tecpatl (flint) knife tipped. She appeared as a beautiful seductive woman or as a terrible goddess with a skeletal head and butterfly wings. Itzpapalotl was the mother of Mixcoatl associated with the moth. She was also associated with birds and fire. She was the patron of women who died in childbirth. Her nagual (symbol) was a deer.

Part II

Matriarchy

The web describes matriarchy *as a social system in which women hold the primary power positions in roles of authority.* In a broader sense it also extends to moral authority, social privilege and control of property. The Oxford Dictionary says *it is a form of social organisation in which the mother or the oldest female is the head of the family, and descent is traced through the female line.*

So in matriarchal societies, women at the head of the families/clans/tribes, decided and ruled the norms of their matrilineal society. They were responsible for everything from politics to economics and all broader social issues.

Ancient warrior *Spartan Warrior*

Ancient Barbarian warrior woman   *Ancient world warrior woman*

Prehistory

The myth of the Goddess is the oldest myth we know; the evolution of that myth tells the story of how our understanding of ourselves—as we have achieved it through the images of our goddesses and gods—has developed over the millennia of human history. Yet today the Goddess seems to have disappeared, and only the God remains. But it has not always been so. (Baring and Cashford, 1993).

At the very beginning women were honoured and revered for bearing children. The worship of Mother Earth was all encompassing. Her legacy stretches back to thousands of years. It is understood to exemplify the evolution of nature worship which is clearly visible through the art representations, religious rituals, poetry, mythology, archaeology and literature of ancient times according to Baring and Cashford, 1993. The matristic epochs were regarded as the sacred feminine centred on societal values of nurturing, care, cooperation, protection, partnership, mutual respect, reciprocity, and connectedness to **Mother Earth** from which all things come. All goddesses were held in high esteem, respect and worshipped. *They trace the image of the Great Mother Goddess of the Palaeolithic and Neolithic times through the Bronze and Iron Ages to the Virgin Mary, 'Queen of Heaven'* (Cashford, Jules & Baring, Ann 1991). But over time societies, turned towards patriarchy, till now, in our modern societies, it is pervasive. However, though the goddesses were undervalued, debased, pushed aside, they did not disappear. They went underground. After all, the universe is an organic, living, sacred entity from which the Goddess-Myth just could not be completely eradicated. This rejection of the goddess led to an imbalance in the psyche, according to Baring. As we saw earlier, the gods and goddesses lived in harmony and their 'sacred marriages' maintained harmony e.g. Inanna and Dumuzi in Sumeria, Ishtar and Tammuz in Babylonia, Isis and Osiris in Egypt, Cybele and Attis in Anatolia, Aphrodite and Adonis in Greece.

Many books by great writers have been written on this issue. Jung (1963) wrote about the existence of the essential principle of feminism in the spiritual development of the individual and collective evolution of humankind. His student

Neumann (1954, 1955; 1983) studied extensively the period on the Great Mother as the most fundamental stage in human history. He portrays the **Great Mother** as the primordial image of the human psyche. Early rituals, mythology, art and records of dream interpretations show this outward expression of their cultures through prehistory. The great feminine has been represented as goddesses in many olden cultures to show the aspects of her maternal nurturing and the fearsomeness when her wrath is aroused.

It was during that time that humans attained the first transpersonal levels of consciousness particularly in shamanic trance. This heightened spirituality is expressed through personified forms of *figurines representing certain deities, priestesses, and other mythical personas* (Gimbutas and Dexter 1999, pp. 4). And today what we consider animism was very much a part of their world. It predates even paganism and is still practised today in many traditional societies. Animists believed and believe all things animate or inanimate were/are suffused with spiritual qualities. Devereux, S (2000, pp. 20) says *the most ancient of religious impulse was that of animism, in which natural phenomena and the land and all within it, animate or inanimate, were seen as being suffused with spiritual qualities, as being ensouled.* The oldest symbol of Mother Earth are the stones: The Cybele stone of Pessinus, moved to Rome in 204 B C, the Kaaba of The Muslims in Saudi Arabia, the Dome of the Rock located on the Rock of the Temple Mount in Jerusalem, the navel stones found in many parts of the world according to Neumann (pp. 260) like that of

Omphalos, considered the navel of the world in Delphi, as well as rocks, mountains and of course the waters.

Bachofen's seminal book (*Mother Right*, 1861) caused great controversy surrounding the idea that matriarchy had begun in prehistoric or primal times. But if we look at the animal world, the herd is a matriarchy led by the dominant matriarch and all band together to teach and protect each other and all the young. Still his book has inspired many ethnologists, though some (like Uwe Weisel) thought it was untenable. After him Jane Ellen Harrison 19th century classical scholar and some generations of scholars suggested that ancient societies were probably matriarchal and they probably existed even prior to ancient cultures based on their studies of myths, oral traditions, and studies of female cult-figures. Others disagreed. In short there was a lot of controversy around the topic. Many researchers have studied matriarchy in ancient times but the basis was laid by the idea of a *woman-centred* society that Bachofen formulated in his 3-volume book: *Myth, Religion, and Mother Right* 1861 which impacted among others, Arthur Evans, Walter Burkert, and James Mellaart (Ruethter, 2005, pp. 15). These classicists looked at Bachofen's evidence of *matriarchal religion* in pre-Hellenic societies. Historian Susan Mann, says that since 2000, (2005, pp. 835-862), *"few scholars these days find a notion of a stage of primal matriarchy persuasive."*

Palaeolithic and Neolithic Ages

One speculative theory is that put forward by Friedrich Engels in 1884. He claimed that society was matriarchal because group marriages were the norm and the paternity of the child could not be clearly established. But with the advent of agriculture and a more settled life, wealth came from the possessions of land and cattle and men wanted the wealth they accumulated to be passed on to their progeny. Along with that they needed labourers for their land. Women fitted the bill. So the status and influence of women deteriorated sharply and patriarchy started becoming stronger. Women *became mere objects in the exchange trade between men.* (Engels, 1984 pp. 70).

But Bertha Diener (originally published 1930 writing under the pseudonym of Helen Diner (1965) published the first book to focus on women's cultural heritage and things changed. She is regarded as the first classical feminist to focus on the matriarchal aspect. She believed the first societies were all matriarchal but in time shifted into patriarchal societies and degenerated. The controversy was further strengthened by Robert Graves' publication of his book *The White Goddess* (1948) along with his analysis of Greek Mythology and earlier myths. In the 1950's Marija Gimbutas (*Old European Culture pp. 324*) developed the theory that Neolithic Europe was matriarchal, later replaced by the Proto-Indo-European patriarchal society in the Bronze Age. Epstein (1991 pp. 113) commented in his book that 20th century anthropologists said: *the goddess worship or matrilocality that evidently existed in many paleolithic societies was not necessarily associated with matriarchy in the sense of women's power over men. Many societies can be found that exhibit those qualities along with female subordination.* From the 1970's these ideas became popular with the second-wave feminists and built on by Margaret Murray in the *Goddess Movement*, the feminists *Wicca* by Eisler and Elizabeth Gould Davis and Merlin Stone.

Epstein (1991, pp. 172-173) further commented that *A Golden Age of matriarchy was encouraged.* This was presented by Charlene Spretnak, Merlin Stone and Raine Eisler but was refuted by others like Cynthia Eller (2011). But then there is Del Giorgio (2006) who insists that Palaeolithic society was based on a matrifocal, matrilocal, matrilineal culture.

Bronze Age

Rohrlich, (1977, pp. 36-59) says: many scholars are convinced that Crete was a *matriarchy, ruled by a queen-priestess"* and the *"Cretan civilization"* was *"matriarchal"* before *"1500 BC,"* when it was overrun and colonized. He also says: in the early Sumerian city-states *'matriarchy seems to have left something more than a trace'* (1977, pp. 39 quoting Thomson pp. 160). Scholars like Stone and Eisler believe that the Semites were matriarchal whereas the Indo-Europeans were patriarchal. Stone in *When God was a Woman* believed Yahweh was an Indo-European conception superimposed on an ancient matriarchal Semitic people. But evidence from the Amorites and pre-Islamic Arabs show them to have been a patriarchal and patrilineal society. This is again refuted by the

Biblical scholar Raphael Patai, who in his book *The Hebrew Goddess* (1990, pp. 38-39) shows that right from the beginning, the Jewish religion was not a monotheistic one. It had many elements of polytheism, like **the cult of Asherah**, a Canaanite goddess worshiped in 12th century BC as evident in the Biblical *Book of Judges* was adopted by the Hebrews who intermarried with the Canaanites. She was publicly worshipped and represented in carved wooden poles. Also many carved, nude, female figurines were unearthed all over ancient 7th century Palestine and Hebrew texts of the time, invoked her aid during childbirth.

Another ancient goddess was **Shekinah,** the feminine Holy Spirit embodying compassion and divine radiance, who was called upon to comfort the sick and dejected. She accompanied the exiled Jews and interceded on their behalf with God for mercy rather than to mete out retribution. Shekinah appears in the slightly later Aramaic translations of the Hebrew bible in the 1st or 2nd century CE texts. Patai (1990, pp. 96–111) believed that initially she was portrayed as the presence of God but later became distinct from God taking on well-defined physical male characteristics.

The Indo-Europeans had multiple succession systems with clear evidence of matrilineal customs, especially among the Celts and Germanics than was evident among the ancient Semitic peoples.

In Sparta women were always in total charge while the men were at war. In Crete too, women held a high place of honour.

Iron Age to the Middle Ages

From the Iron Age to the Middle Ages in a number of North-Western mythologies, like the Irish (Macha and Scáthach), Brittonic (Rhiannon), Germanic (Grendel's mother Nerthus) to name only a few, all have ambiguous episodes of primal female power which has often been interpreted as matriarchal attitudes in Pre-Christian times in Iron Age societies. These were powerful women but the later Christian religion found this female power disturbing and soon replaced it with patriarchal power and dominance. Even in the 1st century AD female power was visible as can be attested to by women leaders like **Boudicca** and **Cartimandua**, **Cleopatra VII** of Egypt, **Elen Luyddog**, ruler of Wales, **Zenobia** of Palmyra, among others, who exercised explicit power, autocracy and equality quite in contrast from that allowed to women in Athens or Rome.

In the Middle Ages it got much worse (see CHP III).

20-21st centuries

In modern times patriarchy is all pervasive and matriarchy has been eroded, demeaned and pushed aside. Most men genuinely believe that they are superior to women and their rights, demands and desires are more important than women's. Many women have been trained to accept this wrong perception of their place in the hierarchy to a great extent. Andrea Cornwall (2001) says her research has proven that in South Eastern Nigeria many women prefer not to work outside the home if their husbands can provide for them, reaffirming how strongly they are affected by the patriarchal view of their place in society. In these modern times, women are again reasserting themselves but the path is very difficult as men do not want to surrender the place patriarchy has given them. This is true around the world and not just in Africa and Asia. But these ideas are social constructs in place since patriarchy took over. They are incorrect assumptions.

Yet there are places where matriarchy still exists and women, indigenous or modern, call the shots. Social norms and rules are made by them. Most matriarchal systems are matrilineal. Here are a few matriarchal / matrilineal societies around the world **today**:

Moseau are an ethnic Chinese people in **Southwest China** (in the Yunan and Sichuan provinces). They are a well-known matriarchal society, though some assert that they are matrilineal rather than matriarchal. The child's patrimony is not known. It is not regarded as important nor is there any stigma attached to it. The children belong entirely to the mother's family. The people practice what is called a 'walking marriage' where the couple do not live together but spend their free time together. Even in 2016 daughters were the only inheritors of property (Kuhn 2016, NPR, Xinhua News Agency 2000, ProQuest web 2021). There are about 40,000 to 50,000 of them living near Lake Lugu at the foothills of the Tibetan Himalayas. And they practice Tibetan Buddhism. The women don't usually marry, but can choose to live together with a partner. However, the mother plays the primary role in the children's life. She is called Ah Mi. The matriarch has absolute power. Every decision in all spheres is made by her. Daughters follow their mothers in this role, sometimes even adopted daughters take on the role. These people have faced severe challenges in a patriarchal world from outside and at one point their culture began to erode — between 1966-1976 during the Cultural Revolution when matrilineal societies were banned, but they held on, somehow. Then from 1990 tourism began and their livelihood picked up. In fact, The News agency says: *tourism has become so profitable that many Mosuo families in the area who have opened their homes have become wealthy.* This financial boost helped the people back on their feet but simultaneously it changed the fabric of their society always having outsiders looking down on their society and cultural practices.

Umoja: In **Kenya,** in 1995 says Emily Wax, (Washington Post, 2005) the village of Umoja was established with 36 women under a matriarch. But there seems to be a controversy here as many others claim it was founded in 1990 by Rebecca Lolosoli and 15 other women. Umoja in Swahili means unity and is the language spoken most widely in Kenya and other places in East Africa. It is a women's refuge. Lolosoli strongly advocated women's rights in a place where women had no rights. It was founded on an empty piece of land in Samburu County in Northern Kenya by women who had fled their homes after being raped by British soldiers in Kenya (Faith, Karimi, CNN news, 2005, online) as well as women escaping gender-based violence, sexual assault, forced marriages from the area of the Rift Valley. Prior to this, they had belonged to the Samburu tribe of Kenya where women were the property of men with no rights at all. It is said that they could be and were beaten not only by family members but also outsiders. They had no voice. But now, in this true no-man's land, where the women have settled, men are banned. Men from the same village set up theirs opposite the women's questioning their right to have a matriarchal society and suing them to close them down. Since 2019, 48 women who escaped rape, violence, gender mutilation live in Umoja with their children in this village (ibid). Many of the women had to flee because they had been stigmatised due to the violence committed **against** them (NBC, 2021). In Umoja the women practice collective economic cooperation (NBC, 2021). They learn crafts like jewellery making which they sell to visiting tourists. Sons are forced to leave the village when they turn 18 (CNN, 2005). Men have been banned from the centre. The villagers protect each other and have done a lot towards gender equity in Kenya and their message has spread. NBC says: *Lolosoli's passion for gender equity in Kenya has carried her to speak on social justice at the United Nations and to participate in an international women's rights conference in South Africa.*

Bribri (Costa Rica): this is an indigenous community that live in the regions of Costa Rica and Panama. They live in the mountains of the Talamanca region and are divided into clans. All children are raised by the clan and belong to the clan. Here only women can inherit land as well as prepare the ritual cacao used in tribal ceremonies. The population of Bribri was estimated to have been between 12,000 and 35,000 in 2015. The origins of the matrilineal inheritance and customs are said to be bound up with the legend that speaks about how a woman was turned into a cacao tree by a Bribri God named Sibu. This is why only women can prepare the ritual drink called Theobroma cacao. Men in this clan have very specialised roles like the awa, whose job is to sing funeral songs. These are the only people who are allowed to touch the dead bodies. The awa has to train for up to 15 years, when he turns 8. It is then that he begins his awa apprenticeship to an older awa. In this way tribal knowledge is passed down from one awa to the sons of his female relatives and the traditions kept alive. Men do not train their children but only their sisters' children. Land passes from the mother to the daughters. Women are highly revered in this society.

Khasi, (India): Still another matriarchal society is to be found in Meghalaya, in North-East India among the Khasi people (Banerjee, 2015). Some believe it is a matrilineal state but Banerjee says: *to assess and account a matriarchal society through the parameters of the patriarchy would be wrong"* and that *"we should avoid looking at history only through the colonizer / colonized boundaries".* (Ibid)

All the clans of the Khasi people trace their lineage through the matriarchs. A Khasi husband is expected to participate equally in the children's upbringing. The married couple does not have to live with the bride's parents unless she is the youngest daughter. The men do get a small part of the property but the bulk is always passed on to the daughters. One woman, Passah, comments: (the man) *"would come to his wife's home late at night. In the morning, he's back at his mother's home to work in the fields,*" it shows the man's role consists of supporting his wife and family in Khasi society (Rathnayake, 2021, vol 1-2, no.4, pp. 46). Traditionally the youngest daughter cares for the ancestral property. She is called Khadduh. The Khasi still practice many female-led customs. Wealth and property pass through the females (Ibid). In 2011, according to *The Guardian*, this matriarchal society's population was about a million. All children are looked after only by the mothers and mothers-in-law. Men are not entitled to even attend family gatherings. In this tribe, when women marry, their surnames, not their husbands', are passed on to the children. Khasi people are a part of the mainstream society and are one of the modern matriarchal communities. They adhere to the constitution and laws. Many of them follow Christianity because, since the arrival of missionaries they had converted.

Minangkabau (Indonesia): This is the largest matriarchal society in the world today. This tribe is indigenous to the Minangkabau Highlands of the island of West Sumatra. The population is 4.2 million. It is often speculated that these people share a pre-history with the Malays as they share many commonalities of language with them. Land ownership and family name is passed on from mothers to daughters. Some men are involved in politics but only with the women's consent. The tribe is mostly run by women. The legend is that a Sumatran king died leaving behind three wives with three young sons. The first wife took charge as her son was too young and this set the precedence for matriarchal rule that the Mingkabau follow till today. The other reason is the role of distant land and the Diaspora. Men leave the homeland in search of opportunities and education abroad, leaving the running of community and the leadership to women. Anthropologists who have studied these people have found that traditionally the social norms have been very advantageous to women here.

Nagovisi (New Guinea): They inhabit a large tropical Island in New Guinea called South Bougainville. The main focus for these people is food production and women play the dominant role. The husbands are generally assigned to clear the land. Every Nagovisi woman is entitled to farm her ancestral land and the right is passed down from mother to daughter. Nagovisi women are very proud of the food produced by them. Any refusal of that food can become dangerous as it shows disrespect and can even lead to divorce.

Akan, Ghana: These people are also a matriarchal society known for their matrilineal system. Major positions in the financial and political ladder are determined by the mother's side of the family. Maternal ancestry decides the norms of inheritance and succession. The men can play an important role in the lives of their sisters' sons but not in that of their own. This is a polygamous society where men are more associated with the upbringing of the female family members and the women are associated with the running and management of the entire clan.

Garo India: This is another Indian tribe that resides in the hills of the North Eastern states. Garo people are an indigenous Tibeto-Burman group. They are the second largest tribe in Meghalaya. The Garos have similar practices to that of the

Khasi people. Their children inherit the name and properties from their mother. Men move to their wives' homes after marriage. The tribe believes in gender equality. Hence, the properties are owned by women but are governed by men.

Patriarchy

Patriarchy, as we know it today is only **5,000 years old**. Civilisation began 90,000 to 80,000 years ago by homosapiens or humans in a matriarchal world, a world in which goddess worship predominated all over the world. We often wonder how patriarchy began and pushed out matriarchy reducing womanhood to a servile position. In this part we will look at the works of Lerner, French, Wagner, and Stone among others.

Gerda Lerner (1986) says: *It* (patriarchy) *began with the conviction, shared by most feminist thinkers, that patriarchy as a system is historical: it has a beginning in history. If that is so, it can be ended by historical process.* She queries why women had been excluded from the historical process and the 3,500 years delay in women realising their subordinate position. She examines ancient cultures and civilisations especially in the Near East to discover the origin of the gender metaphor that we practised and still do so in the Western world, can be traced back to Mesopotamia, (The Fertile Crescent). By 4000 BC the men of Sumer (southern Iraq) had claimed ownership over children and wives. It appears from her research into antiquity – literary, archaeological, artistic — evidence that patriarchy was incorporated in the Western world and from that point on dominated. I concur. Before that, my research showed, for millennia it was a matriarchal world that functioned very well, mostly in harmony. Lerner explains the origin of misogyny in ancient Mesopotamia. And though patriarchy as a system is *out dated,* she says, it will not go away easily. She offers the first coherent theoretical framework for women's history. Patriarchy began with the social organisation of the father or oldest male heading the family/tribe but in time degenerated into male governance and domination, ignoring all female's rights and freedoms. She says: "Patriarchy has gone through many forms," and now exists, as **"an institutionalized pattern of male dominance in society."** This legacy has given the men "advantages that they shouldn't have and to which they are not entitled." Patriarchy she believes was not created maliciously but inadvertently and had unexpected, unforeseen consequences very negatively affecting women.

She further contends that in early societies: *"women's average life span may have been less than 28 years, and when infant mortality was 70 to 75 percent, women were bearing and nursing babies all the time in order for the tribe to survive. So a sexual division of labor was created that was functional and approved of by both men and women."* Unfortunately, this biological division became an oppressive part of that division. **And it was a social invention.** Patriarchy developed in the Near East between 3100 BC and 600 BC with women being exchanged in marriage for tribal reasons and women acquiesced because it was functional for the tribe.

This uprooting of women gave men the idea that their rights were superior to those of women and soon, especially with the more warlike tribe dominating the egalitarian ones. Women and children became the first casualties of war and the first slaves while the male prisoners were killed. From this point female power started disintegrating really fast.

The exploitation of women for sexual and reproductive reason began and the power of the men to make this happen led to class distinction that the *"slave women and children were the first property in these societies"* leading to the idea of female enslavement and the concept of human property.

Lerner rejects Engels theory that patriarchy was a sequel to owning private property. Instead, patriarchy shows *"that the whole system of hierarchical governance and structure is inextricably involved with gender, and that race, class and gender oppression are interconnected and have been from the beginning."* She continues: *"Patriarchy is not based on a biological difference"* between men and women, *"but on a stage of human development when women had to nurse babies all the time."* 'Now with science and longevity of life and a very low infant mortality in most countries, she believes Freud's statement that anatomy is destiny is wrong, now she says 'Anatomy Once Was Destiny'. That makes sense. Technology has replaced anatomy in that sense.

Patriarchy, she believes and I believe so too, *is a human creation*. It has, I believe, outlived its use (if there was any value in it in the first place) *it is not functioning very well now*, and it can (should) be ended. *We can't do that as long as we believe that patriarchy is natural or God-given.* It is not. Patriarchy is not natural or God-given.

Her views drew criticism but there are always critics of any theory. And most men and some women would and do, of course criticise it. Lerner says: *"We need now to shift from an androcentric view of the universe to one in which we always think of both men and women as central to events. This could transform our entire historical body of knowledge."* Her views and those of many other writers mentioned above, coincide. After all, to have humanity one needs both the male and female to procreate together.

For the greater part of human existence society has functioned under matriarchal, not patriarchal rule. The first to be worshipped were all goddesses, not gods. Even today many goddesses are worshipped, some in secret and some openly. Wicca and other similar women movements are gaining momentum in the present world.

Ella Beau (2018) says: Today, *most anthropologists would agree, regardless of their stance on issues such as the universality of male dominance, that an entirely different order of male dominance became associated with the rise of the large and populous agricultural states organized in terms of classes. The patriarchal systems that emerged brought women for the first time under the direct control of fathers and husbands with few cross-cutting sources of support. Women as wives under this system were not social adults, and women's lives were defined in terms of being a wife. Women's mothering and women's sexuality came to be seen as requiring protection by fathers and husbands. Protecting unmarried women's virginity appears to go along with the idea of the domestication of* women and an emphasis on a radical dichotomy between the public and the private sphere.

To go back in time, Sumer in Mesopotamia, the cradle of the oldest civilisation had a matriarchal and matrilineal society. There was no patriarchy at its inception. It began when society changed from subsistence living to agriculture, the building of cities and militarisation. Societies became patriarchal through transition to agriculture or through colonisation. And the full force of patriarchy came to be felt with colonisation much, much later. Howard Zinn 1980) describes the Haudenosaunee (Iroquois) before the Europeans arrived. He says:

Women were important and respected in Iroquois society. Families were matrilineal. That is, the family line went down through the female members, whose husbands joined the family, while sons who married then joined their wives' families. Each extended family lived in a "long house." When a woman wanted a divorce, she set her husband's things outside the door."

In these societies, children inherited from the mothers. Sons, husbands, brothers all had access to property through their female relatives who were their guardians. And in most matrilineal societies (which were also matrilocal) — women inherited the land, men helped raise their sisters;' children and young men left home to marry into another matrilineal clan. Women's political status matched their central role in society. Gabriela Ngirmang explains in Zohl deI Ishtar' *Daughters of the Pacific* (1994):

> *In Palau [Belau] women play an important role in issues of policy. Women traditionally own land. We control the clan money. We traditionally select our chiefs – women place and remove them. Having observed their upbringing closely we are able to decide which men have the talent to represent our interests.*

Wagner (2001) says it was no coincidence that the American women's rights movement was born in the territory of the Haudenosaunee (Iroquois). Three women's rights leaders had connections with the Haudenosaunee people: Elizabeth Cady Stanton, Matilda Joslyn Gage and Lucretia Mott and they, says Wagner, *"believed women's liberation was possible because they knew liberated women, women who possessed rights beyond their wildest imagination: the Haudenosaunee women."*

In an 1891 speech Wagner says, Stanton informed the National Council of Women how misbehaving Haudenosaunee husbands *might at any time be ordered to pick up his blanket and budge.* She said she envied *How Indian women* ruled the house" and how *"descent of property and children were in the female line."* She continued:

> *The women were the great power among the clan, as everywhere else. They did not hesitate, when occasion required, 'to knock off the horns,' as it was technically called, from the head of a chief and send him back to the ranks of the warriors. The original nomination of the chiefs also always rested with the women.*

Prior to colonisation these tribal women lived by horticulture and hunting. Villages had longhouses in which 25 families could live. These quarters had partitioned off sleeping areas and a shared fireplace with the family living opposite. The food farmed by the women was stored at either end of the longhouse and its distribution was controlled by them. Chiefs needed the power and consent of women to depose and to initiate war. Wagner continues that many 18th, and 19th century Indian and non-Indian reporters *contended that* **rape didn't exist among Native nations prior to white contact.***"*

In contrast, **European tradition legalised marital rape and wife battering.** A woman and her property legally belonged to her husband and divorce was almost impossible for women to get. Gage who was working on a book about the Haudenosaunee when in 1898 she died had this to say: *"That the woman of every Christian land fears to meet a man in a secluded place by day or night, is of itself sufficient proof of the low state of Christian morality."* Gage focussed on the position of women in this tribal group of what she termed *Mother Rule*. And earlier (in Gage, 1893) she wrote that in Iroquois society women had true power through matrilineality which led to a more equal relationship.

Before patriarchy, matrilineal societies existed in the Near-East and Middle-East. There is an abundance of relics showing the strong influence of goddess worship in these regions. Stone (2012) says that many historians' routine characterisation of goddess wordship as *fertility cults* has been sexist and oversimplified. Mother goddess figurines as well as other goddess figurines have been found in large quantities in Modern Iraq. The goddess Astarte was worshipped as a very important goddess in Canaan around 7000 BC. Female figurines with a hand raised to their breasts have been found in Jericho. These 7,000-year-old ruins show the existence of matrilineal villages on the Aegean and Adriatic coasts and coasts of old Europe, Czechoslovakia, Southern Poland, and Western Ukraine. Houses here had altars with statues and paintings of a lone woman standing and female animal shapes or things associated with snakes and butterflies. French (2008) says these people lived in peace and stability for thousands of years, farming, raising animals, making pottery, carving, and making bone and stone implements. Set in beautiful, accessible, unfortified sites with good water and soil, none of these villages show signs of war, nor do the graves show stratification.

She continues that in these areas from 7000 to 3500 BC the towns developed complex governing, social and religious institutions, specialized crafts such as goldsmithing, and perhaps a rudimentary script. By 5500 BCE they knew copper metallurgy and depicted sailing boats on their ceramics. 40 shrines dating to 6500 BC have been found at the site of an ancient Anatolian (Turkish) town called Çatal Hüyük. These included figurines of young women, birthing mothers, and old crones. This town had a population of 6-8,000 people living in connected houses. The entrance was at the top of the houses accessed by a ladder. They had mud brick fireplaces, clay ovens and sleeping platforms.

An important precondition for patriarchy was the connection between sexual intercourse and the birth of the child to establish paternity. It was not important in earlier times as descent was traced through the mother, of which there can never be any doubt. But this desire to prove paternity does **not** justify what happened next.

According to French (2008) male dominance came into play when men started to claim ownership of the child and naming right. To do so, they needed control over the women. **The murder of first-born children began from this time as men** wanted to be certain the child was truly theirs. By 4000 BC many villages in Sumer had become patrilineal though women still had some control over the food. Men and women still hunted, fished, farmed, trapped birds together and still worshipped the goddess Innana. But after communities began to trace the paternal lineage, they started becoming patrilocal. French explains this thus in her book:

> *"In patrilocal marriage a woman lives with strangers, isolated from any who love her or will protect her, sometimes even from any who share her language. Often abused and exploited by husbands and their families; in patrilocal groups, women do not possess their bodies, their labor, or their children, who belong to their husbands' lineage. Some patrilocal societies allow wives to leave, but they can never take their children with them. Therefore, most women remain."*

During this **time male solidarity and puberty rites began.** Boys were taught to scorn *"feminine emotion"* and instead to display hardness, self-denial, harshness, obedience especially to elder males and thereby creating a bond of power goals. Women ceased being respected or held in high esteem. French says:

> *in male dominated societies, girls were humiliated, isolated confined and allowed only small amounts of certain foods and drink, taught that her body is powerful but contaminated, a girl learns she has power – to pollute: in such cultures, menstrual* **blood is a source of horror and fear.**

And once patrilineal values were established, with women marrying into the man's clan, escape became impossible. And as agriculture and population increased, men started seeking territorial expansion and greater power. Women lost control over food distribution. All power became concentrated in male hands, including the running of the temples and harvest management. Sumerian temples now started placing gods over goddesses and Inanna lost a lot of her primacy. By 500 AD Christian, Roman and Byzantine emperors closed down goddess temples, though many still worshipped goddesses in secret.

During this time too, began the killing off of male prisoners and incorporating the females into the tribe generally through rape. The women stayed for the sake of their children and there was no protection for them – their tribal males were dead. This disenfranchisement – the capture and **enslavement of women started the class system and private property** ownership. In *The Creation of Patriarchy*, Gerda Lerner contends that it was only after decades of conquering women in this way that tribes learned how to enslave them.

By 3500–2800 BC the military elite were strong competitors with the temple elite. Society became more and more warlike. Warriors became chieftains taking over communal lands for private use. Small states began uniting to form larger kingdoms. The strongest of these chieftains became kings. The temple became the king's property. The kings' or rulers' daughters were appointed to the position of high priestesses. They represented the goddess Inanna and went through a marriage ceremony with the High priest. The people were taught to believe that only the sacred marriage between the Goddess Inanna could bring fertility to the land. And this practice went on for over 2,000 years. The myth cycles clearly show the subjugating of women, the war between the sexes and men's triumph over women – a main reason for that, I believe, was women's dedication to the protection of children. French explains *that goddesses created everything, and Siduri, one of the most prominent, reigned in paradise. Later, a sun god usurped her realms, goddesses were demoted, and, by the later epic of the legendary king Gilgamesh, Siduri was a barmaid.* Later Babylonian / Assyrian creation stories described how the god Marduk defeated Tiamat, the Great Mother to explain male superiority.

Inanna, in the first myths, encompassed everything. She was responsible for birth, death, and rebirth *"as mother, protector and goddess of the vegetation and the weather, of the morning and the evening star."* This changed in later myth of *Enki and the World Order.* When Enki became the primary god, a proper bureaucrat lording it over a lesser hierarchy, he assigned offices to them excluding most goddesses including Inanna (except two). But Inanna's power persisted. She became a goddess of love and war, of healing, of interceding on behalf of mankind and after the Amorite conquest she became a goddess of prostitutes. But her power continued in one form or another.

Kar.kid is the Sumerian word for prostitute. It first appeared in the Sumerian language around **2400 BC**. At this time **the temple priests prostituted female captives and slaves** to draw men (and money) to the temple. Lerner (1986) comments on this too. She says: It is likely that commercial prostitution derived directly from the enslavement of women in warfare. As slavery became an established institution, slave owners rented out their female slaves as prostitutes, and some masters set up commercial brothels staffed by slaves. The ready availability of captive women for private sexual use and the need of kings and chiefs, frequently themselves usurpers of authority, to establish legitimacy by displaying their wealth in the form of servants and concubines led to the **establishment of harems.** These, in turn, became symbols of power to be emulated by aristocrats, bureaucrats, and wealthy men.

Another source **for commercial prostitution** was the worsening condition of the farmers who often now needed loans in times of famine to survive. Debt led to slavery. Children of both sexes had to be surrendered as bond or sold for *"adoption"*. Male heads of families could benefit from female prostitution and so they did. Women might end up as prostitutes because their parents had to sell them into slavery or their impoverished husbands might so use them for the same purpose.

From 2350 BC slavery became a permanent feature of their social order and of male property. Private property ownership now emerged. **Women were degraded and termed 'property' and judged by different legal and moral standards.** Between 1792 and 1750 BC, Hammurabi, a Babylonian king compiled and amended previous law codes and engraved the Codex Hammurabi — sanctioned by the god Shamash. These laws had already been in practice for hundreds of years, administered by communal judges and elders forming a tribunal. It was based on *an eye for an eye.* There were three distinct classes: the patricians including priests and government officials; the burghers and the slaves. Class determined the punishment. If injury was done to a person of a higher class the punishment was more severe than vice versa. A man could send his innocent slave to bear his punishment for his crimes. By the Codex, the father had unlimited authority over his children. Of 282 laws, 73 concerned marriage and sexual matters. E.G. a wife had to fulfil her role to her husband's satisfaction or he could reduce her status to that of a slave or divorce her, he could take another wife if he felt she did not comply. Women had no recourse to divorce. Property was passed from male to male. Head of the family was a male. The main potential of a daughter was a bargaining chip as a bride and virginity was an absolute condition for marriage. If a bride was found not to be a virgin she could be divorced immediately. Girls were always under very strict supervision.

Learner writes: ***By the middle of the second millennium B.C., prostitution was well established as a likely occupation for the daughters of the poor.*** And not just this, sexual regulation of females belonging to the richer class became firmly entrenched. A virgin daughter became a financial asset **and commercial prostitution became a social necessity to meet the male sexual needs.** The problem was in distinguishing the respectable from the non-respectable females and discouraging men from socially associating with the latter. Law 40 (MAL) dealt with these two points. One way of distinguishing respectable from non-respectable women was: all married and respectable women had to cover their heads in public. All non-respectable women had to go with uncovered heads. Any breach of this law led to very severe punishment like being flogged naked and then being covered in pitch.

In the 1595 BC, Babylon was sacked and by 1300 BC a highly militaristic Assyrian Empire arose named after its previous capital in Syria. The Middle Assyrian Code 40 (MAL, as above) was much harsher than the previous Babylonian code. 59 out of 112 laws dealt explicitly with marriage and sexual matters. E.G. if a virgin was raped, she had to marry her rapist and he could never divorce her. If he was married then he had to pay the girl's father by surrendering his wife to be kept as a slave or concubine. No one considered the girls' or women's points of view.

One of the harshest punishments was for abortion. Any woman who performed abortion or aborted a baby, was impaled and denied burial. Adultery too was a crime but punishment was only for the woman, not for the guilty man. And if a man hit a pregnant woman, not his wife and caused her to miscarry, then he must allow his pregnant wife to be treated in the same way. **The men always got off scot-free. The point of the abortion law was to reinforce the power of men over women.** They were to decide which child lived or died. A wife could not be allowed to usurp the man's right.

Andrea Dworkin in her essay *The Rape Atrocity and the Boy Next Door* succinctly sums this up. She writes: Women belonged to men; the laws of marriage sanctified that ownership; rape was the theft of a woman from her own. The crime of rape was a crime of theft, of abduction, of taking another man's property outside of any agreed arrangement or transaction. This is what made adultery only possible on the side of the wife; divorce difficult for her to initiate; and forceful resistance to rape both punishable, and necessary as evidence. Ultimately, she says, *"Rape was a crime against the man who owned the woman".* Dworkin studied these laws late last century because they remain *"the basis of the social order as we know it."* Like Stanton and Gage and the first wave feminists who came before her — she wanted to change them. Strange how our "very developed society" still harks back to Hammurabi's ancient laws in regard to women, abortions, rape and so on!

Conclusion

To wrap up, patriarchy with all control centred in male hands, has dominated our world for a long time now about 10-12 thousand years. But this was not always the case. Social system and social order began with matriarchy. There was much less war, more equality and much more stability and morality in the world. There was no rape or prostitution. **Rape and prostitution both became popular without any punishment for the male, with patriarchy. Brothels began with patriarchy; wife bartering began with patriarchy** — all these were ways of demeaning and controlling women. Many theories have been put forward over time as to why things changed and patriarchy began and does not want to let go of any control. With patriarchy women have been very badly abused and male bigotry has at times, reached unbelievable heights of malice and demeaning of women. But it is a fact that many well-developed ancient societies ruled by matriarchies advocated rights and freedoms for all. There was no slavery or prostitution or brothels or discrimination in these societies. Men were not demeaned or discriminated against or treated as only sperm donors. These were much more equal and contented societies.

There have been advocates who opined that only underdeveloped societies had men as superior. Historical evidence does not support this (Bennet, 2011, pp. 25). We do not have sufficient archaeological evidence to give us further insights. What is supportable is that patriarchy, since it took over, has been an inseparable part of most civilisations. In the still existing matriarchal societies today, there is still much more equality between the men and women. One wonders why men felt the overwhelming need to discriminate. Was it their fragile egos? A weaker intellect? Fear of women? Or what...?

Some conceptual theories to explain the dominance of patriarchy in the past and now are the following: the **biological theory** which contends that women are inferior to men because they are physically weaker. But this is highly questionable as there are (and were) women who were and are physically as strong or sometimes stronger than men (e.g. Khutulun, Amazons, Celtic warrior women, Slav & Teutonic warrior women etc.). In ancient times the women warriors were easily a match and often better warriors than their male counterparts like the above-mentioned groups and more (See Part III, *A Matter of Honour* (2024) by Sophia Z Kovachevich). Then again 'weaker' is a word of perception. Weaker? How? In having less bone mass or in the ability to bear the excruciating pain of childbirth, in the ability to multitask or be quicker in grasping a point or even in physical movement? Bennett (2011, pp. 31) says*: Strength must be measured in endurance and mental ability* and this would prove that there are many examples in the past and present, where women have been much stronger. The single fact that women are the central point to reproduction and its painful birth-giving characteristics, proves that the amount of pain is much greater than men have ever felt. According to these criteria, women are definitely superior. There are many other reasons.

However, some theorists say that women's child-bearing ability makes clear their weakness as well as their role in raising the children and in the family. Firstly child-bearing is extremely difficult and secondly many men make excellent parents and are often better at parenting than are many women. The only indisputable fact is that women get pregnant and men don't. The rest is really a matter of individual intellect, desire determination and societal demands. Lassen (2011, pp. 10) says historically there is evidence of numerous men better at parenting than their female counterparts. This is proof that gender roles are for the greater part, socially constructed.

Another theory put forward is that patriarchy arose due to the **inherent competitiveness of men**. And women decided which man they wanted / desired to continue the existence of civilisation. A woman wanted a strong, healthy man who could invest mentally and physically in her child. And one who had resources that would guarantee her child's future. Their competitive spirit was aroused. Men therefore established a social role based on strength, ability to overpower other men and thus they decided on a world of raw power. And this information to be all powerful was passed down from generation to generation of boys and men. But then why did they need to make women powerless, subservient? They believed that women would favour the strongest, most successful and resourceful man. Here was no need to disempower women to prove their strength. This cannot be the only reason to disempower women.

Monotheistic Religion from the start began the aggressive disempowerment of women. So men were in a position of power in society backed by religious views about male superiority and female inferiority. The Bible, Torah, Quran all cite God as a He and since then almost all earthly rulers have been males. Women are often precluded from inheriting the throne because of their gender, irrelevant if they are better suited to rule. All three religions of the BOOK denigrate goddesses and regard them as witches. In all three religions women could not attain to any position within the religious hierarchy – no matter how erudite or capable or holy. Only men could, some of them extremely corrupt (Kovachevich 2024, pp. 117-124). Coffen (2007 pp. 66) agrees about the role of Christianity and adds that popery has always been patriarchal.

Civilisation made a serious mistake in putting or allowing so much power in the hands of only one section of society. That is why power has corrupted men who wield it. Men's arrogance has given many women an uncalled-for inferiority complex, feeding men's unfounded superiority complex. It has also affected many males adversely. Now many men would change their sexual orientation as would women. It has been the case for very long and has got even worse in modern times in some respects. Men and women have equal capacities in different ways and should be equal partners. But women too are guilty of not breaking free earlier. Instead, this inequality has created a lot of problems and divisions. **There is nothing positive about male dominance** and who knows how much better civilisation would have been if society had continued to be matriarchal. Or even if they had been allowed a greater say in all familial, national, international and global affairs!

It is unfortunate that once male domination began women have consistently been attributed negative qualities to boost male egos. The abuse and bigotry that women have been suffering for centuries, have led to women's rights movement and anti-discrimination laws that are present in the modern society (Lassen, 2011 pp. 260). In spite of the crumbs thrown to women in recent years, our world is still very much a patriarchy, dominated by males in every sphere of life. And they would also interfere and forbid abortion like in Hammurabi's time, thousands of years ago. So how advanced are men today if their conception and ideas are the same or similar to those of a civilisation that existed in 1750 BC?

Just consider the following points:

- Women today are still paid much less; many positions are closed to them, promotion is hard to come by,
- Rape and child molestation, is rampant,
- Wife-beating is a common occurrence.
- Women and girls are kidnapped or tricked/coerced with false promises into leaving their country and then become sex slaves.
- Male physical and mental abuse are commonplace.
- There are many men's only clubs and educational institutions

So, how are we more advanced today? We are only advanced in our killing and destructive abilities and in fomenting murder, genocide and mayhem in every corner of the earth. We are good at destroying the fabric of society, the earth, the sky, the waters, the environment — in short everything. We are excellent at creating extremely destructive weapons, in technology which is fantastic but detracts from our freedoms. Our modern kids are growing up to rely not on their intellectual abilities but on their iPad and computers.

Research shows there is no difference between male and female intelligence or capabilities The biological and genetic 'evidence' that some presented has also been easily and completely refuted. **Women are not inferior to men in any way**. Nor have they ever been. They are often stronger psychologically, emotionally and sometimes even physically, more resilient, as always.

Bennet (2011, pp. 154) says: The modern intellectual development has also shown that there are neither conceptual nor environmental perspectives that define men as being stronger or more superior to women. It is certain that the present days have much changed and there is a great shift in the way masculinity and femininity are viewed. Patriarchy is, supposedly, becoming less dominant and the roles are merging. I'll believe it when there is true equality between the sexes in the world.

The exact origins of patriarchy are lost in the mists of time, but its effects are still very much felt. It has divided society in very unfair and negative ways. It will take a long, long time to root it out if we really want civilisation to survive.

It is safe to posit that one reason for patriarchy was the **male ego** — to have absolute proof of paternity. In the absence of the modern research methods available today to determine paternity, men had really one recourse which soon became a rule, a norm, a tradition — kill the first born if in doubt, seclude (imprison) women ensuring no other man or men could have access to her. Any straying from this narrow path would lead to the woman, never the guilty men — to be ostracised and punished, often, in earlier times, stoned to death. And religion helped the men greatly in this earlier, now our legal systems also do the same. Marital rape was not considered wrong as a woman belonged – body and soul — to the man and he could use her as he wished. It was not a crime in a man-dominated society. **In the 1970's women could not own businesses or hold credit cards in the USA. She could be fired from her job just for being pregnant.** Many colleges Ivy leagues, law firms declined to even interview female applicants. For example, **Ruth Bader Ginsberg** faced serious obstacles when she first tried to enter the legal profession as did **Sarah O'Connor.**

Until 1993 rape was not even a crime in most US states and around the world. It is still an accepted part of life. If and when the woman complains, she is forced to relive the episode, publicly over and over again. At the end there is seldom any redress. The man continues to rape as he sees how easy it is to get away with it. In the sphere of economics, women work harder, longer hours at the office and at home for much less pay, having the same qualifications and experience across the board, be it in an office, in a coffee shop as a cleaner or whatever. Even now, the social system regards men differently, more positively than women. They are regarded as more intelligent, competent capable. It is not really always so!! In the US there has never been a female president and Kamila Harris is the first female vice president whereas there have been in Europe, a large number in Asia, in Africa and in many Muslim countries. USA is perhaps the most patriarchal country in modern times. It is crassly unfair and unequal. We certainly **do not** live in an equal society.

Take the example of the earth. Throughout history it has been perceived as a female entity. Since patriarchy and down through the centuries, males have destroyed it to a great extent, gouging into it for gold, oil, minerals, jewels or whatever for greed and to prove their domination over the land. *In Canada and the States religious women were pressured to oversee programs devised by male leaders in civil society, which attempted to destroy the culture and distinctive identity of Indigenous children* (Good Faith and Media, web). How is this acceptable or fair? Or even morally right?

Patriarchy is basically a dominance system. It is not only detrimental to women but also to men who do not belong to the hierarchy either through wealth, power or birth. And in the modern Western world, more specifically the USA, a 'macho' man, whatever that might mean, is highly valued. Physical prowess has become the norm with body building taking a very high place. But while they build their bodies, their mental capabilities suffer severely. Most entertainment is based on the feats of macho men or criminals or killers (again mostly men). Children's cartoons follow the same pattern to brainwash them from a very young age. Bullying in schools has skyrocketed. Physical and monetary power tops everything else. The world has become a place for bullies and corruption in the mad desire for dominance and control. Women too, are to blame for the present situation. They went along with patriarchy and even maintained it by their direct and indirect support. Women who rebelled against patriarchy were ostracised, excluded, rejected by many women who were afraid to *upset the apple cart*, so to say. So patriarchy was allowed to dominate and get stronger and stronger. In modern times there is now a resurgence to take control by females of female destinies. Matriarchy once ruled the world very successfully and for a long, long time. It can do so again but perhaps not in its pure form but more as a shared endeavour with males having more of a say. Patriarchy is a new experiment and I believe not a very successful one. Society has very rigid norms and there is no scope for expansion or individuality. Those who try to break the mould pay a high price. Yes, civilisation has developed at a very fast rate but it has the lost many things in the process perhaps even its soul!

Part III

Women and religion

In the Middle-Ages

In all olden religions, women played a vital role in all aspects of religions. The earth Gaia was mother earth from which everything living was born, women ruled the fates as they wove the lives and deaths of mortals; goddesses were very powerful. No man dared to insult or slight a goddess with impunity. This was true of all religions around the world.

Besides goddesses, holy shrines and oracles were tended by women priestesses to whom all from the king to the lowliest man owed homage. They were not to be trifled with whether they were called priestesses, druids (Banduri according to Tacitus) prophetesses (völva), who were the arbitrators in tribal conflicts, or (*Eirik's Saga*) shamans. Change began with agricultural societies, speeded up with organised religion and changed drastically during the Middle Ages.

In Europe

The concept of women and their role in society changed drastically during the Middle Ages (Allen 2006) as Catholicism gained strength. The position of women got weaker and much more restricted perhaps even going back to Judaic times. During the Middle-Ages, as organised religion got stronger, men asserted themselves as the ones to be in control. From the 5th to the 15th centuries society became more and more patriarchal and women came under the rule of men regardless of class (Middleton 1981). In this strongly patriarchal society, women lost their positions greatly. Misogynism was not only tolerated openly but also widely commended. Women were now becoming relegated to the position of being a man's possession back to the time of Hammurabi and the earliest patriarchies. Warrior virtues, physical strength with weapons, intellectual pursuits, ruling her lands on her own became qualities to be frowned upon. They were not 'womanly virtues.' Women were "weak vessels", mentally and physically and, it was now deemed they needed male guidance. A very good example of this was the fate of Eleanor of Aquaitaine, a very strong, educated, intelligent, capable rich heiress whose second husband, Henry II imprisoned her for 16 years till his death. Women were not allowed into the priesthood; the First Council of Orange in 441 AD in the Western Roman Empire forbade the ordination of women as deaconesses. This ruling was upheld by the Council of Epaone in 517 AD held in The Burgundian kingdom and the Second Council of Orléans in 533 AD (Thurston).

More than any other, the Roman Catholic Church played a large part in this with its unifying cultural influence. The Church was now the only reservoir for the preservation of the art of writing. Scribes were church men trained to write their point of view. Women scribes were not allowed. In fact, most women were not encouraged, but generally forbidden to be literate. The role of priesthood became only for men and female druids and mystics were regarded as witches and to be cleansed generally through burning or drowning especially in later centuries under the Spanish Inquisition (for both sexes) from 1478 at first mainly aimed at Jews and Muslims but later to include Protestants and all scientific knowledge suppressed in the latter 19th century; the Salem witch trials; and the nationwide manhunt for witches in England between the 15th and 18th centuries. The only role in the religious sphere open to women at this time was to choose a monastic life but never to wield power. They could never become bishops or cardinals or popes. They could be nuns and abbesses always under the power of churchmen.

The main role of women was to bear children and be wives and mothers. Women were allowed to work in the lower classes as washer women, baking bread, milking cows and so on. Some women also worked as jewellers, spinners, parchment makers or helped their husbands with their jobs. Women were not encouraged to be literate. Some very wealthy women were the exceptions. They were educated like Eleanor of Aquitaine but ultimately their power and possessions passed to their husbands on marriage. Eleanor was imprisoned by her husband Henry II till his death (for 16 years), for helping her son rebel against him and for Henry's inability to break her spirit or control her actions – in spite of all his power.

One woman badly maligned by history and swept under the carpet, a taboo subject is **Pope Joan or John** as she called herself. There is even controversy about her very existence but it could be because she was an embarrassment to the church. That is why her records have been expunged and doubt about her existence has been created. Joan became pope in 855 masquerading as a man, at a time when women were not allowed much freedom. Two years later she got pregnant and towards the end of her term it was discovered. Some say she was murdered quietly, others she was torn apart by the mob, others she was banished, which was very unlikely. It depends upon the source. But the very fact that such a person, at such a time, had existed says much both from a feminist and historical point of view. I believe she did exist but because it was uncovered that she was a woman, who had fooled the whole church and all men, the churchmen and the elite would deny her existence.

There are documents detailing her life even books and plays on the topic including by the famous Renaissance poet Giovanni Boccaccio placing her among 106 Famous Women (*De claris mulieribus*, no. 51). To add to the mystery in St Peter's square there is a carving of a woman wearing the papal robes and crown while giving birth.

According to the Catholic Church, Pope Joan is an urban legend. Some scholars like Prof. Valerie Hotchkiss of the Southern Methodist University believes Pope Joan's story in the book: *History of Emperors and Popes* by a monk, Martin Polonus (see note below). Some say it was added in later and the trend continued. Whatever the truth, there it is — women did assert themselves in whatever way best suited them at whatever cost, but were maligned or outright denied existence. They were embarrassments to the male-dominated society of the times. I believe Pope Joan did really exist. Records prove so.

I have to digress here a little to show what competent, intelligent and capable women were up against in a strongly misogynistic society, by delving a little deeper in Pope Joan's history.

According to legend, as they say, **Pope Joan** or Ioannes Anglicus, reigned as Pope from 855 to 857 AD in the Middle-Ages. That can be verified. Her exact reign is hidden in the mists of cover-up. She first appeared in the 13th century Chronicles that spread throughout Europe showing her abilities, masquerading as a man, reigning as a Pope, giving birth while in a religious procession and being murdered — the culprits either many or a few.

Since then, no church procession has been allowed to take that exact route. The Vatican expunged all mention or reference to her in their rituals and implemented new rules to establish that no other women could EVER do so again (Rustic, 2006, pp. 1-2; Noble, 2013, *Catholic Review*). In the 16th century there was a bust of St. Joan in the Sienna Cathedral among the other pontiffs. It was removed after protests in 1600 (Rustic, 2006, pp. 12-13).

The first mention of Pope Joan was in a 1250 Chronicle by Jean de Mailly. It inspired a number of works, the most popular and influential of them being the 13th century *Chronicon Pontificum et Imperatorum* by Martin of Opava or Polonus. His views were accepted till the 16th century when

Catholics and Protestants started the debate about her existence. Protestant scholars, David Blondel, (in Hotchkiss 2012, pp. 69), and Duffy (1997) attempted to discredit her totally, even her very existence. That disbelief has continued till today by many. **It was the fragile male ego. They could not countenance a woman outwitted all of them and only nature (childbirth) gave her up.**

After the Protestant Reformation of 1517 begun by Martin Luther at Wittenberg Germany, many works at deconstructing Pope Joan began, the first led by Florimond de Raemond a magistrate in the *parliament of Bordeaux* in 1587, followed by others. **Then in 1601, Pope Clement VIII officially declared Pope Joan to be untrue. A famous bust of her, inscribed *Johannes VIII, Femina ex Anglia*, carved in 1400 to commemorate a series of Popes in the Duomo di Siena, noted by many travellers, was either destroyed or recarved and relabelled and finally replaced by a male figure, that of Pope Zachary (Stanford, 1990).**

Pope Joan has become a popular figure in fiction since 1886. Some are: plays among others by: Ludwig Achim von Arnim's: *Päpstin Johanna (1813)*, a fragment by Bertolt Brecht (in *Werke* Bd 10) and a monodrama, *Pausin Johanna*, by Cees van der Pluijm (1996).

Some plays, novels, films and other works on Pope Joan are the following: Emmanuel Rhoides' 1866, by Mark Twain and Alfred Jarry (transl. Lawrence Durrell):*The Curious History of Pope Joan* (1954). The American Donna Woolfolk Cross's 1996 historical romance, *Pope Joan*, (German musical

& film); Wilhelm Smets' *Das Mährchen von der Päpstin Johanna auf's Neue erörtert* (1829), Marjorie Bowen's *Black Magic* (1909), Ludwig Gorm's *Päpstin Johanna* (1912), Yves Bichet's *La Papesse Jeanne* (2005) and Hugo N. Gerstl's *Scribe: The Story of the Only Female Pope*, (2005).

Two films based on her story: *Pope Joan* (1972): entitled *The Devil's Imposter* was in the US. In 2009 recut to include more of John Briley's original script: *She... who would be Pope*. Also in 2009, another film with the title *Pope Joan* was released, this one a German, British, Italian and Spanish production directed by Sönke Wortmann and produced by Bernd Eichinger, based on Cross's novel. The 1982 play *Top Girls* by Caryl Churchill featured Pope Joan as a character, to discuss the restriction of feminism in the past. In 2019 a theatrical show in Malta featured Pope Joan as the main character. There are also video games depicting her. For a person who may not have existed, that is a lot of exposure. Fictional or not, her legend continues till today. **The Oxford Dictionary of Popes declares that there is *"no contemporary evidence for a female Pope at any of the dates suggested for her reign"*, but nonetheless acknowledges that Pope Joan's legend was widely believed for centuries, even by Catholics.**

Another woman whose reputation has suffered at the hands of male-dominated society is **Mary Magdalene.** She was a good, pure woman who believed in Jesus and so followed him even into the desert. She was his strongest disciple. She was the first person to witness his resurrection and take and spread the news to all others. Yet she was and still is in many places, maligned as an adulteress, a fallen woman, a whore and a sinner. She was none of these. In recent years there are some movements to clear her names and give her, her rightful due. What she was, was a believer in Jesus and she was strong enough to defy all to show it. That was her crime.

Other literate females were Herrad of Landsberg, Hildegard of Bingen, and Héloïse d'Argenteuil. They were influential abbesses and authors. Hadewijch of Antwerp was a poet and mystic. Both Hildegard of Bingen and Trota of Salerno were medical writers in the 12th century. From the 14th to 16th centuries there were women who played significant roles in theology like St Catherine of Siena and St Teresa of Ávila, and the mystic Julian of Norwich.

Very rarely a woman exercised political power in those times. Some who did, were: Eleanor of Aquitaine one of the most powerful women, married to two kings – Louis VII of France and Henry II of England; mother to two others; Constance, Queen of Sicily, Urraca of León and Castile, Joan I of Navarre, Melisende, Queen of Jerusalem, Isabella of Castile, Catherine of Braganza and other queens' regnant exercised political power. There were others too.

In 1210 Pope Innocent II had this to say regarding the role of women: *"No matter whether the most blessed Virgin Mary stands higher, and is also more illustrious, than all the apostles together, it was still not to her, but to them, that the Lord entrusted the keys to the Kingdom of Heaven"* (Innocent III, Epistle, 11 December 1210). Christine de Pizan was another noted late medieval writer on women's issues. Her Book: *The City of Ladies* attacked misogyny, while her *The Treasure of the City of Ladies* articulated an ideal of feminine virtue for women from all walks of life ranging from princess to peasant's wife (Allen 2006, pp. 646). She recommended in her book, that princesses should consider very carefully their advice on going to war as war only brings death, destruction mayhem and hate, always keeping in mind their husband's honour. The outcome of wars is always terrible.

Women during this time were rarely able to lead armies with impunity. One glaring example is the extremely brave, spiritual and honourable Joan of Arc (French: La Pucelle d'Orléans) who for all her troubles and valour in saving The French throne was burnt as a witch by the English and the machinations of the Duke of Bedford with the help of Bishop Pierre Cauchon, counsellor to Henry V of England and the Church.

Towards the end of the Middle Ages, more and more restrictions started being placed on women's work. Women were no longer allowed guilds, female property rights also started being curtailed (Erler & Kowaleski 2003 pp. 198). Medieval marriage was a private and a social matter. Canon law dictated, the law of the Catholic Church according to which, marriage was a concrete exclusive bond between husband and wife. It placed all power in the hands of the husband (McDougall 2013, pp. 163-178). Men were the elite in Western Europe but not only in law, theory and practice but also in domestic law, culture, labour, land, property, economy, gender, holiness, sexuality and the interplay of continuity and change throughout the Medieval Age from 500 to 1500 CE in the main religions Judaism and Christianity but not yet in Islam where women held political power and played a significant role in all spheres including Ayesha, the prophet Mohammad's wife. Meantime the Church began replacing the power and voice of the elders in the kin in traditional religion by that of the Church authority.

Note on Martin Polonus: He was also known as Martin von Troppau, Martinus Oppaviensis, and Martin Z Opavy. He was a Dominican Monk in the 13th century. He was ordained in Prague and later was appointed Archbishop of Gnesen (Poland) by Pope Nicolaus III. He left behind a collection of ecclesiastical writings besides his history - *Chronicon pontificum et imperatorum*, which is a chronicle of the popes and emperors until Nicolaus III in 500 manuscripts, he also wrote the most important chronicles of the mendicant orders. He is the most respected Medieval Chronicler. The Manuscript itself is proof of its durability. It begins with an account of Christ and Emperor Augustus and records the events of Christ's life beautifully written and decorated. He gives credibility to Pope Joan.

Difference in Western and Eastern Europe in the status of women

The status of women differed greatly from region to region. There began a move to later marriages and greater celibacy. This helped control the power of patriarchy to a point. The rise of Christianity and manorialism created incentives towards keeping the nucleus family. Marriages took place later and the marriages laws instituted by the Church undermined kinship and enlarging the family including by adoption, polygamy, divorce, remarriage, and consanguineous marriages adhered to earlier, to maintain clans and clan power throughout history (Bouchard 1981, pp. 269-270). It did however forbid marriages in which the bride did not agree to the union (Greif 2005, pp. 2-3). Brides rarely dared to do refuse.

In Eastern Europe, things were different often specific to the region where the status of women was concerned. In the Byzantine Empire, the Bulgarian Empire and Kievan Rus, most women were educated and had a higher social status than their counterparts in Western Europe (Levin 1995, pp. 96-98). There was equality in family relations and the right to family property for both sexes, recognised by law with the Ekloga issued in 726 from Constantinople and the Slavonic Ekloga in Bulgaria in the 9th century (Levin 1995, pp. 137, 142). In some parts of Russia, the average age for girls to be married was between 12 to 15 (Levin 1995,) and the traditional Slavic patrilocal customs (Levin 1995, pp. 225-227) led to a more inferior status for women (Mackenzie, G. Muir pp. 128). In some South Slavic rural areas, women married much younger men than themselves. This continued into the 19th century (Mackenzie, G. Muir pp. 128). The manorial system did not reach Eastern Europe and this had a lesser effect on clan system and cross-cousin marriages (Mitterauer 2010, pp. 45-

48, 77). Orthodox laws banned marriage between relatives closer than third or fourth cousins (Levin 1995, pp. 137-139).

The Bandraoi or Bandruí (female druids)

Druid is an Indo-European term from the root *deru* meaning truth or true. The position of a druid was a very honoured one in Celtic society. They were the intellectual elite. The druids were the religious leaders of the Celtic people in ancient times. They were responsible for organizing worship and sacrifices, divination, the judicial process and they were exempt from military service. They were the philosophers, scientists, theologians and holders of sacred knowledge in their culture. They were healers and planners of military strategy. They were active in negotiating treaties and wars. They mediated quarrels and participated in assemblies. Extensive training was required to become a druid and the training period took 19 years! Pomponius Mela (45 AD) Roman writer and geographer had written that virgin priestesses who could predict the future lived on the island of Sena, in Brittany (ed. Chisholm Hugh 1911).

Julius Caesar was fascinated by them and wrote about their extraordinary status and their knowledge of philosophy and theology. Most Roman writers ignored them, unfortunately. Strabo wrote about a group of druidesses who lived on an island by the River Loir. In the *Historia by Symmachus* (425, in the book by Matthew pp. 58-99) there is a description of the problems faced by Diocletian, Alexander Severus and Aurelian, from the female druids. Tacitus also mentions the slaughter of the female druids by the Romans under Suetonius on the island of Mona in Wales. The unarmed druids defended the island black-robed all unarmed, with curses as weapons were forbidden on Mona during this festival and were all slaughtered. Suetonius planned it thus. All were slaughtered. There was no distinction between the male and female druids, in fact according to Tacitus the female druids were very powerful. Cassius Dio mentioned a famous Druidess named Ganna who went to Rome on an official trip and was received by Domitian, son of Vespasian. At the Battle of Moytura, between the Tuatha Dé Danann and the Fir Bolg over the sovereignty of Ireland, druidesses played a large part. Another famous druidess was Fedelma who was in the court of Queen Medb of Connacht in 10th century Ireland. Then of course there was Boudicca the most famous of all druidesses. Rome killed a great many druids and the Catholic Church years later, burned many as witches and sorcerers in league with the devil. Saint Patrick burned more than a hundred Druid books and destroyed many places where the druids had flourished. He, like the Catholic Church feared druidic influence. The Catholic Church was completely male dominated and would not allow any power to women. In fact, one woman, Pope Joan (Ioannes Anglicus, 855–857, see above) outwitted everyone in the Vatican and reigned for two years as Pope in the Medieval Ages. She was finally found out and killed.

There is a misconception that druids were only males. Most of the Romans and Greeks who wrote about Celtic society may not have taken note of women in power, since the Romans and Greeks had a patriarchal culture and could not countenance the power of womanhood. This misconception continued into the 17th and 18th centuries when the Druid Reformation took place. The founders of this movement had a Romantic view of the druids and not very much historical evidence to work with. The Druid orders that were founded during these years were for men and men only.

In Celtic myth itself, there are many mentions of females being involved in druidry, as well as other magical and religious functions. The information below details female druids in myth and was taken from *"The Female Druid"* on *Druidcircle.org*:

- In the story of Fingen Mac Luchta of Munster, Fingen would visit a Druidess every Samhain who would foretell the events of the coming year.
- The Second Battle of Moytura mentions two Druidesses who promise to enchant the rocks and trees *"so they become a host and rout"* their enemies.
- Prior to the famous Cattle Raid of Cooley, Mebd the Queen of Connacht, consults a Druidess named Fidelma who predicts the outcome of the coming battle with the Ulstermen. *"How seest thou our host?"* asked Medb. *"I see the host all becrimsoned..."* replied Fidelma.
- The most famous of all was Boudicca. Her mother too was a banduri or druidess. Boudicca led a mighty uprising against Rome at the height of its power. Some people dispute Boudicca was a druidess. But she trained as one.

- Dio Cassius mentions a Druidess named Ganna who went on an embassy to Rome and was received by Domitian, younger son of the Emperor Vespasian.
- Pomponius Mela in De Chorographica speaks concerning nine virgin "priestesses" who lived on the island of Sena, in Brittany, who *knew the future.*
- *The Historia Augusta (The Scriptores historiae Augustae* (LCL 139-140, 263) which was written in about 400 A.D. by Aelius Lampridius mentions a Druidess foretelling the defeat of Alexander Severus. *Go forth but hope not for victory, nor put your trust in your warriors.*
- Then of course, there are the keepers of the eternal flame at Kildare, which was for a long time a pagan temple dedicated to the Goddess Brighid. The flame was tended by Druidesses and later by Christian nuns, in honor of Saint Bride.

In the modern practice of druidry today, there are a good number of women involved. Men too are represented in their ranks.

In all olden religions, women played a vital role in all aspects of religions. The earth Gaia was mother earth, women ruled the fates as they wove the lives and deaths of mortals, goddesses were as powerful if not more so than gods. No man dared to insult or slight a goddess with impunity. This was true of all religions around the world. Besides the goddesses, holy shrines and oracles were tended by women priestesses to whom, all, from the king to the lowliest man owed homage. They were not to be trifled with in any way.

Following are some examples of female role in Greek society:

In general, most Greek women could occasionally have a say in politics and only through personal wealth. In case of divorce the husband retained all the communal property though the dowry was returned to the wife. Husbands were legally allowed to have concubines and prostitution was legal. Many slave girls took to prostitution in order to buy their freedom faster. Upper class Greek women got some education. Others did not. There were women poets like Erinna (218 BC); Aristodama (Smyrnian woman granted Aetolian citizenship); Sappho (630-570 BC). Stoics and all dominant philosophical schools of thought excluded women totally. They only emphasised women's traditional sex roles. However, the Epicureans and Cynics admitted women into their society. One named Hipparchia taught publicly with her husband (Malherbe, 1977, pp. 54-55, 78-83, 94-95, 172-175, 282-285).

Sparta

The status of women in Sparta was quite different to that of most other Greek city states like Athens or Corinth. In comparison, Spartan women had a lot of freedom and equality not just among the Greek city states but in the ancient world.

- Spartan women had social equality, financial freedom, power and influence.
- Spartan women owned 40% of the land and exercised great political and economic power (1st century AD).

- Girls participated in sports same as the boys.
- All were equally educated and taught the use of arms and warfare.
- Both also received spiritual training (*Plato and Protagoras*).
- Women were encouraged to have strong opinions and speak their minds freely, even when they did not agree with their husbands. However, they did not participate in elections. Still, they had a lot of freedom. In many ways they were even more emancipated than modern-day women.
- When in other city states the birth of a girl child was not always welcome and many were exposed, in Sparta this was not the case. As long as the child was healthy, they got the same care as boy children.
- Again unlike others, Spartan girls were neither pushed nor forced to marry. One reason for this may have been to avoid psychological and physical scarring of the girls by early pregnancy and childbirth. They were expected to want to marry at the time it suited them. Force in the marriage bed was not an option. A very modern view. Spartan women unlike others again, were never forced to marry much older men. The age difference between the two was usually about 4-5 years. This was to enable them to have strong, healthy babies.
- There was no marital rape or wife beating allowed in Sparta
- When the Spartan men went to war, the women were left in charge of everything. They needed to be literate in order to do so. They were a very warlike

people and spent most of their lives at war or training for war. It was up to the women to run the household, businesses, finances and see to the welfare – schooling, training of the children and protecting the city in their husbands' absence. This gave them a lot of power.

- Spartan boys left home by the age of 7 for their martial training by the state. But as the old adage goes: *'Behind every great man, there is a woman'* it is equally true that behind every man is a strong woman. This is especially true of the Spartan women. They were the backbone of their warrior kingdom. It was a warrior society with a firm belief that strong women produced strong sons, so the health of both men and women were of equal importance.

- In 600 BCE Sparta conquered the southern half of the Peloponnese. These conquered people were called 'helots' and they were the agricultural backbone of the land and so the Spartans were left to train for war. This also made Sparta self-sufficient and not needing to import goods, they became quite isolated. They also feared uprisings by the helots. For this reason, Sparta became an armed state where men and women were equally trained for war and for women to keep the state safe in the absence of the men. The Spartan women also had much more autonomy than women in other Greek states.

- Infanticide was common in the ancient world, generally of female children. But in Sparta, all weak children were weeded out girls or boys. All healthy children were equally well-fed and well-cared for. It

was all a state decision. All received military training including wrestling, and horseback riding.
- Plutarch wrote that *the men of Sparta always obeyed their wives*. Aristotle (*Politics*) went further saying the influence women had in politics was too much and arguing that it contributed to the downfall of the state. Women did not have a vote in the assembly but had a lot of influence behind the scene. Plutarch says of Spartan women that they were strong and wealthy enough to refuse to bear too many children. He portrayed Spartan women as being heroic and proud.
- Sparta tried to do away with dowry and believed a strong, healthy woman was a better dowry than money and wealth. Women had the right to divorce their husbands and remarry.
- All property was state owned and so it was never a problem. All children irrespective of who the biological father was, was accepted fully.

When a warrior left for battle his mother would say, "Come home with your shield or upon it." They became known for their confidence, resilience, and assertiveness.

Athenian woman: *"Why are you Spartan women the only ones who rule over their husbands?"* **Queen Gorgo:** *"Because only we are the mothers of men"*. (Plutarch, Sayings of Spartan Women).

Women rulers were rare in Greek city states but some did have them like **Gorgo** of Sparta and **Aspasia** of Athens. Some won acclaim **Sappho** poetess of Lesbos, **Arete** of Cyrene philosopher, **Agnodice** of Athens, physician. Sparta gave a lot of freedom to the women and so, Aristotle claimed, the Spartan constitution should be rejected. But because women were such a harmonious part of society, Sparta became great, monopolized the sovereignty and was always considered the *City of Brave Men*.

Athens and other states

The status of women among the Greek city states differed. In Athens, the city where democracy began, albeit a very flawed democracy, the women had very few rights. They were excluded from education and political life. In the 6th **century Solon legalised prostitution thereby socially accepting a double standard.** Women were at the beck and call of the men, their fathers, brothers, husbands. Prostitutes and concubines were an integral part of their society. Women in this profession had a lot more freedom than any other women in Athens and many slave girls chose this life as a quick and easy way of buying their freedom. In many other Greek city states women's role in society was much **more equitable like in Sparta, Thessaly, Delphi, Crete, Gortyn and Megara**, as records show. They owned land, the most prestigious form of private property at that time. But not so in Athens, the city where democracy was born.

Scholars have debated whether the earliest social and religious structures were matriarchal. Matriarchy itself can take different forms: where men and women are equal or where men are subordinate to women, as among the

Amazons. But their records, epics, all show that at first goddesses predominated. Priestesses dominated the religious lives of the people. Things started to change from around 700 BC. Hesiod's *Theogony* shows how power started shifting to the male gods like Zeus who then established patriarchy among the gods and freedom to exploit goddesses and earthly women for their pleasure.

On the other hand, we have Homer's *Odyssey*. In the Trojan War (late Bronze Age) there were many strong and powerful female rulers in Greece. Like Helen, Clytemnestra, Penelope, Andromache, Aspasia, Gorgo of Sparta, Artemesia I, Anyte (poet and writer), and others. Inheritance was matrilineal — through the female. Helen's choice of Paris could not be challenged but her husband, Menelaus' right to the Spartan throne came through her. **That is why the Greeks went to war — not for love of Helen but for the throne of Sparta.** Agamemnon sacrificed his daughter, Iphigenia to appease the gods. His wife Clytemnestra could not forgive this betrayal. In his absence she took a second husband and killed Agamemnon on his return.

Still for Homer, sons were more valuable than daughters. And not just Homer, Mycenaean tablets report that food allotment for men at that time was two and a half times more than for a woman – pregnant or not. Most of the women's voices are silenced in the texts of the Trojan War from antiquity. This was because it was most probably so in reality. One example of this would be how Hector's wife Andromache's concerns were arbitrarily dismissed by Hector.

According to Homer, Hector says: *Go home*, and *attend* to *your* tasks, *the loom and spindle, and see the maids work hard. War* is a *man's concern, the business of* every man *in Ilium, and mine above all.* And so, she does as was expected of Late Bronze Age Aegean women. (Homer: The Iliad Bk VI: 440-493). Kassandra (Cassandra) the princess dedicated to Apollo's temple had the gift of prophecy but was fated by Apollo never to be believed. So when she warned against bringing the Trojan horse into the city or dire consequences would result, no one heeded her. And the Trojan horse was full of Greek soldiers who slaughtered Trojans all that night long when one of them opened the impregnable city gates to the Greek army. So fell great Troy. Not in battle but by betrayal.

In Plato's view, women in general were expected to obey men. In his *Republic (1X, 579)* he noted that the place of women was in the home. Aristotle had an even lower view. He said it was based on the law of nature that clearly showed men to be superior, able to think, philosophise, be virtuous. Women should only obey and be silent. Pericles (430 BC) went even further saying women should not be spoken about at all, but kept in the shadows, secluded and silent. **Greek thinkers did not have a high regard for women at all.** There was a saying in ancient Greece, attributed variously to Thales, Socrates and Plato, in which man thanked the gods that he was not uncivilized, a slave, or a woman (Diogenes Laertius I, 33). They should all be ashamed. They would not exist if not for a woman.

Prostitution was rife. Men married at around 30 years of age but they could not indulge in liaisons with daughters of citizens. So brothels flourished. It was also good in many instances for the women as many were slaves and in this way they could buy their freedom fast. Single men could move their favourites into homes as common law wives. Prostitutes also had much more freedom than other women. They were also financially independent. One group of working women called the *hetaerae* were well-educated, artistic escorts for males and attended parties and mixed with other men as their wives could not. On the down-side, children of these unions, no matter who the father was, were never considered Greek citizens. Many were aborted for this reason.

Laws differed in different parts of the Hellenic empire. Whereas in many Greek states, women's role was very restricted in others it was not so like Sparta, Crete and others. In **Hellenic Egypt,** women had the right to make contracts and wills and the obligation of taxation. Greek women required a male guardian in order to make a legal contract; Egyptian women did not. In Greece though women had the right to conduct business, make loans and manumit slaves, it was only with the approval of their male guardians.

As Hellenic influence spread, changes began in societies due to these interactions. Women started to exercise more power including in politics. Some women became competent in music, art, oratory, philosophy, poetry, medicine and craft. Class barriers started breaking down. Family institutions started weakening. Traditional sex roles began being challenged mainly because women had more economic power. Queens of some Greek states, of Syria and Egypt held real political power. E.g. Macedonian queen Olympias, Alexander's mother ruled Greece; Arsinoe II co-ruled with her Egyptian husband, Ptolemy II, Cleopatra VII ruled in her own right.

There were at least 9 very well-known female poets during that time, among them Corinne and Sappho. They were upper class women who had the leisure to write. **None of them lived in Athens.**

In Greece, women in religious positions were always honoured even publicly. The Ancient History Encyclopaedia says: *The priestesses of Greek religion enjoyed a great many perks that other Greek women did not.* Placating gods was important and society depended on the priestesses to do so. These women had property and commanded respect, often seen as role models and even famous. They were often consulted on important state matters and in a way equal to men. They did not pay tax, had bodyguards were given the best seats at competition and had many legal benefits. When they died, they were honoured with lavish funerals.

Greek priestesses could have children and sometimes were even expected to be married. When a cult expected the women to abstain from physical relations, they chose an older woman for the position.

The position of priestess could be inherited bought or won through election. It was a busy job. There were 170 festivals and priestesses were responsible for 85% of them. They sacrificed animals, led complicated prayers, and were responsible for holy vessels and relics. The Oracle at Delhi was interpreted by the most powerful priestess. Priestesses had a pretty good life. They were out of the control and sometimes the cruelty of men.

There were priests and priestesses in the cult of Dionysius and their celebrations were wild. But again, it was a political office and one of their women-priestess of Demeter was the one responsible for performing marriage ceremonies.

During the Hellenistic period many women converted to the mystery religions where women had a much more powerful role. The usual social and sexual roles were ignored. Foreigners were also accepted as were slaves. One such cult was the **Eleusian mystery cult** of the 4th century BC. Some women were married. Others lived in celibate communities of like-minded women. They wanted to free women from being just sex objects, and child bearers.

According to the Oxford Research Encyclopaedia, there were many festivals that men were totally banned from participating in. It was a time when all women could leave the house freely to participate in these festivals. The largest of these was the **Thesmophoria** festival. Men were expected by law to pay for their wives to attend. Unmarried girls could not attend. Then there was the fertility and agricultural rites where women took over the men's assembly hall. All men were forbidden to be there. This was a yearly festival and lasted for three days in Athens. Women at these rites elected their officials who would preside. It was the closest they could get to political life.

Women's festivals were shrouded in mystery. It was a time when they could let loose and speak as they wished. It always ended in a feast.

Minoan Crete

The power and presence of Minoan women was pervasive in society not just in the religious and social spheres. They were at the heart of the society. They were said to be brave, graceful, beautiful, intelligent fully deserving of respect and honour. The Cretans exemplified all this through their treatment of women. **A reason for this could be that the Cretan Minoan civilisation was about 1000 years older than that of other Greek city states and the matriarchal influence is thus more apparent.** This is also seen in their portrayal of the twelfth God in their system displayed in the Throne Room of Knossos. She is the Great Goddess who is superior to the male gods. This is the Sun goddess, the goddess of Fertility and Queen of the Pantheon.

In the games that all Greece is famous for, **the women played an equal role with the men,** though today most of us do not know that. Both boys and girls were bull dancers and their grace, beauty and courage are also depicted on the frescoes and wall paintings. A telling extract from: *In the palaces of Knossos* by Nikos Kazantzakis is: ... *Krinus, with the shaking of what the bull did, took turns and jumped softly like a feather on the back of the bull. She stood firmly on her* *hands and struck her feet twice in the air and suddenly she put all her power and she made air flip and fell behind the bull (Kazantzakis: In the palaces of Knossos).*

In Minoan Crete women held a different position to elsewhere in Greece. They were at the heart of the social and religious life. The women were depicted as brave, graceful and gracious, beautiful and strong. They were proud and respected by all. They represented the culture of Crete. The Throne Room in the place of Knossos is both a secular and religious place. This is exemplified by the Great Goddess (secular aspect) and the Priest-King (religious aspect). The Great goddess is the one that rules all the gods in the pantheon, not the young male god. She is very powerful. She is the Goddess of the sun, of Fertility and Queen of all. Hers is the last word. She always sits on the throne while the male god stands by her side. Many researchers have suggested it is a mother-son combination and not a husband-wife as is usual.

The Cretans honoured the Mother Earth and the Sea by organising festivals and sorting activities, followed by feasts. The stars of the celebration were the omens and girls including the daughters of the king, like beautiful Ariadne and Faedra who danced with snakes beautifully and gracefully to show the connection to Mother Earth. The climax of the celebration was the Bull-dancing (*Tavrokathapsia*). It showed craft, skill and courage. It was a way to honour the bull, a sacred animal, Taurus while also expressing faith in and the ability of the young to perform on the bull. This was a very difficult and dangerous exercise. Both girls and boys participated. They ran to the bull grabbed it by the horns and vaulted on it through the air landing on the ground behind the animal. There are many frescoes at the palace of Knossos depicting the bull dancing.

For Cretans, power ultimately lay with women, who were the real rulers. According to the **Law Code of Gortyna, Crete,** women had the right to own, control and inherit property. A certain percentage of what she produced through her work belonged to her. In divorce a woman retained half the property. In Athens, it went to her family.

Women were also stars at the festivals to honour mother earth where the king's daughters like the beautiful Ariadne and Faedra (daughters of King Minos) danced not only with snakes underlining their closeness with nature but also with the bull at the climax of the festival (*Tavrokathapsia*). This was a great honour reserved for the best and bravest. The bull was a sacred animal to them.

Ancient **Cretan** paintings always show women priestesses in ornate robes in sacred groves as part of the religious cult. They are surrounded by female dancers. If there are men, they are dressed similarly. **Male oracles or priests were extremely rare**. But from the time Zeus became the chief god, men tried to cut out or exclude women from all religious rites. Even in the rites of the female goddess, men tried to dominate. For example, **the oracle at Delphi,** dedicated to Apollo was a woman priest always called Pythia who gave the oracle but it was now interpreted by a **male priest** who acted on his political perceptions to answer the questions from this point on.

An exception was the oracle of Athena. It was always a woman. It was an influential and political post and it was hereditary. It was a noble woman of the same family who became the priestess on the demise of the old one.

Roman Empire

Rome produced many unforgettable women of strength. Some were wise and faithful wives. Some were ruthless, ambitious women. Many factors played into their roles. What was important was her **marital status:** married; to whom; unmarried; a born Roman citizen or a foreigner; from which family; who was her father; free or a slave, the time she lived in. If it was the Archaic Age, things would have been extremely hard, father's control to husband's control. And extremely important also was her education, character and desires.

In general, Roman women were relatively better off than in many Greek city states. They could even participate with their husbands at banquets and ceremonies, unlike the Greek women of the same time. During **Emperor Hadrian's rule** they had even more freedom – they could refuse the man chosen for them, draw up their own will stipulating their own terms and conditions, which shows that they had at least some education. Plutarch says women could also give funeral orations and eulogies as that was not gender-based.

But fertility in women was a very important issue. If they could not produce children they could easily be cast aside, discarded. Still all women were expected to have certain qualities and characteristics like morality, frugality, and dignity that were highly praised and encouraged in women, as they were the first teachers of all young Romans.

Though women had more freedom, they seldom wielded outright power. That belonged to the male domain. **It was a macho society.** They could not become the Caesar, but they could rule in the name of their husband or son as many women did or advise the ruler behind the scenes. Some were virtuous women and some had their competitors for power ruthlessly assassinated. Though they were very different in the way they wielded power what united them was they were living in a man's world where they faced many injustices including social, moral and legal ones. But these women had the strength to overcome the limitations imposed on them and achieve their ends — good or bad. They demonstrated what one can do, if they have the will to do so. They achieved fame or infamy depending on how you look at it, in a world that did not value them, regarded them as inferior. They shaped history through their political strategy, romantic liaisons, grit, determination and champions of their husbands or sons and most important of all how much power they could wield behind the scenes.

Note: People are much influenced by their upbringing no matter their education or cultural exposure. Often, we carry with us the initial attitudes we perceive and learn in our childhood. And these come through in our interactions, governance, traditions, philosophies, laws and in our writings for posterity.

Three such examples are the following:

Philo: a Hellenistic, Jewish philosopher, much influenced by his culture and traditions, living in 1st century Alexandria where women were highly honoured, resisted the influence of his environment and continued to see women as inferior and evil (*Hypothetica* 11, 14-17); their place belonged in seclusion and subordination to men, to be ruled by the father, husband or brother (*Flaccus, 89; De Spec.leg 111, 169-171*) because he believed that women were controlled by sensual desires whereas the men were controlled by reason (*De opif. mund.* 165, *Leg.all.* 38-39). Physical desire or sex was evil (*De spec. leg.* III 113). Contact between the spiritual and material was evil (*De opif. mund.165, Leg.all. 38-39*). Males/men he considered spiritual and female/women as sensual and contact between them should be avoided as much as possible. However, he believed women should have some education.

All extant works of Philo the 1st century Alexandrine philosopher was preserved by Greek priests, some only survive in Armenian. These titles: *Apologia pro Judaeis Hypothetica: Apology for the Jews; Flaccum: Flaccus* –Jewish persecution under Caligula *and De specialibus legibus: The Special Laws I, II, III, IV; De opificio mundi: On the creation and legum allegoriae: Allegorical Interpretation I, II, III)* quoted above are the Latin and English translations as used in reference works.

Josephus is the other example of the same phenomenon. He was a Jewish Palestinian historian who spent part of his later life in Rome. As a Jew, he accepted the inferiority of women but living in the Roman Empire at that time, he came across many influential women, some of whom he described in his historical works (*Antiquities VII 11, 8, XI 3, 5, War I 5, 1* (Queen Alexandra), *VII 9, 2* (Masada). He acknowledged the natural resentment of Alexandra, Queen Mother of Mariamne the Hasmonean, who was engaged to Herod's son, found her movements strictly restricted by Herod. Still he reiterated in his works the subservient position of women, their segregation from religious worship, the nullity of them as witnesses and other such rules. Throughout his works, it is the Jewish traditions and beliefs that emerge. Women were inferior, evil and so they must be subservient to men. *The woman,* says the Law, *is in all things inferior to the man. Let her accordingly be submissive, not for her humiliation, but that she may be directed; for the authority has been given by God to the man* (Josephus, *Antiquities V 8, 15.11*).

Plutarch: Also, from the 1st century there are the works of Plutarch (*Bravery of Women*) that explains ancient Greek customs reflecting the same ambivalence towards women as do Plato's works. For example, there is the ideal woman who helps liberate her city state and then withdraws into seclusion, never participating in politics again, returning to her voicelessness, weaving and keeping to her household chores. In marriage, even if she contributes the larger portion of the estate, the entire state then belongs to her husband. Wives are only meant to be seen in the company of their husbands, or they are to remain secluded and silent. Unlike Thucydides, he believed women should have some grounding in Philosophy, literature, geometry and astronomy but they should be taught these by their husbands only. This should make for a more fulfilling life discussing such topics together. And in case of arguments and disagreements, husbands are prompted to use reason and not force to convince their wives. They should share mealtimes, according to Plutarch.

In Plutarch's works there is also a reference to female prophetesses and poets, pointing out that there was literacy among married women and sometimes they also had political acumen, and played a role in politics, which he praised. Most of the women in his book do not belong to Athens but from all over Greece where women had more freedom than in Athens. He may also have been influenced by the Roman and Hellenic society of his own times.

Rome:

In ancient Rome the official state cult was that of Vesta – goddess of the hearth, family life, its continuity and that of the state, and domesticity. But the strange thing is the head of this **cult of women – the Vestal virgins, was called <u>Pontifex Maximus</u>** – a male, and females could never attain that position. The females were always excluded from the highest religious offices in Rome.

The job of the vestal virgins was to tend the fire of the sacred hearth of the state. They had to be virgins and stay that way. Any mistake led to public flogging or being buried alive.

There were six vestal virgins and all had to be from noble patrician families since the time of Augustus Caesar. They all had to be Roman. They were chosen from a group of 20 and had to serve for 30 years. Then they were free to marry. However, most vestal virgins preferred to continue, especially as their authority increased with seniority. Also, these women were independent of paternal control. They got a share of property on induction. Their roles were highly public affairs as they rode through the city, attended banquets and theatres as important guests and were entrusted with important political documents and wills. They even influenced some emperors but their authority only came from the male pontiff.

The flaminica was the wife of the flamen dialis and a priestess of Juno. When she died, he lost his position. When empresses were elevated to divinity, priestesses were chosen to tend their shrines. But there were also male cults like those of Mithras and Hercules where only men were admitted. There were many cults for many purposes in Rome.

Rome imported Greek priestesses to take responsibility for the **cult of Ceres**. It was an all-female cult. Men were not admitted nor were women of a lower class. These women were granted Roman citizenship. Rome also had the cult of Isis which had 26 sacredotes (priests), 6 of them were women. All classes were accepted. This cult was regarded revolutionary by the Romans and was suppressed a number of times.

In Rome, female influence even in religion was controlled by the men in order to reinforce the subordinate position of women. Breaches of conduct were very harshly punished often leading to horrendous deaths.

Celts:

Ancient Celtic society was matrilineal and women in that society *were highly honoured, female symbolism formed the most sacred images in the religious cosmos, and the relationship with motherhood was the central element of the social fabric, the society was held together by common allegiance to the customs of the tribe loosely organised around the traditions of goddess* (Condren, 1989).

Celts were a polytheistic people. They had many deities, female and male. Some were worshipped only in small communities and some over a much wider area. Some deities were referred to by different names in different places. Over

200 deities who were venerated have survived, that we are aware of (Cunliffe, B, 1997 pp. 187).

Celts were a society of warriors. War was a natural way of life and as they mixed with other societies they took their beliefs to them. Goddess worship spread. On the eve of battle druids — male and female performed rituals and ceremonies for the success in battle. Offerings were also made to the war goddess. After a successful battle some of the best warriors were chosen to wed the goddess of the land before they could claim dominance over the conquered land.

First the Romans eroded Celtic deities and then the Church destroyed them, but they had been immortalised in the myths and legends by the bards and so live on till today in works like the Mabinogion (including stories of Cerriwidwen, Arianrhod, Rhiannon) and the Tales of the Ulster Cycles. Today we still know who Morrigan, Badb, Catha, Eostre, Macha and others were. Their heroes and heroines also live on like Boudicca, Rhiannon, Cú Cuchlain and so on. Tradition dies hard. Some goddesses changed to fit in in Christianity like Brigd who became the Catholic Saint Brigid and Epona the Celtic Horse goddess was adopted by the Romans.

Recently there has been a revival of druidism and pagan movements in Europe including the Wicca movement.

Women and religion in pre monotheism

Pre monotheism women not only played the traditional modern roles of wives, mothers, and homemakers, but at the same time they were also property owners, defended their homes, went hunting, were trained in the arts of combat (warriors), went on raiding parties, led armies, ruled nations and traded goods in their own right. They had at least equal social, economic and religious standing as the men. More often they were the goddesses and worshipped and revered by all. Both contributed to the welfare of the society equally. Women were very important but they did not dominate the men as it happens conversely today. With post-monotheism the imbalance in society led to an imbalance in the natural order of things, in my opinion. No one is using their potential to the full. When men relegated women to a lower status, they did themselves harm thinking it was showing their power and dominance. It was the opposite: it showed up a lot of their weaknesses because the two, men and women are two halves. Together they make a whole. They fulfil each other. In modern society, some of us have realised that but we still have a long way to go to become true equals.

In the ancient origins of civilisations, women played very important roles. Female figurines were the deities people worshipped: they were the creators, the givers of life and abundance for millennia, long, long before organised religions. The oldest civilisations venerated woman as the supreme creator.

Once humans started living together and religion began playing a part, the role of women had been an important one. In ancient and matriarchal societies, it was a very important role. The first deity to be worshipped was the Great Goddess the Mother Earth, Gaia. In the rituals of birth and death too, women always played a major role. However, with the appearance of patriarchal societies the male gods in ancient religions started abrogating power, female power started dwindling. Then with the appearance of organised religion, women began being pushed to the background, to a minor, even servile, position and in many ways even excluded from religious rituals. Organised religion gave it the coup de grâce. We will only consider a few of the well-known religions and the place of women in them. Most organised religions have used religion to empower patriarchy and the status of men over women. Religion is often portrayed using religious doctrines with a strong gender bias.

To the Abrahamic religions belong Judaism the oldest monotheistic religion, followed by Christianity and finally Islam. All three are strongly patriarchal religions. They will be discussed in more detail later.

Monotheism: changing role of women

Monotheism began with the Abrahamic faiths, beginning with Judaism and the teachings of Moses, its first Prophet. According to both the Bible and the Quran, Moses was the leader of the Israelites and lawgiver to whom the authorship, or "acquisition from heaven," of the Torah (the first five books of the Bible) is attributed. Judaism, the first monotheistic religion originated in the Bronze Age among the polytheistic, ancient, Semitic religions most specifically the Canaanite religion then co-existing with the Babylonian religion and the syncretizing or harmonising of elements at that time with the worship of Yahweh as it appeared in the early prophetic Hebrew Bible. This broke away and evolved into the worship of Yahweh, one Canaanite god while suppressing all the others. It became a strict monotheistic religion excluding all other gods. They had very strict guidelines for moderating all aspects of life especially as it regarded women. In monotheistic Judea where religion was concerned, women were expected to know the basics and their place in it. Women were cut off from participating in the priesthood and most religious ceremonies and even in mainstream life.

Judaism

The role of women in Judaism is based on the Hebrew Bible, the Oral Law (corpus of rabbinic literature) by custom and by cultural norms. Little had changed over time and a lot now changed. My question is what caused Moses to take the leap from a matriarchal, polytheistic religion to a very exclusive, male dominated religion that had no previous history to fall back upon? And where one strata of society was totally disenfranchised. Different female role models are mentioned in the Hebrew Bible and women are treated differently under different circumstances. The Old Testament presents us with two views about creation and man's place in it. Genesis 2 describes how man (Adam) was created from dust and a little later, almost as an afterthought, woman (Eve) was created from Adam's body. Then in Chapter 3 we learn about The Fall and Eve's part in it, Adam is held blameless. The subordinate position of woman is set and her sinful, evil nature. But one overlooked point is: if Eve was created from Adam's body, **she had no means of being anything that did not come from Adam.** So where did the evil in women come from? Only Yahweh and Adam were involved.

The other presentation came about several centuries later. In the story of Genesis, it is written that Adam and Eve, man and woman were created at the same time and both were fashioned in the image of the creator. But who had seen the Creator to know the image? Both are blessed and commissioned to fill the earth and rule over it by Gods decree. How do you fill the earth with children without physically procreating and procreation is considered 'original' sin? Which view is man to follow? So are we to sin to fulfil God's commands? Or were they to have abstained from procreation and let the human race die out? Judaism like other Abrahamic religions is a misogynistic religion. Now, most religions are misogynistic. From the start of monotheism, women were held to be the property of men and **all God's addresses were only to men. Why? Why not to both?** Yet men are ordered to honour both parents **and as a crumb,** to allow women to rest on the Sabbath.

The primary role of women was always unquestionably, in Judaic culture, that of wife, mother, child-bearer and keeper of the household. This was and is the most important role for women. There is a saying in the Talmud that when a pious man marries a wicked woman, the man becomes wicked, but when a wicked man marries a pious woman, the man becomes pious. So it appears that men are weak and cannot think for themselves but follow women's lead. If that is the case, why are women subordinated to men who are so easily swayed??? The family unit has been and is the nucleus of the Jewish community. In Traditional Judaism, being Jewish, Jewishness is passed down through the mother though children are identified through the father like Dinah daughter of Jacob in the Torah.

Very few women are mentioned in the Jewish Bible compared to men. They are generally mentioned if they played a pivotal role in subverting some man-made power structure. Some of them are regarded today as feminists. Some of these women are: matriarchs Sarah, Rebecca, Rachel and Leah, Miriam, and Huldah, the prophetesses; Deborah, the Judge; Abigail, who married David and Rahab, and the Persian, Jewish Queen Esther.

In **Biblical times** women had a lower status than men. Women could not divorce men but men could do so very easily. There were many practices that put women in inferior positions to men like that of chalitza. There are many gender differences, suggesting women were subordinate to men. Society prized the continuity of family unity and property most of all. Women were economically dependent on men and could not own property except if there was no son. But even in that case, she was constrained to marry within the tribe to keep the land within the tribe. The dice was loaded against women.

In **Talmudic times (70-640 CE)** women had more protection and men and women were treated almost equally in many ways. They were allowed to be educated for one thing and to continue to educate their children even if the husband died.

Again, very few women are mentioned by name except those having a positive influence on their husbands like Bruriah, Rachel, Yalta and Ima Shalom. The first three were all married to rabbis.

Some few women mentioned in the Old Testament who functioned in a religious capacity were: Miriam, Deborah, Huldah, the wife of Isaiah, and Noadiah. Women were also sages and did compose religious hymns. But they were totally excluded from being priests.

The Torah specified that women were impure during certain times of the month each year and after childbirth for 40 days for a male child and 80 days for a female in The Book of Leviticus. Any contact, even the slightest, rendered the man ritually unclean also. Women during this time could not prepare meals and anything they touched became unclean. They were not allowed to participate in anything at all. In synagogues women were never allowed to sit with men. They sat in a different part of the synagogue when they were allowed to attend. **But this contradicts the very laws of nature. If a woman is unclean during the monthly cycle, then no children should ever be born as the cycle sets conception in motion, and without conception there is no childbirth.**

In the **Middle Ages** it was believed three factors affected how women were perceived: the biblical and Talmudic heritage, Jewish women living within a non-Jewish society, their economic situation in it and finally women's role in supporting the family. There was a conflict between the expectations of their religion and the reality of the society they lived in. It was similar in many ways to that of other women there too. Jewish women prayed separately from the men because it was believed they would be a distraction to men. Are Jewish men that weak? They were allowed to learn the Torah. Around the 13th century they still sat separately. They were not allowed to officiate or become rabbis. They were totally excluded from any religious office.

All in all, according to the Old Testament, women were considered the property of men: before marriage of her father, then of her husband, as a widow of her brothers-in-law, sons and sons-in-law. Polygamy was common as women were regarded as spoils of war. She **had to** be a virgin when she was first married.

In the Ten Commandments the exhortation that Moses received from God: *You shall not covet your neighbour's wife*, or his male or female servant, his ox or donkey, or anything that belongs to *your neighbour* (The Book of Exodus 20:17) and in the Bible (Book of Deuteronomy) it is clear this is addressed to men, **that women are no better than possessions** — same level as a donkey or ox.

Women who produced sons were respected while women who could not have children for 10 years were regarded as sterile and could be easily divorced. Sarah and Rebecca were especially revered as the mothers of Israel for the many children they had. With time Hebrew women led a harem-like existence, confined to the home. Restrictions increased with time and penalties for transgressing were added. The patriarch ruled the house and the tribe or clan. Inheritance passed from father to son. Women were still not allowed to divorce. Women who bore male children did achieve some social status. Some were even leaders like Deborah who led the people of Israel as judge and as military commander against the Canaanites; Queen Athaliah who ruled the southern kingdom for six years after the death of her son, Ahaziah and a late Hellenistic book that presents a literary portrait of another Hebrew queen, Esther, in legendary Persia.

Judaism had to preserve all its values against the encroaching Hellenistic thoughts that had spread world-wide through the Roman Empire and its overseas acquisitions. This led to them becoming even stricter in their observances. Women became objects of evil, temptresses and the only contact with them should be for procreation which too, was an unclean act being the outcome of the monthly cycle. Foreign women were the worst and would lead man down the path of damnation. Society became even more misogynistic. Divorce of sterile women became compulsory. Male children were preferred to female and men gave thanks in the synagogue for being born males.

Women were strictly confined to the home, had to cover their heads before the males in the family, could not participate in family meals, or when guests came. They were not allowed to be educated, conversation between males and females became very restricted, they could not testify in court. They were supposed to be silent most of the time. Their position was truly difficult, terrible. In short it was worse than in olden times, worse than ever before or after.

However, attitudes towards women differed in different sects. The Essenes were a celibate community and women had no place whatsoever in their community. They lived in the wilderness. John, The Baptist, was an Essene.

The Jewish diaspora, conversely had more contact with the Hellenistic and Roman worlds. The Jewish women in Upper Egypt could own property, participate in business ventures and even initiate divorce. They were also taxed and could be called up for military service. The Essenes in Egypt were also less strict than those in Palestine. This was in consequence to the high position that women held in Egypt.

Rabbinic literature too, expressed a very misogynistic attitude towards women. They were generally painted as evil-temptresses, witches, nymphomaniacs, and also as lazy, greedy, vain and frivolous – to allow men to control women and their activities. It was a monogamous world but polygamy was allowed only to the men, divorce was compulsory if a woman could not bear a child within 10 years and male children were infinitely more valuable and preferred to female children.

Modern Judaism

In Orthodox Judaism male and female roles are clearly defined. According to the Torah women were only expected to have a general understanding of practical aspects, relevant to running a household. They were not permitted to participate in many aspects of life, like in religion, social gatherings, education and so on as explained earlier.

But change was in the offing. The world was shrinking due to technological advancements like the printing press, radio and so on and information was much more easily accessed. Women's movements around the world also had a strong effect a little later but now the Jewish women came to know much more about the roles women were playing in the world. They were no longer circumscribed within a small circle. This did not sit well with the Rabbis who tried hard to discourage women.

Jewish women had to follow a very strict code of dress: heads had to be covered before all men; they were allowed to wear skirts but not trousers as that was considered very immodest. Women were cut off from all contact during their periods and after childbirth. Jewish women still did not sit with the men in the synagogue but were divided by a large space so that men could concentrate on the service and not get led astray by the presence of women.

In the early modern period, there were Jews scattered world-wide like in Italy, Poland, UK, Lithuania, Ottoman Empire, US and many other European countries. Where they lived affected their way of life too. Women became educated and published writers; they became butchers which they were not allowed to do previously. But this was allowed only to women qualified to do so and in order to supply food for the family. Women also acted on their husband's behalf as agents, moneylenders, manufactures of cosmetics and other such things. But this was done privately. Women in business, was still a controversial topic.

They were still not allowed to worship alongside their husbands and could not read the Torah. But translations began and women were able to get their hands on them. They started demanding a voice.

Some women were educated, though it still was not a general thing. These educated women became teachers, went into healing, midwifery and teaching Hebrew to the new generations. Once the girls became teenagers, around 14 years, their fathers arranged their marriages. Men married when they were 24 or over. Finances were an important part of the marriage agreement. The girl brought a dowry and the man vouched for the sum of money she would get if it ended in a divorce.

To conclude, this section, in Greece, Rome, Judea and part of the Mediterranean world the position of women in the first century, though it differed from culture to culture still was that of a subordinate. There was little equality in these places- some a little more (Greek and Roman worlds), some none (Judea). Egypt was different and women had a lot of freedom and rights in politics, economic and religion. But Judea under

Roman occupation could not completely ignore the secular culture. They had to react negatively or positively. And so they did. It was more negative than positive to begin with but change came as it must – always.

Into this highly charged, complex, traditional, syncretistic world, Christianity was born. The voices of the women in these worlds had been silenced. Their achievements and contributions were rarely recorded. In the writings of the times women's roles were glossed over, or even overlooked. Only a few managed to be heard in the Mediterranean areas except Egypt. On the other hand, **women** in many cultures like the Celtic, Germanic, Slavic, Mongolian and in many Asian countries like China, Japan, the Middle-East and others women had a lot of freedom and also led armies into wars very successfully. In reality the women were neither subordinate nor silent as many women demonstrated. It was only in some societies and even there, women had started to question and demand their rights. They challenged the norm and a lot of these challenges took place in the social setting in which the New Testament (written much later) was formulated.

Christianity

Christianity developed as a sect /branch of Judaism. Jesus was a Jew before he founded Christianity in the 1st century AD. The early Christian men therefore, had been brought up in the Judaic faith, values and beliefs in which women took a subservient place as portrayed in the Hebrew Bible (Old

Testament). The Book of Genesis begins with the story of creation and Eve's position is apparent.

It is widely established that the role of women in the establishment of early Christianity was vital and the women who figured most of all were: Mary, mother of Jesus, Mary Magdalene, Mary of Bethany and her sister Martha. The women's roles were more assured and stable until the third century AD and the publication of the New Testament. Mary Magdalene is especially important and has been brutally demeaned by Church history. She was pivotal to the spread of Christianity, Jesus' closest disciple, the first who saw the resurrection and took the news to all other disciples; the first woman to give up all and follow Jesus and yet she has been and still is, in many quarters, in Western Christianity, infamous, a harlot, a sinner, repentant but a sinner still. Stories about her abound. I believe an important reason for this was her strength in breaking the mould, in challenging established norms to follow Jesus into the desert. Karen King (Prof. of New Testament Studies & the History of Ancient Christianity at Harvard University in the Divinity School) discovered new texts in Egypt and with sharper insights have now proven that Mary Magdalene's portrait has been vastly, inaccurately portrayed. That in fact, she was a prominent disciple and leader of a wing of the very early Christians and that she had promoted women's involvement and leadership. She also says new evidence found in the neglected texts show that many other women besides the three Marys and Martha named above contributed towards the establishment of Christianity in the earliest years. Some of the other women were Joanna and Susanna who also accompanied Jesus and supported him during his ministry financially (**Luke 8:1-3**). Jesus talked publicly and privately to women and even took their advice (**Mark 7:24-30; Matthew 15: 21-28**). A Jewish woman honoured him by washing his feet with perfume. Jesus frequently had meals with Mary and Martha and taught there. Women were among his earliest and staunchest followers.

After his crucifixion, at first women continued to play a prominent role, attested to by Paul's letters in mid 1 AD, in his greetings to many women, Jewish and Gentile (**Romans: 16:3, 6, 12, 15, and Philippians 4:2-3**). It is apparent women did missionary work establishing Christ's message.

Paul's letters are also an important source for the workings of the early church. Most adherents did not meet in churches but in designated homes possibly because it was a forbidden religion by the Romans who ruled Judea and also due to the expenses. Homes were women's domain and without their active participation such meetings would never have been possible. Women did take the leadership roles attested in **Philemon: 2** (Apphia); **1Corinthians 16:19**, (Prisca); **Acts 16:15**, (Thaytira), **Colossians 4;25**, (Nympha and Laodicea, the deacon Phoebe) **Romans 16:1**, (Euodia and Syntyche) **Romans 16.6, 12** and many others. These women taught, preached and led prayers, offered the Eucharist. These, according to the **Didache**, were the duties of Christian prophets.

The most prominent among the women was Mary Magdalene even in the second century. References to her is scattered throughout the bible. She was Jesus' most unwavering convert and was there with him throughout, even in the desert. She is mentioned, among other chapters, in **the Acts, Luke, Mark, Matthew, John, Gospel of Peter** and even has a gospel of her own: the **Gospel of Mary**. Mary has a vision and tells it to others. Levi writes it down confirms and concludes: that indeed the Saviour loved her more than the rest of the disciples (18.14-15). While her teachings do not go unchallenged, in the end the Gospel of Mary affirms both the truth of her teachings and her authority to teach the male disciples. She is portrayed as a prophetic visionary and as a leader among the disciples (Karen King).

Jesus though born a Jew gave women a lot of power and equality with men. But women's prominence was challenged and questioned at every point. Society at that time was strongly patriarchal and misogynistic. Finally ancient Christianity ruled women's leadership was heretical and all evidence was to be erased and suppressed. So, many oracles, works, collections were destroyed. Texts were changed, at least one woman was turned into a man. In Paul's Epistle in Romans 16:7, she is called Junia and her husband Andronicus. Junia, a female apostle became Junias, a man.

Mary Magdalene

Sometimes the stories were rewritten. From the 4th century Mary Magdalene, one of Jesus' closest apostles, became the sinner who anointed Christ's feet (**Luke 7:36).** Mary of Bethany **in John 12:1-8** did that, not the Magdalene. This set the stage to paint Mary Magdalene as black as possible, to destroy the perception of her purity, strength, belief in Christ and support of him. She was a woman and could not be allowed such high standing. This fiction, says Karen King, was invented at least in part to undermine her influence and with it the appeal to her apostolic authority to support women in roles of leadership.

With the discovery of the discarded texts, a new picture is presented not the one-sided version we have always read. The rediscovered **Gospel of Mary** shows that leadership was supposed to be based on spiritual maturity, not on gender, whereas in **1 Timothy** women's salvation lay only in bearing children, their voices were to be silenced. Leadership positions were not for them.

This silencing of women and curtailing their participation damaged them greatly. They were no longer allowed to hold any position within the church hierarchy. They still continued to contribute but they were reduced to be subservient to men and their views. This worsened in the Middle-Ages and only in recent times are Christian women finding their voices again.

Other Christian women

There are many, many women who contributed to the spread of Christianity and some few of them in literature are the following: There was **Thecla** a virgin Martyr converted by Paul who became a missionary. She was threatened with rape and twice put in the ring as a martyr but she persisted in her faith. In the **Chapter on the prophets** there are numerous references to women leaders – **Mary Magdalene, The Corinthian Women**, Philip's **daughter Ammia of Philadelphia, Philumene,** the visionary martyr, **Perpetua, Maximilla, Priscilla (Prisca), and Quintilla.** The last two inspired a Christian movement in Asia Minor (the new Prophecy) in the 2nd century that lasted for four centuries. In the **African Church** there was a woman prophet, said Father Tertullian in his congregation who had visions, served as a counsellor and healer. Another unnamed woman in **Egypt** spoke in the first person as the feminine voice of God (*Thunder, Perfect Mind a gnostic manuscrip*t). These papers were discovered in **1945**. Around that time women were ordained as presbyters and bishops (**Montanists**). In the third century African Bishop Cyprian tells about a woman prophet in Asia Minor who celebrated the Eucharist, performed baptisms. Second century Roman Governor Pliny tells about two slave women he tortured who were in fact deacons (**Letters to Trajan 10:96**) Women were also ordained in Italy and Sicily in the 5th century. Many women died as martyrs, most famous being Perpetua who kept a diary while imprisoned by the Romans. There was great fellowship among the Christian women awaiting death at Roman hands. Threatened with physical violence, Perpetua relinquished her roles as mother, daughter and sister in favour of defining herself in spiritual terms.

Early Christian Women's Theology

This was based on the views of diverse women like the Gospel of Mary, theology of the Corinthian women prophets; the Montanist women's oracles, Thunder Perfect Mind, and Perpetua's Prison Diary. In brief they were:

- Jesus was primarily a teacher and mediator of wisdom rather than ruler and judge.
- Theological reflection was based on the risen Christ rather than the Crucified Saviour. This is also true of Perpetua's view. Instead of identifying with the suffering Christ, she encounters the risen Christ in her vision.
- Direct access to God is possible for all through receiving the Spirit.

- The unity, power, and perfection of the Spirit are present now, not just in some future time for all Christians.
- The spiritually advanced should share freely with all without claiming hierarchical power.
- Ethics of freedom and spiritual development is emphasized over ethics of order and control.
- A woman's identity and spirituality could be apart from her roles as wife and mother or slave. Gender is regarded as a "natural" category before the power of God's Spirit at work in the community and the world. This means that potentially women (and men) could exercise leadership on the basis of spiritual achievement apart from gender status and without conformity to established social gender roles.
- Overcoming social injustice and human suffering are seen to be integral to spiritual life.

From Women in Ancient Christianity: The New Discoveries by Karen L King

Women's Changing Roles

Women's roles in Christianity have changed through the passage of time much like that of the other Abrahamic religions. At the inception women had a much stronger voice and much more freedom to preach and much more leadership roles. With time that changed as male dominance in the Church grew stronger. Interpretation of the Bible became male-orientated. Organised church prohibited women from leadership roles, preaching and in participating actively in religious affairs in the Roman Catholic and Orthodox Churches. Only men could serve as priests, elders (bishops, deacons, presbyters); only celibate males could serve in senior leadership positions (Popes, Patriarchs, Cardinals). Women could only rise to the position of abbesses and consecrated virgins. But they served under male authority. Even the apostles, Peter and Paul who held women in high regard, tried to get them to follow the *Patria Poestas* (Rule of the Fathers). Patriarchal societies gave the males the authority in marriage, government, society. The New Testament records the names of the 12 Apostles of Christ, yet women were the first to see the resurrected Christ, the ones to house the meetings of the apostles and help Jesus in spreading the Word. In *Dialogue of the Saviour*, Mary's affirmations make it abundantly clear that Mary was to be counted among Jesus' disciples as she well understood, better than the others, Jesus' words and commands.

In Church practice again, it is male designation that is used – Pope (Papa) Abbot (abba) both meaning father. There is none designating mother anywhere. Women are excluded. It is an exclusive male-dominated church. Women, to signal their subordination to the male, had to attend church veiled and they had to be silent in Church.

In the **Apostolic Age**, women were important members of the movement and participated fully. They did a lot to spread the new faith. The Apostolic Age ended with the death of the last Apostle John in 1st century AD in Anatolia.

In the **Patriastic Age (1 to 8 AD)** around the 2nd century, however, women began being relegated to a subordinate position. It was at this time that Tertullian (155-220) 1st Christian author from Carthage, Africa: wrote: *"It is not permitted to a woman to speak in church. Neither may she teach, baptize, offer, nor claim for herself any function proper to a man, least of all the sacerdotal office."* Origen of Alexandria, (185-254 AD) concurred, saying: *Even if it is granted to a woman to show the sign of prophecy, she is nevertheless not permitted to speak in an assembly. For* (as Paul declared): *"I do not permit a woman to teach,"* and even less *"to tell a man what to do."*

The Eastern Church allowed more participation to women but all leading roles were for men only.

From the **Middle Age** (from the Fall of Rome 476 CE to 14th century) there was a marked change in women's involvement in religious affairs. The Church grew stronger as did patriarchy. Women became even more powerless. Yes there were now convents to escape to from the role of marriage to spend a life in prayer and meditation but no nun could rise to any position of power within the church. There were many individual Christian saints but their power did not extend over men nor in Church affairs. It was at this time that Joan of Arc was burnt as *a witch and heretic, three times in one day,* for daring to dress as a man and lead the French to **victory** over the English. True she was canonised centuries later in 1920.

It is true that there were many female monarchs from this time on but they all had to either convert like Olga of Rus or queens who backed the papacy like Matilda of Tuscany and the Eastern Church or like Jadwig of Poland and Elisabeth of Hungary. They were not encouraged to participate in the religious life in any important capacity. Elizabeth I of England refused to bow to the Church of Rome so was excommunicated and all the English especially the clergy, were encouraged by Rome to work against her. Elizabeth won and England stayed Protestant.

The Post Reformation period saw a lot of upheaval in the relationship between church and rulers. A ruler's religion became of paramount importance. Protestantism and other schisms had already begun in Europe. The Pope Clement VII refused to annul Henry VIII's marriage to Catholic Catherine of Aragon in favour of Protestant Anne Boleyn. England left the Catholic Church and formed the Anglican Church of England. In Rome females, were not valid inheritors to the throne. In England and other Protestant countries, Catholic convents were closed down, their treasures removed. But women's roles continued to be subservient. Protestant Martin Luther declared: *the wife should stay at home and look after the affairs of the household as one who has been deprived of the ability of administering those affairs that are outside and concern the state* (Lecture on Genesis 3:11). The majority of Protestant Churches upheld women's traditional roles of subservience. Among the reformers who upheld the power of the male at this time were John Calvin who believed: *the woman's place is in the home.* John Knox was adamantly against the rule of women *(First Blast of the Trumpet Against the Monstrous Regimen of Women)* and he, more than anyone else was responsible for the dire state of Scotland and the troubles of Mary, Queen of Scots.

Some **Quakers and Pentacostal movements** were the exception as was **John Wesley's** Salvation Army and **Adam Clark**, the Methodist, **John Gill** the Baptist Theologian and **Matthew Poole,** The Puritan Theologian who all upheld women's right to speak publicly on religious affairs under the influence of the spirit.

Many women both Catholic and Protestant were martyred during this period for their faith. Many women were stripped of their babies and children so they could be raised as Catholics in institutions.

Modern Times have been covered later. In the late 18th and 19th centuries women missionaries had to work under male guidance. Things started changing and are still in flux.

Islam

Islam is the newest and youngest of the monotheistic, Abrahamic religions and came into existence within the context of historical, political, economic and social issues in late antiquity in the Middle East in Mecca and Medina in Saudi Arabia. The end of the 6th century saw a lot of political upheaval in the region and it was time for a change. Muhammad, the prophet of Islam was born in Mecca in 571. Orphaned early, he still managed to get the nickname of *trustworthy* for his great honesty in all his dealings with others. Soon he was sought out by merchant to safeguard valuables and as an arbitrator for his fairness.

Islam as a religion began in 610 AD. So it is a comparatively new and modern religion. At its inception, it brought hope to having a fairer society where women could voice their opinions, concerns and so on.

Women in pre-Islamic areas are not our concern here but for the record, like other societies of the time around the world, they had very few rights. They could not inherit and were considered the property of the men with no rights of their own. We shall only consider their position in the context of Islam.

According to the web *Women in Islam,* it is generally assumed that all Muslim women are:

Oppressed, inferior, and unequal – for many people, these are the first words that come to mind when thinking about women in Islam. These stereotypes confuse Islam with cultural practices and fail to recognize that Islam has empowered women with the most progressive rights since the 7th century. In Islam, women are not inferior or unequal to men. This article shows the actual teachings of Islam regarding the rights, roles, and responsibilities of women, with a special focus **on gender equality in Islam**.

Pre-Islam Arabia, like most other countries in the world exposed female children or buried them. Women were men's possessions to do with them as they would, like around the world of the times. With the advent of Islam women's position in the Arabian Peninsula improved vastly. **They were honoured, protected, educated, allowed a say in their lives and in the functioning of society. They were returned their identity, could divorce, own property work, vote and participate in civic and political activities.**

The Prophet Muhammad, when reforming the pagan Arabs set about first reforming their mindsets especially concerning their attitudes towards women. He

- Raised the status of women in society;
- Stopped the killing of female children.
- Proclaimed, according to the Quran: *that all human beings, men and women are born in a pure state.* It is up to them to maintain it *by shunning evil tendencies and beautifying the inner being with virtuous traits.* (Quran: Chp. on Women).
- Went on to say men and women are not only equal in God's eyes but *the: most noble of you in the sight of Allah* (God) *is the most righteous* (49:13).

Still, he recognised though they were equal they were not identical, as men were better equipped with physiological and psychological attributes. Each man and woman was to contribute the best towards the general good. Both are to appear modest but again through different manifestations; their responsibilities are also different. However, all this was understood and applied through the prism of culture and tradition and not always quite as it was taught to them. Islam does not believe in original sin. All children are a gift from God. They are all born pure. Sin is the wrong one does later.

To summarise very briefly, the following aspects were seriously addressed:

Education; The prophet Muhammad had declared unequivocally that the pursuit of knowledge is obligatory in both men and women—clearly stated and implemented throughout Islamic history, beginning with Muhammad's family. Their oldest Mosque and university the Al-Qarawiyin Mosque and University, in Morocco in 859 CE was funded by a woman, **Fatima Al-Fihri**. There were many Muslim women who contributed to different branches of thought from the very beginning of Islam.

Motherhood: Mothers are given a very high status for all their sacrifices in childbearing and mothering. Prophet Muhammad said: *Heaven lies under the feet of your mother*, (Hadith) implying the respect in which they should be held, and in the Quran, *Sura Luqman 14* (31:14) it says: *"We have commanded people to be good to their parents: their mothers carried them, with strain upon strain, and it takes two years to wean them. Give thanks to Me and to your parents — all will return to Me."*

Political and Social services: Women were active participants in all areas of service, whether in the marketplace, tending the wounded on the battlefield, participating in battle, in advisory capacities, in law, scholarship, teaching or any other sphere. Caliph Umar appointed a woman, **Shaffa bint Abdullah**, as the supervisor of the bazaar. Women were encouraged to participate fully in the running of the state.

Inheritance: Before Islam, women were themselves property and as such had no right to any property. Muhammad changed all this. **He introduced the shocking, revolutionary concept that women could and ought to inherit, own, and be responsible for their own properties.** He decreed whether she is a wife, mother, sister or daughter, she has the right to inherit part of the property, depending on other factors like relationship. And not just that, but she could use the money without accounting to any one, as she wished. An example was Muhammad's wife **Khadija** who was a very successful businesswoman. She even supported her husband on his missions.

Marriage: Women were no longer possessions. She had the right to accept or reject a proposal and no marriage contract could be signed without her consent. She had the right to seek divorce. **This was a cultural shock to many at that time.** Men were expected to love, respect and honour their wives. Marriage was based on mutual love and respect. Abuse was not allowed in marriage, physical, psychological or in any other form. One Islamic tradition states: *"The best of you are those who are best to their wives."*

Protection from harm: Domestic violence is strictly forbidden in any form. It is an old cultural norm to be discarded and revoked. Islamic law protects all God's creations equally. No one has the right to maltreat or mistreat another human being. I personally think being macho is a sign of weakness where men have to prove their strength because they suspect they do not have it.

A lot of information here is from the Wikipedia.

However, over time cultural norms and traditions have interfered greatly with the teachings of Muhammad and women's position in society has been made extremely difficult. They have, in many places around the world, been rendered voiceless, helpless and just a possession. This has started to change in some countries and to worsen in some.

Islam has had an extensive tradition of protecting the civil liberties of women based on the guidelines set forth by God and His Prophet. Women are empowered with many rights and protections under Islamic law and are honoured with a dignified stature in society **supposedly**, but not always in practise. Women's status in many countries has deteriorated from the time the mullahs (clergy) gained ascendancy.

Women and Religion in Modern Times

What religion determined and cultural norms ended up by dictating are vastly different. In our modern society it is more cultural practices and traditional roles that now decide the role of women but thankfully this is changing around the world; women are recovering their voices: to an extent. It will take time, patience and a lot of mutual give and take between the traditional roles and modern demands to satisfy both parties, I believe.

In most olden religions, women had a very respected and valued place but over time that changed. In **Hinduism** (the oldest religion) they held very high status and respect. They could participate in all spheres of life without fear or favour. It was their right. But with time that changed. In many regions they began to be relegated to the background and men began to be portrayed as superior. Women became incidental to creation in some religions even giving birth and producing new life was *'unclean'*. For example, in Judaism, after childbirth and during the monthly periods, women had to be segregated or they might contaminate others with their uncleanliness. This, I believe, was a cultural outcome shocking as it is and not what religion really dictated.

Hinduism

In Hinduism women in the Upanishads had a lot of respect. Women were a form of Shakti – energy. Disrespect to a mother was unforgivable. One Hindi scripture even states: *"All other sins are expiable but he who is cursed by the mother is never liberated"*. Another Hindu scripture values a woman over that of a man stating, *"An outcast father may be forsaken, but not the mother, she is never an outcast to the son"*. But what about a daughter? That is not mentioned at all. According to some writers like Kramarae, & Spender, (2004 pp. 1059) there are still matriarchal societies in India, as discussed earlier.

Over time female power and respect has dissipated due to many factors beginning with the colonisation of India and the input / influence of Western ideas and values in which women did not have a high place at that time. That influenced and changed the cultural and traditional norms practised by the people of the land. Hindu women today may have a career but all money belongs to the man, all major decisions are taken by men, women are expected to obey. In marriage, even now, if a woman leaves the marriage, she is disinherited by her family and her husband's and all her dowry stays with him. She becomes a pariah. I had students who told me so. Socially too, their lot today is very ambiguous, often miserable. In theory it is very good, in practice, not so. Many men until very recently married more than one woman, all living in the same house. All had to obey the man implicitly. They were not allowed to socialise except with other female members. Their laws too are very male-centric especially in the *Manusmriti*, which is extremely discriminatory and harsh against women. Girls are still often married off to much older men. They are seldom allowed to choose their spouses. Love marriages are rare and dangerous as the couple can be killed on the basis of honour, even by the parents especially if they live overseas in Western countries. But widows have a better time now. They are no longer forced to be burnt on the pyre (Sutee) and cremated with their dead husbands and can even remarry. Suttee was abolished in India in 1829 (*The Bengal Sati Regulation XVII*) and it was made illegal under Governor General William Bentinck. Sutee plays a very small part in Hindu culture today according to Kotak, (2003, pp. 294) but it is given a very prominent place. Women today have a greater say in the choice of their spouses and more freedoms especially in cities. Rural areas still lag behind.

There is a strong movement to change things. Life for Hindu women overseas is sometimes much better than within their own societies in their countries. But there have been cases around the Western world where parents, relatives of a loving couple have killed them in the name of Honour. Whose honour? What honour?? These are the questions. Some Hindu women have stepped forward to promote the rights of women and many charities have worked hard to raise awareness and promote the well-being, inclusion and rights of women. One charity which has devoted itself to the campaign for women's rights is the *Manushi organisation* and they have had some influence in changing things for the better for the women there. Still there are many problems women face. Some more important ones are:

- Dowry problem, which is acute in certain castes and communities.
- Parental interference in marriage and career matters.
- Domestic violence and abuse.
- Violence against women which often goes unreported or ignored.
- Bride burning and dowry deaths.
- Gender based abortions.
- Gender inequality in the treatment of children.
- Dwindling sex ratio. Sex ratio in many parts of India has fallen considerably in the last few decades due to gender discrimination. AUN sponsored report (2013),

says it may take at least 50 years for a state like Haryana to return to the usual sex ratio.
- Trafficking in females. According to the same UN report (2013) female feticide worsened the sex ratio in Haryana to such an extent that it has led to the trafficking of women from various parts of India to that state where they are turned into domestic workers or forcibly married against their will. Girls who are forced into such marriages against their will are called "Paro."
- Sale of women. Every year, hundreds of women and young girls are either bartered or sold into sex trade, the modern form of slavery popular around the world today.

Indian women are far less emancipated in many ways than earlier.

Buddhist

In **Buddhism** there is very little distinction between the sexes. They do not recognise women per se but as a part of the human race. In one scripture the Visuddhi Maggi says: *Reverend Sir, have you seen a woman pass this way?"* And the elder said: *Was it a woman or a man that passed this way? I cannot tell. But this I know, a set of bones is travelling upon this road"* (Mohr, & Tsedroen, 2010). But in reality, it is a different story. In theory men and women are equal but Buddhist teachings have undermined women's access to religious spaces and roles according to Gethin (1998). For example, in Buddhism women are not considered as a complete entity and cannot attain enlightenment and become Buddha. To do so, their bodies must first be reborn as a man. On the other hand, they say women are better suited to enlightenment. It is very ambiguous. In some Buddhist societies as in Thailand, Sri Lanka and Burma their position is much better with more freedom and equality (Dewaraja, 1994). Even now in Thailand which is 90% Buddhist, women can only become white-cloaked nuns but not monks. This role in actuality is that of a glorified temple housekeeper. To circumvent this, many have travelled to Sri Lanka to receive full ordination.

Historically, Buddhism has in fact been a male dominated society and its literature reflecting this has been highly androcentric. Women's voices have never been heard or always silenced. Even now there are very few exceptions. Some of these are: I.B. Horner, (1930): *Women under Primitive Buddhism;* L.S. Dewaraja (1994): *The Position of Women in Buddhism;* Kajiyama, Yuichi (1982) *"Women in Buddhism, The Eastern Buddhist"* in which she refers to Mahayana and Indian texts that show how they discriminate against women on spiritual grounds. Early *Mahayana* texts developed further in *Pure Land Sutras* show that women were denied Buddhahood until they changed sex through reincarnation to attain Buddhahood. Gross, Rita M. (1993): *Buddhism after Patriarchy: Feminist History, Analysis, and Reconstruction of Buddhism* show the issues that led to the subordination and control of women across Asia in history, conceptually. Barnes, Nancy, J (1994): *"Women in Buddhism:"*

In Today's Woman in World Religions (ed. Arvind Sharma) focuses on the shifting roles of women in contemporary Buddhist societies including full ordination for women in Buddhism which, where it had even existed, had lapsed with the new Japanese religious movements like the Thervadea Meditation groups and movements for social justice in Tibet and Sri Lanka. And also Willis, Janice's (1985): *"Nuns and Benefactresses: The Role of Women in the Development of Buddhism,* in *Women, Religion, and Social Change,"* (ed. Yvonne Haddad and Ellison Banks Findly).

Today, it is an opportune moment to discuss the necessary change of female role in Buddhism. Women should, actually must, have a voice in matters concerning them.

Judaism

The role of women in ancient and Middle Ages has been covered earlier. The role of women in modern times has changed quite drastically in comparison. In 2006 two women received rabbinic ordination, (*smicha*), a thing that was unbelievable once. However, the ultra-Orthodox Jews have still not accepted this change. In modern times, Jewish women are serving as advocates in rabbinical courts, in Orthodox congregations (without the title), at bar Mitzva ceremonies, wearing the traditional *tallitot* and a Jewish woman, Golda Meir, a teacher and politician, served as the fourth Jewish president from 1969 to 1974. To a great extent, this change was also due to the position of women in Western society and the education of women mandatory in all countries including

Israel, and around the world. No one wants to be left behind still in darkness while the world marches forward to a different beat. This change has also affected the Ultra-Orthodox Jews. Women are now allowed to study the Talmud, once totally forbidden, even in schools. The views of women like **Nehama Leibowitz** on the Torah are accepted as authoritative and they are allowed to teach men and women alike. This is a major step forward.

The Talmud Menahot 43a, recorded that *"All must observe the law of tzitzit: Priests, Levites, Israelites, converts, women and slaves".* This became a law only since Rabbi Shimon bar Yohai (2nd century) ruled that women were exempt and Rabbi Yehuda bar Ilai (2nd century Tanna from Usha) demanded that his household women attach tzitzit to their garments.

In the *Tenkh* and *Talmud* the male and female roles are specified. In modern times there have been a lot of changes and a forward movement. Women have more freedom today, can choose their own life partners, get an education and have a career. Their clothes have also changed and like other parts of the world, they dress the same as other females everywhere and not only in traditional clothes. They can also join the forces and train as soldiers, sailors and so on. Actually, Israeli Defence Forces or IDF conscripts women into the ranks as a mandatory draft law. In fact, in 2021 women made up about 40% of the IDF conscript soldiers and 25% of officer corps. In 2018 over 10,000 women served in the IDF on a permanent basis (Jewish Encyclopaedia - The Shalvi / Hyman Encyclopaedia).

Religious values: have also changed over time. There has been a sharp decline in religious marriages and increase in non-religious ones. In the 21st century most marriages take place in a secular setting.

Cohabitation: is acceptable now and about 60% of marriages are preceded by cohabitation. Many believe that marriage is a life-long commitment and a stable marriage is necessary for a healthy and stable life. So cohabitation is now openly accepted by society.

Note: Tzitzit are the fringes or tassels worn on traditional or ceremonial garments by Jewish males as reminders of the commandments of Deuteronomy 22:12 and Numbers 15:37-41.

Christianity

It is the second Abrahamic religion. It is based on the life and teachings of Jesus of Nazareth, the Messiah sent by God, who was crucified and rose again to give eternal life to those who believe in him and follow his teachings. Christianity divided into different denominations over time – historically, always over power. As one strong group wanted more power and to follow a different path, they broke away from the mainstream. This led to the Great Schism of 1054. Other schisms followed.

The Great Schism: In 286, Roman Emperor Diocletian divided the Roman Empire into the East and West co-equal blocks to keep the empire stable after the disastrous civil wars and the disintegrations of the third century. They co-existed equally under two Caesars except for the rule of Rome — Emperors, **Constantine I** ruled from 306-337 and was the first to convert to Christianity and **Theodosius I** ruled from 379-395, and was the last Roman Caesar to rule over both the Eastern and Western halves. He divided the empire between his two sons one governing from Ravenna and the other from Constantinople. In 476 the Western half collapsed after the disastrous battle of Ravenna at the hands of the Germanic tribes. Still, it was viewed as a polity for administrative expediency. In 554 the Western part was formally dissolved. The Eastern part continued till 1453. In 800 the Frankish king **Charlemagne** became the emperor of Rome and revival of the Western half began. This would lead to the **Great Schism** of 1054.

At the heart of the problem (Schism), lay the claim of the Roman Pope Leo IX to universal jurisdiction and authority. Byzantine under Michael Cerularius, Patriarch of Constantinople was ready to honour the Pope in Rome but believed ecclesiastical matters should be decided by a council of bishops, and refused to grant unchallenged dominion to the Pope in Rome. So the problems in a nutshell were ecclesiastical, theological, political, cultural, jurisdictional, and linguistic. The schism divided the churches into the original Orthodox Church in the East (Constantinople) and the Roman Catholic Church in the West (Rome). At first, they remained on friendly terms but later it led to bitter rivalries and since the Sack of Constantinople by the Catholic Crusaders in 1204, the schism has not been mended till now. Efforts to do so were attempted the last being in 2014 by Pope Francis and

Patriarch Bartholomew who signed a Joint Declaration affirming their commitment to seek unity between their churches and again they talked about it in 2015 and then in December 2021 in Nicosia, Cyprus. The final outcome is still to come.

The Orthodox denomination: as such started in the 1st (first century AD). The Orthodox and Catholic denominations share a lot of common characteristics. It consists of a community of churches each governed by a bishop. The Orthodox Church does not accept the modifications that the Catholic Church brought about and stays with the original ones. It is the Orthodox or *right belief* because it maintains the original creed as the origin of the Holy Spirit.

It does not accept the modification of:

- the existence of purgatory,
- the Immaculate Conception of the Virgin Mary, and
- the concept of Original Sin that the Catholic Church has adopted.
- Women are not and cannot be ordained as priests even now. In other ways they are free to participate in church events. Traditionally women have been ordained to the diaconate but not to the priesthood or episcopacy. The order of deaconess existed in the Church, in some areas surviving through the eleventh-century. The Church emphasises, that women are the **backbone of the Church** and in their parishes and homes. They form an important part of the Church choir and as supporting members. A man married to a woman of good repute can be ordained as deacon.
- Priests are usually married.
- Altar girls are generally not allowed to serve liturgically in the church sanctuary. In October 2004, the Chancellor of the OCA issued a statement forbidding this practice and citing the position of the OCA's Holy Synod. Ladies' societies abound in every parish, raising funds for the church, doing good deeds, teaching in Sunday classes and so on. Parishes would not function so well without their input.

There are many women saints in the Orthodox Church and some are *equal to the apostles.* Orthodox theology of priesthood emphasises the character of the priest, not his sex, and understands the priest as representing the people to God rather than representing Christ or the Father to the people. An emphasis on the priest as *'in persona christi'* is more characteristic of Catholic theology.

The countries that practice Christian Orthodoxy today are Russia, Serbia, Greece, Rumania, Bulgaria and Ukraine (majority in all), Belarus, Georgia in Europe; Ethiopia, Egypt (minority) in Africa. USA has all denominations including Orthodox (World Atlas).

The Catholic denomination: separated to become such in 1054 (11th century) (see above). It is the branch of Christianity formed by the Roman Catholic Apostolic Church in Western Europe. Its base is the Vatican and holds the Pope to be the supreme authority for most existing churches. They converted aggressively wherever Europe colonised unlike all other branches of Christianity and in 1214 had the most adherents of all Christian denominations. **Convert or die** was the unspoken motto of the Catholic Church – not of Christ or other Christian denominational churches.

The Catholic Church gives a lot of importance not only to Jesus but also to the Virgin Mary and the Apostles. It argues that it is <u>the only church founded by Christ</u> and was entrusted to the Apostle Peter, and that is why it is claimed as a *"sign and instrument of intimate union with God."* But, the doctrine of the Catholic Church has been based on **doctrines and concepts that are not present in the Bible and that are transmitted only through their apostolic tradition.** This is one of the main reasons for the separation with Orthodox and

Protestants and later other denominations. The main rites and sacraments are: baptism, communion, the Eucharist and marriage. Christianity came much later to Rome than the East and Byzantine. **When Byzantine was Christian, Rome fed early Christians to the lions and put unarmed men and women including Christians into the arena to die.** And not just that, early Christians were hunted and hounded in Rome. They could not live in the sun. They inhabited the dark, dank catacombs under the city of Rome.

The role of women here is very complex. The Virgin Mary a central figure in the life of Christ, is exalted but other women are denigrated. Mary of Magdala, a good woman, is often denigrated, regarded in Christianity as a harlot for her courage in breaking the expected pattern of feminine behaviour. In 591 Pope Gregory I first pronounced her a *"sinful woman"* contrary to the evidence in the canonical Gospels. The epithet stuck, even though in the Bible she was simply a woman from Magdala in Galilee who became a female disciple and was the first witness to Jesus' resurrection, the cornerstone of Christianity. The label *prostitute* sticks till today in spite of Dan Brown, Margaret George and others to dispel this false assumption of her.

Catholicism has remained a strongly male dominated organisation at all levels of institutional leadership with harsh consequences. The celibacy of Popes began in 1074 when Pope Gregory VII imposed it. It was reinforced in Norman times in 1139; marriages of the clergy were strictly repudiated. However, many Catholic Popes broke the rule spectacularly and had children (many illegitimate, born while they were Popes) some of whom followed their fathers as Popes (A *Matter of Honour* Sophia Z Kovachevich pp. 70-73). They did not honour their own decrees nor bide by them.

After the Second Vatican Council, the role of women was re-evaluated, including the ordination of women into the priesthood. But it came to naught. **Women cannot be ordained and become priests, bishops or popes in the Catholic Church** because they claim, Jesus selected only men as apostles, only men can lead the church and perform the sacraments they say. Gender, not spirituality, was to decide apostolic service. They forget Mary Magdalene when so deciding. She was the first of his followers, closest to him. Women could work in other spheres but not in the priesthood, being ordained or in positions of such power. Their roles in the Protestant church that allows women into the priesthood and ordination did have an effect but it seems not enough yet.

During the papacy of Pope Paul VI, there was considerable openness for discussion of women's ordination. No decision was made but then during the papacies of John Paul II and Benedict VI, severe restrictions **even on discussion** of women's ordination were imposed. Discussion re-emerged during the tenure of Pope Francis. Nothing came of that either in Church policy.

The ongoing movement to bring women into the ordained diaconate has been led by female theologians like Phyllis Zagano. This had a better reception within Catholic institutional circles. It led to Pope Francis actually appointing a commission to study the question. But the commission's report failed to have a clear-cut consensus. So, no further action has been taken on the issue of diaconate ordination for women. The door is now closed to any further discussion.

In 1994, Pope John Paul II released an apostolic letter in which he stated that priestly ordination was reserved for men alone. He also stated the presence and roles of women in the church are *"absolutely necessary and irreplaceable,"* even when not linked to the ministerial priesthood.

Since then, many Catholic women have fought to receive the priesthood. Most notable is Women's Ordination Worldwide, an organisation dedicated to *"working for women's equality and ordination in the Catholic Church."*

In 2014, the National Catholic Reporter announced a *"new day is dawning"* as more than 200 women claimed they were official Roman Catholic priests.

Pope Francis released a "letter to young people" in March 2019 where he acknowledged the hardships many female members have faced such as *"a fair share of male authoritarianism, domination, various forms of enslavement, abuse and sexist violence."*

There are also two points of controversy about this matter. **The first** is that women are not interested in embracing a priesthood dominated by male superiority and clericalism that has pervaded the Church for centuries. **The second** is Pope Francis' promotion of *synodality*, a new organisational model for Catholicism. In 2023 a new synod is to convene to discuss this issue. It has come and gone. There are no changes instituted yet.

Protestant denomination: In the 16th century (1517) Martin Luther initiated his break-away movement from the Catholic Church – The beginning of Protestantism. They protested church corruption among other church venialities. There were many reasons for this — **political, economic, social, and religious.** In particular the main causes were: problems with indulgences, the Pope's overwhelming power and interference, and the corruption of the church.

Luther made clear that the Bible is the *"Sola Skriptura,"* God's only book, in which He provided His revelations to the people and which allows them to enter in communion with Him. Catholics, on the other hand, **do not base their beliefs on the Bible alone** but also on canonical scriptures and sacred traditions. The **Catholic Church had also forbidden the possession or reading of the Bible** by lay people according to **The Index Librorum Prohibitorum** issued by the Catholic Church. Luther began printing the Bible for lay people too though anyone caught possessing one could get into serious trouble.

Protestantism was greatly helped by the actions and interference of Henry VIII, one of the most powerful kings in Europe at that time. Henry wanted an annulment of his marriage to Katherine of Aragon, a Catholic Princess of strongly Catholic Spain. The Pope, Clement VII refused and could not be budged from his position. Henry wanted to marry beautiful, witty and young Anne Boleyn. Henry broke away from Rome and became the Head of the Church of England, rejecting all Papal authority. The country was excommunicated, as Rome always does in cases of confrontation. Henry persisted and England became Protestant followed by many other countries. Protestantism is now the most influential Christian denomination. In England it is the most popular, followed by Anglicanism, the Reformed tradition (including Presbyterians), Methodism, Pentecostalism and Baptists.

The Reformation also saw to the Bible being translated into the vernacular by early reformers like John Wycliffe (England), Jan Hus (Bohemia) and others too all following Luther. It also **abolished the celibacy for priests, monks and nuns and promoted marriage as the ideal state for both men and women**. Men could still become clergymen, women could no longer become nuns as convents were destroyed and convent life banned. Marriage became the only proper role for a woman.

But now women could be ordained. They could preach, teach, and become missionaries. But the main role was still the same to raise and teach children, maintain a Godly household. They were however free to have careers in any branch they wished for. They could be presidents, rulers, (not so much) and all else. They are in the defense forces, as soldiers, scientists, doctors, Judges and every other job that they wish to have.

The Anglican denomination is practiced in England and some parts of the United States. They believe that there is One God who exists eternally in three persons—Father, Son, and Holy Spirit. They believe that Jesus Christ is completely God and is also completely human. If a religious group does not teach these two doctrines, they are not recognized as Christians. It is a broadly based fraternity of 40 autonomous provinces that have mutual dependence defined as faith, practice and spirit of member churches following the *Anglican Communion* which are all in **communion with the Archbishop of Canterbury.** It is the largest Christian denomination in the world with over 98 million adherents. The members consider themselves to be part of the One, Holy, Catholic and Apostolic, and Reformed Church. For many it represents a form of non-papal Catholicism or a form of Protestantism without founding figures such as Martin Luther or Juan Calvino (John Calvin). It has deep roots in pre 16th century practices. At its core it is based on the Bible and the 39 articles of the Book of Common Prayer which is a summary of the first five centuries' teachings of Christianity. It rejects all later dogmas and additions of the Catholic Church. It rejects the cult of images. All bishops hold the same rank. The Bible can be interpreted freely and the clergy can marry.

The Anglican Church ordains women to three traditionally holy orders: bishops, priests and deacons. Most Protestant churches allow women to become ministers or priests. In 1992 England's General Synod adopted a Measure permitting the ordination of women as priests (but not bishops) with the requisite support of two-thirds of each of the synod's three

Houses — bishops, clergy, and laity. Then in 2014 the Church of England finally voted, to **allow women to become bishops** and the first women bishops were ordained in 2015. Now there are about 1,380 female priests in Anglican churches around the world. The Episcopal church in the US and Anglican churches in Canada, Australia, New Zealand and other countries have had female priests and even bishops for years. The very first woman to be ordained a minister of a recognized denomination in the United States was Antoinette Brown Blackwell, née Antoinette Louisa Brown, (1825 to 1921).

However, women still **cannot** be ordained in the following Church denominations: the Roman **Catholic Church** and the Southern Baptist Convention, or **SBC**, the Church of Jesus Christ of Latter-Day Saints, known as the **LDS**, the **Orthodox Church.**

There are many other Christian denominations like:

The Church of Jesus Christ of Latter-day Saints (LDS) that do not allow women to be ordained into the priesthood even though they say men and women are equal in the eyes of God. Kate Kelly started a movement to ordain women in 2013. She was excommunicated by the Church in 2014 for this. Today there are over 650 women around the world wanting to be ordained to the LDS.

Jehovah's Witnesses *All of Jehovah's Witnesses are preachers, or ministers, including several million women,* officially. But women do not participate in the leadership of the Church. Resistance against the status of women has begun in different groups of Jehovah's Witnesses. And the Church holds firm that women should be submissive to their husbands, letting them make all important decisions.

Evangelicals: The Southern Baptist Convention **(SBC)** believes women are complementary to men but cannot hold any authority over men. They have women's organisations and female missionaries. The Convention provides monthly women conferences to help women "thrive" in their relationship with God. **A major scandal arose in 2019** when hundreds of sexual abuse victims spoke out against male church leaders. Many within the faith claimed the sexist culture of the church was to blame. Others took the media chaos and used it to bring "new life" to the female ordination controversy. Women used this to push for more equality within the churches. Beth Moore, a popular influential teacher is seen as a threat to those with authority. Evangelical women follow her lead and the number of female influencers in the church grows.

Other Protestants generally have a *"priesthood of all believers,"* according to Rutherford. In some leadership and pastor roles are not ordained to an official priesthood because for them, every baptized Christian is considered a priest already. So they have led the way including women in pastor and leadership roles.

Females can be **Lutheran** bishops, **Methodist** elders, **Baptist** pastors, **Presbyterians** based on the culture of that area. Rutherford believes *"If the culture reflects a lower position of women, then the religion most likely will as well. They tend to work in harmony."* She continues: *religions differ* *greatly in their traditions and practices with regards to women and are so diverse that it's hard to know what each church will do. While some Lutheran or Methodist denominations ordain women, others don't".* Despite the fact that progress for women's status in religions can be "very slow-moving," especially in conservative traditions, *"I think you would have to say in all religions there is a movement forward,"* said (Taunalyn Rutherford, world religions professor, Utah University).

There are many, many more Christian denominations and new church organisations with their own beliefs and ways. And still more are springing up all the time, some very dangerous ones. It is far too many to go into here.

Islam

It is the third of the Abrahamic religions. It is a much-misunderstood religion due to the biases that society has had beginning with the Crusades. It is mostly perceived to have a very negative role for women. In actual fact it was not so to begin with. Stereotypical stigmas often forced women within the Islamic culture to be guarded as these social stigmas infringed on their culture and personality as individuals. In the Khilafah (elected, not a kingdom) the State is obligated to provide women with the highest level of education and view women as valuable citizens of the state. The role of women in Islam is viewed as vital and honourable. But what is expected and what happens in reality are not always the same. The original laws of Islam assured women much more equality and dignity than was available to women in Europe at that time. But it changed in most places for women, in later years, for the worse. In modern times, many Islamic countries are going backward and enforcing very strict norms on all, especially women. In some countries though, they can join the forces and have somewhat more freedom though not as much as in Europe and USA.

Some common misconceptions are that women in Islam are, marginalised, lack power, are oppressed, forced into marriage, forced to wear veils, and voiceless much like Judaism and Middle Ages Christianity. These are fallacies. In all the Abrahamic religions these were rules once. But not so strictly practised anymore. Many women like head coverings and there are modern trends in how to look good wearing them. They could be scarves, hats, veils or whatever. Like women elsewhere in the world, the main role is to raise children, run the household and take care of the family. Most Islamic women have careers alongside this outside the home like all over the world. They can be heads of states singers, performers, politicians or whatever. **Many forget that at least eight countries have had Muslim women as their head of state in modern times, far more than in USA** which has never had ONE woman leader from either – Democrats or Republicans – their two major parties. No female has ever has ever nominated as a presidential candidate. There were and are many females, **Muslim** heads of states in modern times. (see pp. 215)

Modern Feminist Movements

Feminism began as a result of sweeping changes, social, political and industrial and as a result of the World Wars. Women from disparate backgrounds contributed to it but it really originated in France long before the Modern Age. In 1610 a French woman, Catherine de Vivonne, the Marquess de Rambouillet, began a salon for the Upper Class for intellectual and literary discussions which later included social and political discussion too. Women's role at that time was determined by the *querelle des femmes*, (*question of women*) that addressed all women's issue – education, marriage, social mobility, and so on. After the French Revolution, the concept of women's equality was considered but the focus was on the equality of mankind. However, women were now mobilised politically and there was at least a veneer of equality. Early feminism began here.

In 1792 Mary Wollstonecraft published a seminal work on Feminism arguing for the equal treatment of women in her book *Vindication of the Rights of Women*. It was the first book to demand a radical need for change in the status quo regarding women.

All modern women's movements, of which there are many, aim to end discrimination and violence against women; give them back their voices through legal, political, social and religious means. In the USA, strangely enough, it did not begin as an overt gender equality movement but as breaking the image of submissive females. Women threw playboy magazines, pots, pans and bras into trash cans in protest.

These women wanted to protest social issues. From there it went into modern feminism. Some of the most prominent movements in the Western world are the following:

Modern Women's Movement: began in Canada in 1890 followed by Newfoundland in 1970. They strove to end inequalities in gender, law, politics, workplace, society and social reform, like pay equity, pensions, affirmative action, day care, reproductive rights, against domestic and sexual violence, sex stereotyping, for property rights, representation in government, and so on. These movements operate from all levels of society.

Suffragette movement: The first seeds of modern feminism were sown in the US decades before the American Civil War during the 1820s and 1830s when franchise had been extended to most white men. Women and the Blacks were not included. It came into prominence during the Anti-Slavery and Temperance movements in 1848 in Seneca Falls, New York, led mostly by women. The organiser was Lucretia C Mott and the other important women were Jane Hunt, Mary Ann M Clintock, Elizabeth Cady Stanton, and Martha C Wright. In 1840 Elizabeth Stanton and Lucretia Mott were denied seats in the Anti-Slavery Convention in London due to gender. So they initiated the Seneca Falls meeting. Stanton herself wrote the outline for the need for equality between the genders and equal voting rights. The Black African, Sojourner Truth was among the participants. Seven decades later, women won the right to vote. It was a long and hard fight. And not just in the US but all around the world. In the

UK, the movement was established by Millicent Fawcett in 1897 and Emmeline Pankhurst, its strongest voice joined in 1903. Her methods were very direct and confrontational. Membership increased rapidly.

The Americans did not describe themselves as feminists but as suffragettes. Feminism came to the US from France in 1910 (Source: Kelly). It came in three waves: **The first** was concerned with women's right to vote and economic issues. **The second** was about social rights and **the third** which began in the 1990's is a continuation of feminism and focusses on the individual identity instead of laws. It embraces individuality, diversity, the media and the fight against endless violence against women. It is continuing now with the *Me Too Movement* against sexual abuse, sexual harassment, and rape culture practised against women, prevalent today. As men are not just sperm donors, so women are not just sex objects, as they are usually portrayed.

It includes all legal rights for women above and beyond simply gender equality and voting rights. Feminists fought for legal rights, financial independence, and transformation of gender relationships between the sexes among other rights (Woloch pp. 1994, 108). Soon the pure suffragettes and feminists split.

Women's Liberation Movement: Post WW II, more and more women sought work outside the home. There was a dearth of manpower. Women also sought to pursue higher education, and to enter the workforce. But decent careers in the work force were not open to women. Only the lowest paid, menial jobs for equal slots of time, but less pay, was available to them. So the **Women's Liberation Movement** emerged in the late 1960s and 1970s to revolutionise the fundamental aspects of employment, education, sexuality and domesticity. In 1966 Betty Friedman and other feminists formed the **NOW** party (National Organisation for **Women**). This united many diverse women's causes under its umbrella, predominantly white women. Then the **second wave** appeared with **MS Magazine under its founder Gloria Steinem** who pushed for access to the pill, abortion, equal employment opportunities, and reduction/cessation of violence towards women, domestic violence and other related causes. In 1968, two years later, the first Feminist conference took place in Chicago. Even at present there is no real equality in the USA between men and women. Women still make up only 20% of the Senate and even less in Congress; The US has never had a female president or vice president though Hilary Clinton did come very close until Kamila Harris now... Hilary Clinton was defeated by Donald Trump. *The Equal Rights Amendment of the Constitution* pushed for by Alice Paul in **1920** has still **NOT** been ratified; Men and women in same jobs are not paid equally, do not get the same benefits and are not treated the same. **USA is the only developed country where women do not get maternity leave.** Only 22% of CEOs of Fortune 500 companies are women.

Meanwhile there was still another movement of younger, more radical feminists who were animated by two things: The Civil Rights Movement and the Anti-Vietnam War

Movements. A better-known group among them was the **Red Stockings.** They were a loosely organised group but took a very militant stance in their public approach and their demonstrations (source: Echols and Willis). They also had consciousness-raising sessions in which they shared experiences, discussed issues including female sexuality.

Black Feminism: Some feminists criticised the Women's Liberation Movement for its exclusion of non-white women and working-class women. This was accidental not intentional but it spurred on Black Feminism. It led the Black Feminist Gloria Bell Hooks (alias, Gloria Watkins) to decide between joining the male Black Power Movement or the female-led Women's Liberation Movement which exemplified the black feminist philosophies (Tandon). Some black feminists responded by breaking away and forming their own groups like the **National Black Feminist Organization** and the **National Alliance of Black Feminists.**

Womanism: is an offshoot of Black Feminism started in 1970 by Alice Walker, a Pulitzer Prize winner. This group sought to provide a bridge by examining society as a whole rather than problems of different groups in it.

The Feminist Sex Wars: In the late 1970s, the Anti-porn feminist war began led by Catharine MacKinnon and Andrea Dworkin. Pornography has become openly accessible and the portrayal of women as overt sexual objects had negative effects. Most feminists resented this violation of their rights. Anti porn feminist Robin Morgan said: ***Pornography is the theory; rape is the practice*** (D'Emilio & Freedman 1988).

And it is true. Rape cases have been on the increase since then. Anti-Porn theory states that, heterosexual intercourse is a form of male domination and must be totally altered so as not to harm or demean women.

Pro sexism appeared led by Betty Dodson and Gayle Rubin, who saw physical relationships as a mutually pleasurable experience. However, some feminists were not satisfied and wanted woman's total emancipation (Tandon).

Wicca, sometimes known as the Goddess movement, Goddess spirituality, or the Craft, appears to be the fastest-growing religion in America. Thirty years ago, only a handful of Wiccans existed, now, it is popular in many Western European countries also. Its followers practice witchcraft and nature worship and others regard it as a religion based on pre-Christian religious traditions of Northern and Western Europe. It is a modern Pagan religion first introduced by Gerald Gardiner called the father of Wicca, to England in 1954. It is categorised by scholars as both an old and modern religious movement of Western esotericism. Its adherents are diverse – theists, atheists, agnostics... The early Wiccans worshipped the duo – the *Horned God* and *Mother Goddess* as did hunter-gatherers of the Old Stone Age. They believed they were the inheritors of the religion. The Horned god is associated mainly with animals, the natural world and the afterlife. The Mother goddess embodies fertility, spring and a role model for women. They practice witchcraft and nature worship. Their symbol is the pentacle, its five points representing the five elements – earth, air, fire, water, and aether / spirit as well as the human body – head, arms, and legs. The Wiccan High priestess and journalist, Margot Adler said that Wiccan rituals were not *dry, formalised, repetitive experiences* but religious experience that could alter consciousness.

Feminist theology is another new movement found in several religions, including Sanatan Dharma (old form of Hinduism), Buddhism, Christianity, Judaism, and New Thought. The adherents reconsider the traditions, practices, scriptures, and theologies of those religions from a feminist perspective. Some of the goals of feminist theology include increasing the role of women among clergy and religious authorities, reinterpreting patriarchal imagery and language about God, determining women's place in relation to career and motherhood, studying images of women in the religions' sacred texts, and matriarchal religion.

In the Abrahamic religious traditions, God is always imagined to be male, solely because most societies are male-oriented. These theologies give males the dominant and fuller roles in religious worship in churches or synagogues or mosques restricting women's roles severely or not at all earlier. Feminist theologians would change this attitude. They argue that even in theology there is gender politics stated/explicit or implicit.

But women's ordination still remains largely off limits in many traditions, including the two largest U.S. Christian denominations — the Roman Catholic Church and the Southern Baptist Convention, or SBC — as well as the Church of Jesus Christ of Latter-day Saints, known as the LDS, and Orthodox Judaism. It is also off limits in the Orthodox Church. Pope Francis said *"that door is closed"* regarding women's priestly ordination, once again affirming the teachings of his predecessors, including Pope John Paul II and Pope Benedict XVI. Still women's roles in a variety of faith traditions have expanded over the last few decades to include higher leadership and greater authority. There is still much progress to be made for women's role in religions.

To conclude this section, more and more people are striving to find stability, some core belief to adhere to not just in the USA but also around the world. All these movements have spread to many other countries around the world. There are more and more religious denominations, more and more cults and belief systems appearing today. Many are attempting to connect to some higher consciousness, some form of spirituality. Many different cults, belief systems not necessarily religious always, are abounding. Many people are lost in the turmoil; the fear, the cancer of murders and mindless killings in the modern world. We each have got to find our own peace, our own way.

Some Modern Female heads of states

Tansu Çiller, Prime Minister of Turkey, 1993-1996 also served as deputy Prime Minister and Minister of Foreign Affairs. Graduated from the school of Economics Turkey, Ph. D from University of Connecticut, USA

Megawati Sukarnoputri, was President of Indonesia, 2001-2004, currently is leader of the (Indonesian Democratic Party of Struggle). She stabilized the overall democratisation and smooth relationship among legislative, executive and military institutions of the country.

Mame Madior Boye, Prime Minister of Senegal, 2001-2002. Boye is known for her strong feminist ideals, having frequently raised women's concerns during her time in office. On leaving politics, she was appointed as the special representative of the African Union for the protection of civilian populations in countries with armed conflict. She founded and was president of the Association of Senegalese Lawyers from 1975 to 1990.

Atifete Jahjaga, President of Kosovo, (2011-2016) is the fourth and current President of Kosovo, and is the youngest to ever be elected to the position. She graduated from the faculty of law. Before going into politics, she worked in the Kosovo police force, progressing her way up to the rank of Major General. During her presidency, she has led many initiatives for empowering women, including hosting an international women's summit in 2012. It was attended by 200 leaders from Europe, North America, Africa and the Middle East.

Roza Otunbayeva, President of Kyrgyzstan, 2010-2011 was sworn in as President in 2010 after acting as interim leader following the 2010 April revolution that deposed President Kurmanbek Bakiyev. Otunbayeva graduated from the Philosophy faculty of Moscow State University in 1972, and went on to head the philosophy department at Kyrgyz

State National University for six years. Her political and diplomatic posts include being the first ambassador from the Krygyz Republic to the United States and Canada, and the first ambassador to the United Kingdom.

Sheikh Hasina, Prime Minister of Bangladesh, 1996 – July 2001; 2009-2014; 2014-2018; 2019-present: was sworn into office for the second time in 2009. Previously she served as PM from 1996 to 2001. Her father, Sheikh Mujibur Rahman, was the first Prime Minister of Bangladesh. Her political career has spanned more than forty years, during which she has been both Prime Minister and leader of the opposition. She was arrested in 2007 on charges of extortion, however returned as Prime Minister in 2008 after a landslide victory. To date she is the longest serving Prime minister of Bangladesh.

Benazir Bhutto, Prime Minister of Pakistan, 1988–1990; 1993–1996: Benazir – daughter of former Prime Minister Zulfikar Ali Bhutto, became the first woman to be elected as the head of a Muslim state. At age of 29, she was the chairperson of the centre-left PPP, one of the major political parties in Pakistan, and was known for her charisma and intelligence. Her feminist legacy, however, is complicated. Whilst she often spoke for the empowerment of women, many criticize what is seen as her limited action — for example, her inability to repeal the controversial Hudood Ordinance, which implemented a literal form of Shari'at that limited women's freedoms. Despite her controversial tenures, she was globally mourned following her tragic assassination in 2007.

Khaleda Zia, Prime Minister of Bangladesh, 1991–1996; 2001-2006: She was the second woman in the Muslim world to become a head of state, after Benazir Bhutto. She was the First Lady of Bangladesh during the presidency of her husband former President Zia Ur Rahman, and served as PM from 1991 to 1996, and from 2001 to 2006. She was the first female PM of Bangladesh and is currently the chairperson and leader of the Bangladesh Nationalist Party. Her decade-long tenure makes her the second longest serving Prime Minister of Bangladesh.

Ameenah Fakim, President of Mauritius, 2015–2018 was sworn in 2015. She is Mauritius' sixth President, and the first woman to ever run the Hindu-majority country. As well as her successes in politics, Fakim is a highly distinguished biodiversity scientist, having worked in the roles of Dean of Faculty and as pro-Vice Chancellor at the University of Mauritius. Despite having just started in the position, she has already demonstrated a strong commitment to feminist principles, particularly advocating the importance of education for young girls. She has also expressed deep environmental concerns, pinpointing climate change and sustainable development as primary focuses of her tenure as President.

Some other present women leaders around the world are according to *Women, Business and the Law* 2019, recently published by the World Bank are/were:

- Bidya Devi Bhandari – Nepal president (2015) *
- Tsai Ing-wen – Taiwan president (2016, re-elected 2020)
- Ana Brnabić – Serbia prime minister (2017)
- Halimah Yacob – Singapore president (2017) *
- Jacinda Ardern – New Zealand prime minister (2017)
- Katrín Jakobsdóttir – Iceland prime minister (2017)
- Paula-Mae Weekes – Trinidad and Tobago president (2018)
- Mia Mottley – Barbados prime minister (2018)
- Sahle-Work Zewde – Ethiopia president (2018)
- Salome Zourabichvili – Georgia president (2018)
- Zuzana Čaputová – Slovakia president (2019)
- Mette Frederiksen – Denmark prime minister (2019)
- Sanna Marin – Finland prime minister (2019)
- Maia Sandu – Moldova president (2020)
- Katerina Sakellaropoulou – Greece president (2020)
- Rose Christiane Raponda – Gabon prime minister (2020)
- Victoire Tomegah Dogbé – Togo prime minister (2020)
- Ingrida Šimonytė – Lithuania prime minister (2020)
- Kaja Kallas – Estonia prime minister (2021)
- Samia Suluhu Hassan – Tanzania president (2021)
- Vjosa Osmani – Kosovo president (2021)
- Fiamē Naomi Mataʻafa – Samoa prime minister (2021)
- Natalia Gavrilița – Moldova prime minister (2021)
- Najla Bouden – Tunisia prime minister (2021)
- Sandra Mason – Barbados president (2021)
- Magdalena Andersson – Sweden prime minister (2021)
- Xiomara Castro – Honduras president (2021)

- Katalin Novák – Hungary president (2022)
- Élisabeth Borne – France prime minister (2022)
- Droupadi Murmu – India president (2022)
- Angela Merkel, Chancellor of Germany (Re-elected for the 5th term on Mar 14, 2018)
- Kersti Kaljulaid, President of Estonia (elected on Oct 3, 2016)
- Marie-Louise Coleiro Preca, President of Malta (since Apr 4, 2014)
- Sarah Wescot-Williams, Prime Minister of Saint Maarten (St. Martin)
- Julia Eileen Gillard, Prime Minister of Australia (2010-2013)

So between 1988 and 2022 female leaders have been heads of state in Europe, Asia, Africa, Central America, New Zealand, Caribbean and Pacific Ocean Islands and West Indies There have been none in South America. The U S has notably never had a female president. Hillary Clinton came close in 2016, but was defeated by Donald Trump.

Countries where there is **equality** at present are: Belgium, Denmark, France, Latvia, Luxembourg, Sweden, Greece, Iceland, Finland, Norway, Ireland, Canada, Portugal and Spain.

Part IV

Powerful women in history

Many women, intelligent, capable, strong, passionate, courageous and possessing leadership qualities have shaped the course of history, often without fanfare or being given the requisite recognition. Women are always judged much more harshly than men in leadership positions or otherwise. These women have challenged the established status quo and proven themselves. These women abounded much more in olden times than today in spite of us thinking we are emancipated. In the ancient world Africa, Asia, Middle-East, Europe, Native America, Islands, powerful women took the lead and saved their countries, nations, states or tribes. In quite recent history – in the past 5000 years too, there were women leaders and warriors from all over except from the United States. There has never been ONE female leader allowed to lead in the USA until now in 2023, in spite of the US calling itself the most democratic country in the world. In modern times, UK, Germany, Israel, India, Pakistan, Scandinavian countries, even New Zealand, Australia, Africa, Asia and even Islands have produced female leaders to mention only some (see above).

Mary Magdalene or Mary of Magdala: sometimes simply the Magdalene, was a woman who, according to the four canonical gospels, traveled with Jesus as one of his followers and was a witness to his crucifixion and resurrection. She is mentioned by name 12 times in the canonical gospels, more than most of the apostles and more than any other woman in the gospels, other than Jesus's family. She is also the only female to have a place in the gospels — *The Gospel of Mary*. Mary had the honour of being the first to witness Christ's resurrection and see the empty tomb. She took the news of the risen Christ to his disciples before they became his apostles. Christ is said to have shown special consideration and mercy to her. She was the only female who was with him throughout and the one who was with him in the garden just before Judas Iscariot betrayed him. She fulfilled his command: *Go to my brethren and say to them, I am ascending to my Father and your Father, to my God and your God*. And Mary went and announced: *I have seen the Lord.* She became the first evangelist and announced the news of the Resurrection. She broke all the norms of her culture, defied tradition, and was prepared to be ostracised to follow Jesus.

Mary Magdalene

In Rome

Roman women rarely, led armies and fought in the forefront. But they exerted power behind the scenes, often more than the Caesar did. They manipulated the system using any means at their disposal including murder and poison. They were always a force to be reckoned with, more than in any other society of those times. So a portion is dedicated to them here.

Livia Drusilla: (58 BC to 29 AD) was the wife of Augustus Caesar also known as Octavian. They were married for 51 years. He elevated her to the unprecedented position of his advisor and confidante. She was a good wife to him but she is believed to have manipulated the assassination or expulsion of anyone who might have inherited the throne except her sons by a former husband. Augustus had intended for Gaius and Lucius Caesar (his daughter Julia's sons) to be his heirs and adopted them. But they both died soon after. As did his grandson Agrippa Postumus and some other relatives. Livia's son Tiberius became Caesar after Augustus, most believed through the manipulations of Livia, who continued to exert great political power. But this was not the end of her line. Her grandson, Claudius when he became emperor, deified her as Augusta, then her great-grand son Caligula and her great-great-grandson Nero, Rome's two most notorious Caesars also became emperors of Rome.

Some saw her as the epitome of the perfect Roman wife and some as a manipulative person who always got what she wanted. She was strong, intelligent, shrewd, and loyal to Augustus and her sons. Most Romans believed that power was dangerous for women. And it should be denied them. Still some managed to be very powerful like Livia.

She left behind an impressive legacy. She was the first Roman empress to wield such power and the first Western woman to be commemorated over a very long time. No one crossed her and lived.

Julia the Elder (39 BC-AD 14), was the only daughter of Augustus Caesar and step-daughter to Livia Drusilla. In her early life she was conservative, strictly following Livia and Augustus' values. But this period probably sowed the seeds of rebellion in her.

Julia married three times the third time to her step-brother (Livia's son) the future Emperor Tiberius. But she was very unhappy with him and is said to have had numerous affairs. Historical data often focuses on her promiscuity. She got mixed up in a circle of friends who believed Tiberius was not fit to rule. So she was charged with conspiracy, never proven, to assassinate him during the life time of Augustus. He could not be seen to be lenient to her especially with Tiberius' mother, his wife urging otherwise. He had Julia exiled to a small island – Pandateria but was moved from there to Rheigium with a small allowance. When Tiberius became Emperor, he stopped all payments to his ex-wife and she is said, apparently, to have died of starvation. Tiberius' hand was said to have been involved in her death. She was not allowed burial in the family tomb. Julia was a very intelligent person who associated with poets and philosophers. The satirist said of her that she was witty, popular and had a great intellect with a particular passion for Latin literature. Ovid was supposed to have been in love with her. Augustus also exiled Ovid but elsewhere. Her daughter Julia the Younger, Augustus' legitimate granddaughter was also exiled and her child exposed to death on the mountainside. Tiberius was well-known for his scandalous life on the Island of Capri. Like his mother Livia, he was very vengeful.

Most information about her comes from Tacitus who calls her a woman of *feminine rage* and *natural greed*, and Suetonius says she was *incestuous*. Both these writers had their own political agendas as such slurs can be said about a lot of Romans of that time. Like some other Roman women of the time, she was a very ambitious and an unscrupulous mother. Unlike many, she also had the power. Unfortunately, she clashed with an even more dangerous adversary Livia, her stepmother.

Agrippina the Younger (15 AD to 59 AD): was the great-granddaughter of Livia, mother of Nero and sister of Caligula. She became the most powerful woman in Rome. She had great influence on Nero till he turned against her. Like Livia, she was very dominating and pushy. She married her uncle, Emperor Claudius and brought her son, the future emperor Nero with her to the Palace. But Claudius already had a legitimate heir, his own son Britannicus. However, Nero had something that poor Britannicus didn't have – the support of his mother Agrippina like Tiberius had had that of Livia. Britannicus did not stand a chance. He died under very suspicious circumstances after Claudius' death and Nero was crowned Emperor. But Agrippina had strong control of important military and political affairs. Nero became irritated with her control and interference. This came to a head after Agrippina disapproved of his latest mistress. He ordered her murder by drowning. But strong-willed Agrippina survived by swimming ashore. So in March 59 AD he sent his freedman Anticetus and other assassins to stab her to death. She is supposed to have asked them to stab her in the womb for having given birth to such a monstrous son. Nero was just 16 years old at this time.

Julia Domna (193 to 217 AD) was the second wife of Emperor Septimius Severus who was the last man standing during the year of five Emperors – 193 AD. Julia Domna, of Syrian noble descent, was the first Empress of the Severan dynasty and wielded a lot of power after the emperor's death. As empress, she was famous for her political, social, and philosophical influence and received titles such as *Mother of the Invincible Camps*. She was a woman of culture and sponsored many building works. In 197 she became empress consort after the Battle of Lugdunum. When Severus died, her two sons Caracalla and Geta fell out about sharing the rule. They loathed each other. She mediated between them but Caracella murdered his brother and ruled alone. This soured their relationship. Still, she travelled with him on his campaign against the Parthians. He was assassinated there. She committed suicide.

Julia Soaemias (180 to 222): When Julia Domna and Caracella died, the praetorian prefect Macrinus became emperor. He made the mistake of allowing Julia Domna's relatives to retire to Syria. This was a mistake because Domna's sister, Julia Soaemias had a son she believed would make an excellent emperor. Plotting with others and using her considerable wealth she raised a rebellion which soon overthrew Macrinus. She had her son Elagabalus (Heliogabalus) then aged 14, declared emperor. All power was in her hands. She was the first woman who was allowed in the Roman Senate. Soon however, Elagabalus caused many problems. He devalued the currency, worshipped foreign gods, started taking male lovers and then worst of all he married a Vestal Virgin Aquilia Severa, Vesta's high priestess claiming the marriage would produce *godlike children* (Icks 2011, pp. 57-58). This was totally unacceptable. He had to go.

The assassination plot against Elagabalus was devised by Julia Maesa, his grandmother, and carried out by disaffected members of the Praetorian Guard in 222. He was aged 18 years. He and his mother, who clung to him, were both killed – beheaded, stripped and dragged through the streets and then he was disposed of in the Tiber.

Edward Gibbon wrote that Elagabalus *"abandoned himself to the grossest pleasures with ungoverned fury"* Gibbon (chp. VI). His reputation among his contemporaries was one for extreme eccentricity, decadence, zealotry, and sexual promiscuity. The same and worse can be said of many other Roman emperors like Tiberius, Nero, Caligula and others. **Julia Mamaea** (180 to 235) also belonged to the Syrian Severan dynasty. She was the last powerful woman of this dynasty. She was the mother of Emperor Alexander Severus who became emperor at 14 and she remained his chief advisor throughout his reign.

Her son came to the throne through the machinations of Julia Mamesa, his grandmother, after she got rid of her other grandson, Elagabalus. Mamaea was reputedly a very traditional Roman matron but her leadership pushed her beyond that role. She reversed many of Elagabalus' irrational decrees and stabilised the empire. When Alexander came of age, he named his mother as Imperial Consort. He depended greatly on her advice. But when Alexander married, Julia clashed with his wife Sallustia Orbiana, and did not want a rival. She had his wife exiled. But soon, Alexander's relations with the army deteriorated.

In 232 mother and son, after their inconclusive Persian campaign went on to quell the Germanic tribes. But Alexander alienated the Rhine troops with his passivity, lack of military skill and his inflexibility to their pay demands. They blamed Mamaea for this. On March 2, troops were sent to assassinate Alexander and his mother, which they did. He was clinging to his mother at the time of his death. This was the end of the Severus dynasty. The next dynasty put them under *damnatio memoriae* (condemning and erasing their memory).

Ulpia Severina (empress from 270 to 275) was the wife of Emperor Aurelian. Very little is known about her. Her surname suggests that she is from Emperor Trajan's family line and from Dacia. It is assumed she married Aurelian before he became Emperor.

After the fall of the Severan dynasty, the Roman Empire was plunged into a period of rival emperors and tumult known as the **Crisis of the Third Century.** This ended when Aurelian became emperor. He subdued his rivals, reconquered lost territories, drove out invaders and reunified the Empire. His rule though short was important for the stability it brought back. Unfortunately, he was assassinated in 275 by his own officers due to a lie by his secretary that he intended to kill them all. Following this there was a significant period before the next emperor. It is believed that Ulpia ruled at that time and that is why her head is on coins and sometimes she is referred to as "diva" goddess. She may have been involved in the choice of the next emperor. Nothing further is known about her.

Fulvia: was an aristocratic Roman woman who lived during the exciting times of the Late Roman Republic. She belonged to an important political dynasty which led to her marrying important political figures. She married Publius Clodius Pulcher, Gaius Scribonius Curio, and finally Mark Antony, all of whom were important tribunes and supporters of Julius Caesar, and who played important political roles at that time. Fulvia was always very interested in politics and had a strong public voice. She was the first non-mythological woman to appear on Roman coins.

Fulvia was seen as Mark Anthony's partner in his political career, the brains behind many of his policies. Once when Cicero brutally attacked him, she defended him extremely well. It is said that when Cicero died, Fulvia stabbed his tongue in his decapitated head with her golden hairpin (Cassius Dio) for the vile things he had said about Mark Anthony. When Anthony and Octavian (Augustus later) left to pursue Caesar's assassins, she was left in charge of the city. Her daughter Claudia (by Clodius Pulcher) was married to Octavian and she would carry on the Clodian policies later.

Later when Anthony and Octavian fell foul of each other, and Anthony left for Egypt, she stayed in Rome and was a thorn in Octavian's side. She stirred the troops against Octavian, raised eight legions and occupied Rome in the Perusine War for a short time. Ultimately, she was defeated and fled to Greece where she died of illness. Anthony wasn't there to support her. Anthony later married Octavian's sister Octavia minor to heal the breach but he never gained power again. Fulvia was a very strong, politically perceptive, intelligent, virtuous, determined and loyal person. She was one of the very few to be politically openly involved in Rome.

Tullia (535 to 509 BC) was the daughter of Rome's sixth king, Servius Tullius. She married Lucius Tarquinius and along with her husband arranged for the murder of her father and their older siblings. There were two sisters married to two brothers. This pair was the youngest pair. They first got the support of a large number of senators. Tarquinius hurled his father-in-law onto the street where his assassins murdered him. Tullia drove her carriage over his mutilated body – just because he would not give up the throne. The street was thereafter called *Vicus Sceleratus* (street of infamy, wickedness). Tullia returned home covered in her murdered father's blood. In this way they secured the throne for her husband. She became an infamous figure in ancient Roman culture by this action. She was the last queen of pre-Republican Rome. Livy says that the gods were angered and the house was cursed for this act. Their reign ended as badly as it began. There was an uprising led by Lucius Junius Brutus that put an end to this monarchy. The family was exiled. The Romans cursed Tullia as they fled. She appears to have been a very unscrupulous person, very ambitious and with no moral compunctions. She and her husband, who appears to be the weaker person, were similar. They committed patricide and fratricide – both unforgivable crimes. No one knows how they died.

Most information about her is from Livy, a Roman historian, written in 510 BC, Bks 1 to 5 of *Ab urbe condita* that is about the legendary founding of Rome. It is a monumental history of ancient Rome, written in Latin between 27 and 9 BC. The work covers the period from the legends concerning the arrival of Aeneas and the refugees from the fall of Troy, to the city's founding in 753 BC, the expulsion of the Kings in 509 BC, and down to Livy's own time, during the reign of Augustus.

Hortensia (1st century BC) was the daughter of Quintus Hortensius Hortalus, consul and advocate. He was renowned during the late Roman Republic as a skilled orator. Hortensia is best known for a speech she delivered to the members of the Second Triumvirate (Mark Anthony, Octavian and Lepidus) in 42 BC that resulted in the partial repeal of a tax on wealthy Roman women. Cassius and Brutus, Julius Caesar's other assassins, had killed many rich people and confiscated their properties to raise money but it was not enough. So they decided to impose a tax on 1500 wealthy Roman women. The women resented this for a war they had nothing to do with. Hortensia invited the women to the forum and this is part of the speech she gave:

> *You have already deprived us of our fathers, our sons, our husbands, and our brothers, whom you accused of having wronged you; if you take away our property also, you reduce us to a condition unbecoming our birth, our manners, our sex. Why should we pay taxes when we have no part in the honors, the*

commands, the state-craft, for which you contend against each other with such harmful results? 'Because this is a time of war,' do you say? When have there not been wars, and when have taxes ever been imposed on women, who are exempted by their sex among all mankind?"

It was a major feat as women had no say in politics at that time. Hortensia made the men realise the women's anger and do something about it. The women had been furious with the tax but could not appeal against it. Anthony, Octavia and Lepidus were not happy about it but they could not get her to leave the rostrum. Finally, they agreed to tax only 400 women and get the rest of the money elsewhere.

There are many other Roman women who made the pages of history but in general Roman women used their influence and power through and in their husband's names. They were seldom queens or empresses in their own right and they never went to battle or fought. Some did accompany the armies but did not fight unlike many other women of other countries, empires and states. Roman women were expected to be mothers, wives and matrons, though they did advice their menfolk at times. They generally worked behind the scenes and were a power to be reckoned with. Poison, Murders, assassinations were their secret weapons.

Some International women who wielded power

But they were not the only women to do so. Throughout the history of civilisation, women have always been there as a guiding force overtly or covertly in different cultures, religions, ages and societies. When overt power was impossible, they resorted to covert power like in Rome. Some used that power only for good and some did not. Some were a credit to womankind in every way and some were not. But that is humanity. We are all flawed in some way – some in a major way and some not. But we are supposed to do our best at all times. Murder is not the right way but many famous leaders, men and women, kings, queens and commoners committed it in their weakness or greed for power.

Here are other women who exerted overt power and control in different countries. Lack of space leaves me unable to record all of them. There are many, many extremely brave, intelligent, capable and powerful women who flashed across the universal sky and left an indelible mark on the world behind. They often shaped the course of history; they challenged the status quo, when necessary, initiated lasting reforms, ruled over huge tracts of lands and peoples, successfully, saw their lands happy, strong and prosperous and often brought about cultural revolutions. To all these women, I pay homage – forever.

Some few from around the world are presented here. Many more are under specific topics.

Hatshepsut (1508 BC-1458 BC): was one of the most powerful and successful Ancient Egyptian pharaohs. She belonged to the 18th Dynasty and ruled longer than any other woman in Egyptian history. She married her sickly brother Thutmose I in 1492 BC and when he died of illness soon after she continued alone till her death in 1458 BC. She oversaw major building projects, military campaigns into Nubia, Syria and the Levant and rebuilt broken trade networks due to the Hyksos invasions. She also led large scale armies into the land of Punt to the south of Egypt, and successful campaigns to Nubia, Syria and the Levant.

Aelia Pulcheria (399 to 453) belonged to the Theodosian dynasty. She ruled the Byzantine Empire during her brother's minority. Theodosius II came to the throne at the age of 7. Pulcheria was 15 and claimed guardianship on his behalf. She took a vow of perpetual virginity to avoid getting married. The court under them was a pious one. Her brother proved to be a weak ruler and she continued to guide him. When he died in 450 after a fall from his horse, she continued to rule alone. But the people considered it unsuitable for a woman to rule alone and she was forced to take a husband. She married Emperor Marcian but the marriage was never consummated. She died three years later. She did a lot for the church. She was a good queen and a pious woman.

Theodora (500-548): was a highly influential Empress of the Byzantine Empire and a saint of the Eastern Orthodox Church. Unlike most other female rulers, she was not a noblewoman. She was born in Cyprus. Her father was a bear trainer and her mother, an actress. She followed in her mother's profession on stage. There are conflicting accounts about her by Procopius (*The Wars of Justinian*) in which he showed her as a pious, courageous woman who saved the throne for Justinian. But he also portrays her very negatively as a vulgar, mean and calculating woman. He finally contradicts himself by portraying both Theodora and Justinian as pious and conventional. Other Writers were John of Ephesus, her contemporary, who mentioned her in the *Lives of Eastern Saints*; Theophanes, the Confessor; Victor Tonnennensis, who mentions her family connection to the next empress Sophia and Michael the Syrian whose account coincided with that of John of Epheus. Modern writers prefer Procopius' account. It is more salacious though less accurate.

Theodora withdrew from her disreputable profession. When she met Justinian, they fell in love but a Roman law from Constantine's time prevented their marriage. So Justinian after ascending the throne passed a law that reformed actress could become wives of senators and above. So they married. She was a very powerful presence in Justinian's court. She was his most trusted advisor and co-ruler. Many governmental decisions were made by her. She controlled foreign affairs and legislation, put down violent riots, and, **notably, used her husband's reforms to improve the position of women and increase their rights passing anti-trafficking laws and improving divorce proceedings and property ownership for women. She passed laws prohibiting forced prostitution, gave mothers guardianship over children in divorce cases, instilled the death penalty for rape and**

forbade the killing of a wife for adultery. One time when riots broke out over high taxes, religious controversy and political corruption in Nika in Constantinople and it seemed Justinian could be toppled, she argued against fleeing and the riot was controlled. Her protégés all rose to power and high positions. By all accounts she was a very good influence on her husband and the court and a very forward-thinking woman. She did a lot bettering the condition of women.

She made Constantinople into one of the world's most sophisticated cities. She built bridges, aqueducts and churches, the most beautiful being the *Hagia Sophia* built between 532 and 537 AD, an excellent example of Byzantine architecture still admired around the world today.

Empress Wu Zetian (624-705) was born in Shanxi province of China in 624 CE to the chancellor (from a noble and wealthy family) of the Tang dynasty. Unlike most fathers of the time, her father insisted she learn to read, write, and develop intellectual skills. She was very beautiful and the Emperor Taizong took her as his concubine. On his death, his son Gazong became Emperor and Wu Zeitan was sent away to become a Buddhist nun. But Empress Wang, Gaozong's wife had a serious power struggle with his favourite concubine, Consort Xiao. The Empress brought back Wu Zeitan to be her husband's concubine and break Xiao's spell. The plan backfired as Wu Zeitan became the new favourite and the power struggle was now among the three. The Empress and Xiao joined forces against Wu Zeitan to stop her influence over Gaozong. In 654 Wu Zeitan gave birth to a baby girl who died shortly after. It was feared that the child had been murdered by the Empress. Gaozong replaced her with Wu Zeitan as his new Empress consort. The other two, ex Empress Wang and Xiao were accused of witchcraft and executed.

Empress Wu Zeitan of China

Empress Wu Zeitan took control of the empire and became very powerful. Towards the end of Gaozong's life, Wu virtually made all the decisions relating to governing the Empire. Soon after his death, as dowager she had herself crowned Empress in 690 AD and ruled till her death. She began her own dynasty – the Zhou Dynasty. She was the only female Chinese Emperor during the Tang period. She extended China's boundaries far West into Central Asia. Many regard her as one of China's greatest leaders. Her reforms and policies helped make China the most prosperous country in the world at that time. Under her rule, the Chinese Empire not only expanded but had economic prosperity and she also initiated educational reforms. She lowered taxes and increased agricultural production. She was a great Patron of Buddhism and made it the official religion, replacing Taoism. She died at the age of 80. According to her detractors, and rulers always have many, once they are dead, she was ruthless and cruel and carried out political intrigue. That is still to be proven.

Börte Üjin (1161-1230): was the first wife of the famous conqueror and founder of the Mongolian empire Genghis Khan and Empress of the Mongolian Empire, the largest land empire in history. Although Genghis had other wives too, only her children were considered people of the Great Khan and could rule and inherit. She was named the Grand Empress of Mongolia and was one of Genghis Khan's most trusted advisors. As Genghis continued to expand his empire, he had to be away for long periods of time, so he left Börte behind to manage the land. His brother Temuge helped her. She was given total authority to rule and control most of the Kherlen River, which had previously belonged to the Tartars. She was very intelligent and capable.

Borte was abducted by Genghis' enemies the Merkitts and given as war trophy to one of his warriors. Genghis Khan rescued her after several months and accepted the baby as his own. He even wanted to leave the empire to Jochi but the tribe would not accept that because of the shadow over his parentage. So Jochi became the leader of the *Golden Horde*. Börte is one of history's unsung heroes.

Börte Üjin, Mongol Empress   *Eleanor of Aquitaine*

Eleanor of Aquitaine (1122(?) -1204): was one of the most powerful and intelligent females in the Middle-Ages. She was well-educated and used to power and politics. She inherited the titles of Countess of Poitiers and Duchess of Aquitaine at the age of 15 on the death of her father. Aquitaine was one of the wealthiest and most powerful provinces of France at that time and her father had made sure she had an excellent education to rule it. She transformed Aquitaine into one of the largest intellectual and cultural centres in Europe of that period.

She became queen consort of King Louis VII of France and went on the Second Crusade with him — a very unconventional move for a queen in 1147 to Byzantine and then onto Jerusalem. She was involved in some scandal there but she also was responsible for developing trade between Western Europe, Byzantine and the Holy Land. On her return, soon after she had her marriage to King Louis annulled on grounds of consanguinity after 15 years of marriage in 1152. Her daughters of this marriage were recorded as legitimate as it was in the fourth degree. Then she married Henry II King of England in 1154. As queen of England and Duchess of Aquitaine she exerted control too but she and Henry, were both very strong characters and they had many quarrels. When Henry had Archbishop Thomas Becket assassinated, Eleanor was against it and supported her sons' rebellions against their father. Henry had her imprisoned for 16 years but she still continued to have her voice heard. After his death, in the absence of her son King Richard, often she ruled and during his imprisonment in Austria, singlehanded, she raised an enormous sum of money for his release. His brother, John, acting in his stead, did nothing to help. He wanted the kingship for himself and even offered Richard's captors money to keep him imprisoned. His mother, Queen Eleanor, paid more for Richard's release.

Isabella I of Castile (1451-1504): She is considered as one of the most powerful and most controversial figures in Spanish history. She is best remembered for sponsoring Christopher Columbus' voyages; for unifying the remaining independent Spanish kingdoms into one nation **and for initiating the terrible Spanish Inquisition.** She co-ruled with her husband, Ferdinand of Aragon from 1474 until her death.

Isabella and Ferdinand were devout Roman Catholics and Reconquista was nearing its end everywhere. Most of Spain was unified under Catholic power except for the small kingdom under the Nasrid dynasty in Andalusia. From 1485 to 1492, Isabella and Ferdinand forced the Muslim population into exile or death solidifying Spanish Catholic power. At this time too Isabella sponsored Columbus and so contributed to Spanish colonial power and wealth taking Spain into a superpower status.

Spain at that time was a land of diverse religions – Christians, Muslims, Jews. Isabella and Ferdinand felt it was their duty to make Spain a Roman Catholic country only. And so in 1478, they began the **Spanish Inquisition** to bring this about. Thousands of Jews who had converted to Christianity were looked upon suspiciously, at this time. Soon the Inquisition began its work. At least 2,000 Jews were rounded up, tortured and killed or expelled from the country. About 40,000 Jews converted to avoid death, persecution or expulsion. Then the Muslim population of Spain was targeted. In 1502, Queen Isabella issued an edict banning Islam from Castile. It became even worse under the **Grand Inquisitor Jiménez** from 1507. In 1515, Iberian Navarre was annexed and all Muslims were forced to follow Christian beliefs under the Castalian edict. In 1526 forced conversion of Muslims also began in Valencia and Aragon. Then the hounding of the Moriscos, converted Muslims, began and reached its worst point under Philip III when he ordered the expulsion of **300,000 Muslim Moriscos.** This was one of the most brutal and tragic episodes in Spanish history. Spain was the only multireligious, multiethnic, multiracial country before the Inquisition initiated by Isabella. Conversion was carried out by the sword and torture. What shock to Christ who never forced conversion would have thought of this! The Spanish civilisation had developed greatly in art, literature, religion, architecture in the Middle-Ages under the Muslim rule. Now a pall of darkness, torture, death and extreme prejudice descended upon the land. It continued under three Spanish monarchies during the 16th century – Castile (1500-1502), Navarre (1515-1516) and again Castile (1523-1526) all begun by Isabella of Castile. She was known in the Catholic Church as *"Servant of God Isabella"* but not of Christ, who did not believe in forced conversion. She achieved sainthood by this action: *convert or die*. She was a good queen but too fanatical.

Note: The Moors who invaded Spain in 711 AD brought civilisation to the wild, white tribes of the Caucasus. In time they ruled Spain, Portugal, North Africa and South France for over 700 years. Under them literacy rose to its highest point in Spain. Education was universal in Spain when 99% of Christian Europe population was illiterate; where literacy was reserved for the Church and few others. During the period when Europe had only two universities, Spain had 17. **But all this came to an end with Isabella and the Inquisition.** Recent archaeological records and scholarship brought to light what Spain under Isabella and Ferdinand and for generations after have tried so hard to expunge – the legacy of the Moors.

Their advances in art, mathematics, philosophy, astronomy, architecture helped to impel Europe out of the Dark Ages and into the Renaissance. The Inquisition undid a lot of that.

Elizabeth I (1533-1603): was one of most powerful English monarchs and the only female ruler in complete control of England, ever. She never married and kept all suitors dangling because she knew marriage meant sharing authority, power. She was the daughter of Henry VIII and Anne Boleyn, succeeding Mary Tudor to the throne. She was the last Tudor to rule England. She saw what could happen to queens at the hands of husbands and fathers – English history is replete with such examples (Eleanor of Aquitaine, Anne Boleyn, to name only two very strong women). She was never going to be such a victim. Elizabeth preferred to be called the "Virgin Queen," for as she said she was wedded to her land. Elizabeth learnt all about power, diplomacy, strategy and statecraft at a very young age, when her life had been threatened time after time. She learned to read people, to evaluate and manipulate them. She was very intelligent and a born ruler. Though she was a Protestant, she never persecuted the Catholics or any others. Religion to her was a matter of one's own conscience (I believe). Yes, Protestantism became the State religion under her but she did not demand to look into a person's soul – unlike Queen Isabella's Spanish Inquisition. Queen Elizabeth ushered in the Renaissance to England. Her rule came to be known as the Golden Age of England. She ushered in stability, immense progress in many spheres, national pride, huge strides in literature, international expansion, naval power, peace after all the religious turmoil at home. It was also an age of intrigues, adventure, power struggle and intellectual advancement.

Elizabeth was very well educated by the renowned Roger Ascham, a great scholar. She studied Greek, Latin, rhetoric, and philosophy and mastered them. Her court was the centre for poets, dramatists, writers, musicians, scholars, intellectuals, and others. She collected around her such luminaries as William Shakespeare, Christopher Marlowe, Edmund Spenser and other great literary names.

Though a Protestant herself, she did not force conversion or persecute other religions. The execution of Mary, Queen of Scots was something she put off for as long as she could. Finally, her hand was forced. She defeated Philip II's huge Spanish Armada and her reputation sky rocketed. Spain was very strong at that time. Under Elizabeth, England moved inexorably towards becoming the dominant world power replacing Spain. She brought peace, prosperity and advancement in all spheres to England.

Marie Theresa of Austria (1717-1780): was a Hapsburg Empress who reigned for 40 years and controlled a large part of Europe, including Austria, Hungary, Croatia, Bohemia, and parts of Italy. She had sixteen children, who also became key power players like the Queen of France, the Queen of Naples and Sicily as well as two Holy Roman Emperors. After the death of her husband, she made her son Joseph II co-regent in 1765.

When Maria Theresa came to power, Frederick II of Brandenburg-Prussia refused to recognise her power and initiated the war of Austrian Succession by invading the Hapsburg provinces of Silesia, with his allies of mainly Bavaria, Saxony, France, and Spain. Maria retaliated by rallying the Hungarians to arms and they defeated the invading armies and preserving the Hapsburgs as a major European power by the signing of the *Treaty of Aix-la-Chapelle.*

Maria Theresa was a very good ruler. She instituted many economic and political changes to her empire. She increased the size of the army by 200% and increased taxes so that a steady income was guaranteed for the government, specifically the military. She combined the Austrian and Bohemian Chancelleries into a central administrative centre. She started the Diplomatic Revolution in 1756 when she created an alliance with France, a former enemy, to form a coalition against the newly allied Prussia and Great Britain. Her reforms and political decisions succeeded in strengthening the economy and the state.

Maria Theresa believed in the Enlightenment. She promoted education and liberal politics. She supported medical research and demanded the University of Vienna be given money to increase the efficiency of the medical units. She founded the Imperial and Royal Academy of Science and Literature in Brussels to support scientific research. She also instituted civil reforms which included stopping the horrible burning of 'witches', torture, and capital punishment. She made education mandatory. She also instituted reforms in commerce.

Catherine The Great (1729-1796): also known as Catherine II was undoubtedly one of history's most famous women. Born in Poland, a minor German princess of the Lutheran faith and proficient in Russian, in 1774 she moved to Russia to marry Peter III, heir to the Russian throne and converted to Orthodox Christianity. At that time and even now, Russia is one of the largest countries in the world, geographically.

The marriage was a tragic failure. Catherine wanted total power. Peter III was weak and soon Catherine plotted with the imperial guard to overthrow Peter and take over sole rule of the country in a palace coup. It succeeded and Peter III was overthrown and forced to abdicate. He died soon after. Officially, it was stated that he died of a severe attack of *"hemorrhoidal colic"* and an apoplectic stroke. But the general belief was and still is that he was assassinated on Catherine's orders by Alexei Orlov, the younger brother of her then lover Grigory Orlov. No one knows the real truth.

She continued with the work of Peter the Great and Tsarina Elizabeth, in modernising Russia and bringing it in line with Western Enlightenment. Catherine also incorporated these new ideas into politics. She commissioned many art works and improved the foreign policy. She fought and defeated the Ottoman Empire in two major wars and it was during her time the Russian Empire extended over **three** continents, including the colonising of Alaska. It stretched from the Arctic Ocean in the North to the Black Sea in the South, Alaska and the Pacific in the East to the Baltic Sea in the West. She also initiated legislative reforms like local self-government (1775) and Charter of Nobility (1785). She put down the dangerous Pugachev Rebellion led by the famous Cossack Yemelyan Ivanovich in 1773 in the Ural Mountains. After crushing the rebellion, she imposed very harsh restrictions on society. Serfdom became more prevalent than ever before. She never allowed anyone to impinge on her power or impede her in anyway. The punishments were always very harsh. She reigned for 34 years. She was well known for her risqué personal life and her legendary love affairs with mostly younger officers. Her rule is regarded as the Golden Age of the Russian Empire by many.

Queen Victoria (1819-1901) also called Empress of India: is considered by many to have been the most powerful woman in history because not only was she the queen of the United Kingdom in her own right, but also head of the vast colonial British Empire. However, she did not wield actual power in the sense of working on her own unlike Elizabeth I. She had excellent Prime ministers and ministers but undoubtedly, she was a very powerful leader. She ruled over an empire that stretched over **six** continents for 63 years, the second longest reign of a queen, the longest was Queen Elizabeth II who passed away in 2022. Geographically, it was the largest Empire in the 19th century and in history. She ruled over 458 million people at that time. It was a very conservative period in both religious and social attitudes, fashion and politics not just in the UK but also in her colonies including America.

Queen Victoria's rule was a very defining one and it came to be called the Victorian Age. It was said that the sun did not set on her empire because she had dominion over such vast areas. It was said to be 14.2 million square miles, including Australia, Canada, India, New Zealand, Nigeria, South Africa, and Sudan and many others.

Though Queen Victoria shared power with the Parliament, still she wielded quite a lot of power over many political decisions like appointing Cabinet members, and even the Prime Minister, once. She also appointed ambassadors and bishops to the Church of England. The Prime Minister was expected to consult with her on every issue. She contributed massively to social and political reforms. In 1838, under her rule, slavery was abolished throughout the British colonies and voting rights granted to most British men. In 1847 the factory Act was passed reducing working hours to 10 in textile mills. In 1884, she backed the Third Reform Act of 1884 that granted males in every household the right to vote. So, she initiated all these reforms in the conditions of the labour and brought about significant political, cultural, and military changes in her Empire.

Indira Gandhi (1917–1984): was the first and only female Prime Minister of India, serving 4 terms between 1966-1984. She was assassinated by her Sikh bodyguards when she ordered the storming of their holy temple during an insurgency. She was a controversial but very powerful figure, winning a war with Pakistan, which resulted in the creation of Bangladesh in 1971.

Indira was the daughter of Jawaharlal Nehru, a prominent nationalist leader during India's fight for freedom from British rule. She was educated mostly in private schools in India and Switzerland and later she went to Oxford. WWII intervened and she returned to India and soon after married Feroze Gandhi, a politician and journalist. She got deeply involved in politics as her marriage failed and soon she became her father's confidante, advisor and de facto hostess at his prime ministerial residence. In 1959 she became president of the Indian National Congress but continued under the front of a *dumb doll*. No one had gauged the shrewd, decisive, aggressive and somewhat dictatorial leader that lay underneath. In 1966 she became the Prime Minister overcoming all obstacles in her path. She made India a dominant power in the region by 1973. India became self-sufficient in food production; her economic policies transformed the industrial scene. Then when she declared 'a political emergency' suspending all democratic institutions in the country she faced defeat but overcame even this challenge to win a second term as Prime Minister in 1980. She lost her life at the hands of a Sikh assassin in her bodyguard in her response to the separatist movement of the Sikh region of Northern Punjab in 1984.

Margaret Thatcher (1925-2013): was the first female and till now, the third Prime Minister of the United Kingdom. She held office from 1979 to 1990. She was the longest-serving British PM of the 20th century, dubbed the *"Iron Lady"* by the Soviets for her hard-headedness. Her theory which came to be called *Thatcherism* represented a systematic, decisive rejection and reversal of the post-war consensus, by which major political parties largely agreed on the central themes of Keynesianism, the welfare state, nationalised industry and close regulation of the British economy. Her political philosophy and economic policies emphasised deregulation, particularly of the financial sector, privatisation of state-owned companies, and reducing the power and influence of trade unions.

She won a popular victory over Argentina in the 1982 Falklands War, but her economic policies had mixed support, as she promoted a free-market economy and confronted the power of the labour unions.

She died at the age of 87 and with her passed away a great woman. She was a phenomenon – a very hard-working woman who never took vacations. She rolled through the House of Commons and none could stay her passage, with flashing eyes, a steady carriage and a handbag clutched to her side. She made many men very nervous and they instigated a *whispering campaign* against her unable to face her openly. In my opinion, Thatcher was the greatest British Prime Minister since Winston Churchill and the first and only woman to lead a party at the beginning of parliamentary democracy. She was a woman to be greatly admired and I do admire her.

The other two female prime ministers of England were Theresa May and Liz Truss.

Ancient warrior Queens: women and war

The role of women in warfare differed from culture to culture but there is written proof since recorded history of women warriors from about 500 CE. Archaeological records support this.

Following is a very brief outline of active women warriors. Some are queens who led their armies and fought alongside them. From 17th BCE to the 5th century AD there were many famous women warriors. Most of them were queens or military leaders like **Queens Ahhotep I and II in Egypt; Queen Hatshepsut** also in Egypt against the kingdoms of Nubia and Canaan; **Epipole of Carystus** in the Trojan war, **Medea of Colchis**, wife of Jason, **Lady Fu Hao and Lady Fu Jing** in China; **Vishpala** in the Rigveda in India; **Deborah** in the Book of Judges who defeated king Jabin of Canaan; **Queen Gwendolen** who fought and defeated her husband Locrinus for the throne (according to Geoffrey of Monmouth, regarded here to be an unreliable source); burial **mounds of Kangju of Kazakhstan** where rulers were buried with their weapons – swords and daggers; according to Greek legendary history, **Messine** conquered and founded the city of Messina; **Shammuramat (Semiramis) ruled the neo-Assyrian empire, the first woman in history to do so without a man.** She is supposed to have inspired the legendary warrior **Queen Semiramis; Queen Cordelia** on whom Shakespeare based King Lear's daughter. Cordelia is supposed to have fought and defeated her nephews for the throne (again this is recorded by Geoffrey of Monmouth, not a reliable source);

tomb of Armenian women warriors buried with war wounds and war weapons in the Armenian highlands; Arabian; **Queen Samsi who followed Queen Zabibe** to the throne in Arabia was such a good warrior that she was able to face the mighty Assyrian King Tilgath-Pilser III; **Scythian women were brave** warriors, even when young. A 13-year-old female warrior's tomb was unearthed in Russia in 1988. Many other female warrior tombs have been unearthed in Russia. Some others from 580 to 506 BCE were; **Queen Tomyris** of Massagetae an Iranian-Scythian people, led her army to battle against King Cyrus of Persia and defeated him. She wanted his head on a platter and got it; **Pantea Arteshbod** also participated in the Battle of Opis as a Lieutenant Commander in the army of Cyrus the Great (The Immortals equivalent to today's US Special Forces); Greek **poetess Telesilla** defended the city of Argos against the Spartan attack successfully by leading the women of the city under her command; **Lady of Yue** trained the King Goujian of Yue's soldiers for battle; **Artemisia I of Caria**, Queen of Halicarnassus, was a naval commander and advisor to the Persian king Xerxes at the Battle of Salamis. One very warlike female warrior queen, according to Polyaenus of Lampsachus **was Amage, a Sarmatian queen** who warned a Scythian prince to stop his incursions on her Crimean protectorates. He ignored her warning so she rode with 120 warriors and defeated and killed him. She allowed his son to rule under her edicts (Salmonson, JA, pp. 7; David E. Jones, pp. 126).

Queen Sammuramat of Assyria *Warrior Queen Semiramis*

Women warriors in Ancient Times

Since the dawn of time, before established religion took hold, there was more equality in society. Women lived, hunted, fought and died alongside men. There is indisputable proof as archaeological evidence, from East to West from Norway to Georgia, from Europe to Asia, to Africa to American Indians that repeats this fact. This was before societal change and the establishment of patriarchal society began which forced women into a more subservient role and women were forced into the mould of demure passivity and 'helplessness' and relegated to the realm of dependents on male kindness. Men are not kind. But even in the patriarchal world, some cultures maintained the equality of men and women. And in those, women still fought alongside men and led armies and ruled the land. And in some, women proved their prowess **in spite of** men's dominance like Joan of Arc.

War history in our times generally focuses on male warriors. Women are described and treated as "the weaker sex" yet throughout history women warriors, rulers, poets, in fact in all spheres of life have been on a par with men. Warrior women were found in all the continents, Europe, Asia, especially the Middle-East, Africa and pre-colonial America. Very, very few women warriors are well-known today. When we read about a woman warrior, we get the impression that she was an exception and not a general rule. **But that is incorrect.** Men and women in ancient times fought side-by-side, equally courageously; equally well with the same types of weapons. They contributed not only to warfare but also had great political and historical effect on their times. In later times laws and other obstacles had been put in their way and so we rarely heard about warrior women and their exploits.

History commemorates the exploits of great men on battlefields but rarely those of women. However, in spite of everything some warrior women have forced the world to mark their valour on the battlefield and they have become legendary.

From Europe to Asia to Africa some women have left an indelible mark on history in spite of the odds, the common laws and beliefs in general. There have however, been some races that have given women the same opportunities and prerogatives as men. Among them are the Slavs, the Scytho-Sarmatian cultures, some Greek city states like Sparta, Argos,

Crete; tribes in Africa, the Mongol, Kurdish society, Celtic society and the Amazons, the Macedonians, the Scandinavians, the Goths, the Iberians, the Egyptians, the Chinese, the Japanese, the Assacani (Pakistan), the Libyans, the Mayans (Queen K'abel) and many others.

These women epitomize feminism before the concept came into general use. They fought for their beliefs, their homes, their land their people and that won them a place for all time.

Famous Warrior Women groups

In the ancient world heroes were both men and women. In many cultures women fought beside men equally bravely and equally well. World history is full of dynamic, courageous, influential women. They have just not got the same press coverage as men. Some, a very few have been immortalised in plays and films like Cleopatra, Joan of Arc and Boudicca but most have hardly got a passing reference. We will take a quick look at some of these ancient women warriors, druids, priestesses and queens.

Most of us have an incorrect idea that ancient women were powerless, their husband's property. This was not at all the case. The earliest societies were all matriarchal. Women, the creators of new life, were at the top of the chain. She was the socio-political ruler and the productive wife. Only later did society become patriarchal. In such society, yes, women mostly lived in male-dominated societies, their primary purpose being wife and mother to make possible the survival of the race and the functioning of life. But not all societies had rigid rules. Women's roles in many still gave them the choice to participate fully even as a warrior or priestess, druid or queen. In parts of Greece, in Celtic Britain, women ruled in their own right and were famous for their own military exploits. In Egypt women exerted a lot of power in their own right. In Rome many women exerted their power through the males. Roman women were not physically warriors for the most part but rulers still. But in many other races, women fought alongside men as valiantly as the male heroes. Until recent times, women's role in written history was ignored but women played very important roles in the development of their societies in every aspect of life. The oral cultures gave women their due much more than did the later written traditions.

In the East, civilisations like the Akkadians, Hittites, Assyrians, Canaanites (Palestine) had patriarchal societies as did most others. There were exceptions like the Sumerians where women had complete control of properties, education and legally even freedom to take more than one husband. Egypt was another exception and for three millennia they retained their position. Inheritance passed through the female including the throne. Many women were very wealthy and politically powerful. Some women became pharaohs. Egypt influenced both Greece and Rome. Rome was staunchly patriarchal until the contact with Cleopatra of Egypt. Both Greek and Roman societies found themselves between two extremes – the subordinate, secluded women of the patriarchal society and the powerful, rich outgoing women who exercised political clout. These women were constantly challenging the ideal of patriarchal male dominance.

With the beginning of Judaism in the Bronze Age, patriarchy became even stricter, along with monotheism – the worship of one god – Yahweh previously **one of the Canaanite gods** who now took on the role of the **only god.**

In the first century the role of women emerged in the patriarchal society as having no rights, they were the property of men, no social or political role to play except childbearing. The meeting of Judaism and Hellenism led to a change. Some Schools of Judaism became even stricter in their attempt at total seclusion and subordination of women from Hellenistic influence to maintain the purity of Judaism. The other school was those who lived within the Hellenistic culture. There were rich and powerful women here. They continued to ignore the new strictures of the Talmud and Torah, abiding more by the rules of the Hellenistic society.

Into this complex world Christianity was born. It originated in the Judaism of Palestine, where the Hellenistic influence was already present. Christianity spread to other places, Rome, Greece, Egypt. The role of women in the Christian church was thus much influenced by Judaism, Greek and Roman cultures.

Minoan Crete

Women in Minoan Crete held a different role to that of other places. Their presence was all pervasive in all spheres of life – in religious and social life, in fact in Minon civilisation. They were at the very heart of it. Their strength, grace, courage and beauty set them apart from all others and made them the ideal representation of Cretan culture creating strong feelings of pride and respect in the people.

To the Cretans, power was symbolised in the woman ruler. This was most probably a remanent of the matriarchal age as Minoan Crete was at least 1,000 years older than Classical Greece. The twelfth God in the Throne Room in Knossos in their pantheon depicts the Great Goddess and the priest king. She is sitting on a throne while he, the young male stands at her side. This room is both the secular and religious centre.

The great goddess is the Sun Goddess, the fertility Goddess and the Queen of the Patheon all in one. She is the head. She is the one who always sits on the throne. It has been suggested that the young male could be her consort or more, likely her son.

On every occasion, the Mother Goddess or the sea (also a feminine principle) was worshipped in celebratory events, feasts, festivals and sporting events. The stars of these celebrations were always women and girls. The daughters of the king would also participate like beautiful Ariadane and Faedra who would dance with snakes to show the close relationship with mother earth. The Climax of all festivals was the bull dance (*Tavrokathapsia*). Again, the best of the young including the princesses participated in it. It was a most demanding act needing extreme courage, skill and tact. This dance was to honour the bull (Taurus) a sacred animal to the Minoans.

Both men and women participated equally in the games. Many frescoes in the palace of Knossos depict this.

Women did not lead armies as there was little or no war here. They were a trading nation. But it is a fact that women here were very powerful.

This civilisation came to an abrupt end not through war but through an eruption – that of Thera which was a major volcanic eruption. It destroyed the Minoan settlement in Akrotiri that, in turn badly affected the whole civilisation. It was the beginning of the end of Minoan Crete. It was one of the largest eruptions in Europe.

Minoan Bull dance

Illyrian women

One 1800-year-old tablet found in Durres, Albania in 1979 by Fatos Tartari was analysed by Eduard Shehi, an archaeologist. In the tomb was also discovered a book of debts showing the female moneylender was owed 2,000 dinarii when a Roman soldier's yearly income was only 200 dinairi. This lends weight to the ancient historical writings that Illyrian women were of equal status to men as participating in warfare, holding political and military power and leadership positions. They drank with men at banquets and even raised toasts with men, a totally unheard-of thing in Greece or Rome. *When a woman has control over her finances, she has the right to do business, the right to own property and inheritance; she is not a slave to man* (Eduard Shehi). He further says that Illyrian women had more equality than any other women anywhere else in Europe at that time. Actually, that is a bit of an exaggeration.

Another historical proof of this is the record of Cynane, (358-323 BCE) daughter of King Philip II of Macedon and his Illyrian wife Audata. Cynane was well known as an exceptional warrior to the extent that her fighting skills were known throughout the land. She was also an excellent military strategist and master-minded the overthrow of Phillip Arrhidaeus, Alexander the Great's half-brother and led an army against Alexander's general and Philip's regent, Perdiccas. Then she marched against his brother Alcetas, Cynane's former companion, who finally slew her. She was a very remarkable woman in history.

Women of Troy and Anatolia

Artemisa I of Caria (5th century BC) was the queen of Halicarnassus, in modern Turkey and was very well known as an excellent naval commander. She joined the Persian King Xerxes in the Battle of Salamis against Greece. Her fight was regarded as the best against the Greeks. She was decisive, extremely intelligent, especially in her military strategies, ruthless with a strong sense of self preservation. At one point when a Greek vessel was bearing down on her ship, she rammed a Persian ship. The Greeks believed her to be a Greek too and left her alone.

Homer presents the women of Troy as much more skilled in the arts of war than is generally believed. For example, the advice that **Andromache,** Hector's wife gave him, had he followed, it would have been really beneficial. Her name itself means man-fighter. She was well-versed in war tactics. Homer also talks about Penthesilea, the Amazon who came to help the Trojans and died there. Penthesilea, according to Quintus of Smyrna, also got the Trojan women like **Hippodamia** and others like her to take their fate in their own hands. But it was not to be. The women of Troy ended up staying inside the city stopped by "prudent Theano" who reminds them that they have never been in battle before, whereas the Amazons have been trained for warfare. The Fates were against Troy. Penthesilea too, dies there at the hands of Achilles who then falls in love with her. She was buried in Troy.

Amazons:

The Amazons appear in works by the Greek writers Herodotus, and Apollodorus. For a long time, the Amazons were considered to belong to Greek mythology as fierce, female warriors who lived and roamed around a vast area by the Black Sea known as Scythia. They inspired awe and fear in those unaccustomed to them and their ways. They were often described in negative terms as "barbaric" which they were not. There are many stories of them interacting with men, falling in love, having children and long friendships.

They were first documented by Homer in the 8th century and assumed to belong to fantasy. But they existed and appear in works by other Greek writers Herodotus and Apollodorus. And their graves are proof of their authenticity. In the 1900's archaeologists dug up numerous ancient graves in the same area of warrior women. Many of the skeletons showed combat injuries like arrowheads embedded in the bones according to Adrienne Mayor, a research scholar at Stanford University's History of Science Program in the classics department. They also found weapons and even horse skeletons in their graves in the Northern and Eastern Mediterranean region.

The Amazons were believed to be ancient nomadic warriors who finally settled on the left bank of the Tanais (Don) river. On the other side lived another group of warrior women belonging to a tribe called the Scythians. The Greeks did not only speak about Scythian women warriors. They also told stories of Amazons and Amazon-like women. These stories (about Scythian and Amazonian women) included women *from Rome, Egypt, North Africa, Arabia, Mesopotamia, Persia, Central Asia, India [and] China,* Mayor said. **And women who went to war have existed in cultures around the world, from Vietnam to Viking lands, and in Africa and the Americas.**

The Amazons had such a high place in Greek literature that their greatest heroes like Heracles (Hercules), Achilles, Theseus, Alexander the Great, and so on were involved either in warfare or otherwise with Amazonian women. Other cultures were just as impressed by the Amazons and also had dealings with them like the ancient Egyptians, Chinese, Persians, Central Asians, Romans and even the Scandinavians.

In fact, the Amazons were powerful, independent women who inspired awe and fear. This is one reason why they are often depicted in negative ways as barbaric, men-haters and so on. But this is incorrect, especially being men-haters. They had children and there are legends of them falling in love with Greek heroes like Achilles who killed the Amazon queen **Penthesila** in the Trojan war who fought on the side of Troy after Hector's death, then fell in love with her corpse for her courage; Theseus and **Antiope**, the Amazon queen who he kidnapped and brought down their wrath on Athens. There are relief sculptures in the Parthenon on the Western side which display these images. Many of the far-fetched myths about the Amazons have been debunked by archaeology and research. Amazonian graves have been found in Macedon and Philip of Macedon had married two warrior princesses as his wives – **Medea** of Odessos in Trace, Princess of the Geta and **Avdate** a Scythian princess from Illyria. His daughter **Cynane** was a famous warrior in her own right. **Thalestris,** an Amazonian queen met Alexander the Great because she wanted a child by him. This certainly wasn't what men-haters do. Another Amazonian whom Alexander met in battle was **Kleophe,** in the battle of 327 BC. To the Greeks, warrior women were not something out of the ordinary especially when we remember that Pallas Athena, a most revered goddess was the goddess of wisdom, handicraft and warfare with her shield and armour. The women who were warriors were not much different from those that didn't bear arms, the ability to fight in wartime for all women was a given, the norm and not something exceptional or out of the ordinary. Bettany Hughes historian at the British Museum has said that over 800 burial mounds of warrior women have been recently unearthed in Georgia.

These women were not just great warriors and extremely brave, by but they were also very well-balanced, intelligent, powerful, organized and methodical in whatever they did. They enjoyed their work and also motherhood. They fought wars with equal passion that they devoted to love and friendship. They were multidimensional women who proved that women were and still could be perfectly capable and successful on their own in every sphere of life. They are women to be admired and emulated.

Ancient Greek art and legends are filled with these fierce female warriors called Amazons and goddesses – like Athena, Artemis and others. In Greek legend, it seems as if no male hero is truly a hero until he has met one of these warrior women: Heracles kills the Amazonian Queen **Hippolyta** and takes her war belt, Theseus goes into battle against the Amazon queen **Orithyia** after kidnapping her sister Antiope, and Achilles has to face **Penthesilea** outside the gates of Troy among others.

Scytho-Sarmatian

Scythians lived on the other side of the Don to the Amazons. They were there long before the Amazons came, but in time they developed close bonds with the Amazons. They were masters of horseback riding and archery. They lived on a vast territory on the Eurasian steppes stretching from the Black Sea to China from around 700 BC to 500 AD (Mayor, A.: Foreign Affairs Magazine, 2015). They lived hard, supposedly drank excessively unmixed potent wine (when in Greece wine was mixed with water), and fought hard. Frozen mummified bodies preserved due to the permafrost show that their bodies were heavily tattooed with animal shapes.

Many intermarried and from this unions were born the Sarmatian warrior race, which today are the ancestors of some Indo-European races like the Slavs including the Serbs Croats, Poles, Russians, Ukrainians, according to Herodotus, and backed by modern archaeological discoveries. They excavated burial mounds of female warriors, and like the male burials, had weapons in them. Then there is also the Russian folk tales of female warriors, the Polyantis (Polanica) famed for their prowess with weapons at par with male warriors.

Scythian societies were not exclusively female but males and females lived on an equal basis. The girls learned to ride and hunt from as early as 10 years of age as 45 remains of children in one site has shown. So far archaeologists have identified more than 300 female warriors who have been buried with their horses and weapons. More graves are regularly being discovered.

Herodotus had reported that Sarmatian women: ...*have continued from that day to the present to observe their ancient [Amazon] customs, frequently hunting on horseback with their husbands; in war taking the field and wearing the very same dress as the men and he also continued: No girl shall wed till she has killed a man in battle.*

Also according to Herodotus, though how far it is accurate cannot be vouched, for as there are no similar record, Sarmatian women, so long as they are virgins, ride, shoot, throw the javelin while mounted, and fight with their enemies. They do not lay aside their virginity until they have killed three of their enemies, and they do not marry before they have performed the traditional sacred rites. A woman who takes to herself a husband no longer rides, unless she is compelled to do so by a general expedition. This is uncorroborated and probably at least partially, incorrect.

One of the greatest women warriors in Scythian history was **Tomyris,** Queen of the Massagetae in Eastern Persia. She is a byword for heroism. She not only solidified her political position but was an extremely competent warrior – archer, horse-rider in fact she excelled in all the martial arts. She was brave enough to refuse an offer of marriage from the Persian King, Cyrus the Great in 529 BCE. The Persians trapped the Massagetae and killed her son Spargapises. Tomyris went on the offensive to avenge this and fought the Persians killing their leader. She dipped his severed head in blood to show his bloodthirsty nature. It stopped all further Persian incursions into her territory.

In recent years there have been excavations of burial mounds in areas inhabited by the Scythian-Saka tribes and over 300 bodies of warrior women complete with their arms, armour and horses have been unearthed. It can be assumed that these warriors were good with bows and arrows on horseback and on battlefields.

Slavs

Historical records place the Slavic homeland in Central Europe, along the southern shores of the Baltic Sea. The Slavs were much influenced by the Sarmatian culture over the centuries in the East and to a lesser extent by the Germanic cultures in the West. The Slavic warriors are generally described as being exceptionally strong and tall, using a wide range of weapons. They were equally familiar with archery, cavalry, infantry all working in unison. They used speed and were good at ambushing the enemy and using guerrilla tactics. They knew how to take fortified cities using siege weapons learned from the Byzantines, using cavalry learned for the nomadic steppe dwellers, using the longboats learned from the Scandinavians to attack Scandinavian holding in their own lands, thereby giving them a taste of their own medicine.

The Slav female warriors were well known for their courage and their willingness to die to protect their land and family. They were ferocious in battle and this often dissuaded their enemies from entangling with them without major incentives. These virgin warriors were called Polanica in Slavic countries. In Russian folk epic these warrior women or Polyanitsa, (polanica) were known for their prowess and ability to use arms, often superior to that of men. Johannes Skylitzes (Ioannes Scylitzes) 11th century historian writes women participated in the battle in Bulgaria with Prince Svjatoslav of Kiev (971). The Prince was defeated and the Byzantines were amazed to find bodies of women warriors among the fallen warriors.

Russian chronicles also talk about women who participated in the defence of towns besieged by Tartar-Mongol led armies and later by Crusaders, Lithuanians and Poles. The women warriors participated actively. In 1641, during the famous *Azov seats* in the battles with the Turks with the help of the Cossack warriors, the women used archery and caused significant damage. The Cossacks were excellent fighters too.

From the 9th century the Slav conversion to Christianity began (mainly Orthodox). By the 12th century there was a core of medieval Christian states among the Eastern Slavs in Kievan Rus; South Slavs in the Bulgarian Empire, in Croatia, in the Banate of Bosnia, the Grand Principality of Serbia, the West Slavs of Great Moravia, the kingdom of Poland, the Grand Duchy of Bohemia and the Principality of Nitra.

The ancient Slavs rose from obscurity to becoming one of the most prominent forces of the world with their expansion from the 6th to 8th centuries and with their tenacity and stubbornness to hold on to their lands against all adversities down through the ages.

In this tradition women had an equal place with their men be it in battle or in daily living. Women exhibited equal courage and expertise in war as in peace from ancient Slavic, pre-Slavic to modern times (to a lesser degree).

Historical records show that Russian women participated actively in the defense of cities besieged by the Tartars, Mongols and later by the Crusaders, Lithuanians and Poles. This tendency has continued down to the present day. For example: In 1774 a village was surrounded by a detachment of 9,000 Tartars and Turks to be supported by the following army of combatant Cossacks. The town was defended by 150 village women. A Mozdok Commandant described this in *The Slavic Chronicles* of how desperately they fought: *Armed with rifles and other weapons... but also with braids, the women were firing their guns charged up and one of them even had a scythe and cut enemies head and took possession of his gun.* This was also something they carried down from their Scytho-Sarmatian blood line.

Another telling example is that of the campaigns of Prince Sviatoslav Igorevich (943-972 AD) also spelled Svyatoslav. He was a Grand Prince of Kiev who defeated the kingdom of Khazaria, the first Bulgarian Empire, conquered the East Slavic tribes and the Alans among his other exploits. According to John Skylitzes, Russian and Bulgarian women participated in the campaigns and it was realised by the other side only when the scavengers were collecting armours from the battlefield and found many of the warriors to have been women.

In the famous Azov battles with the Turks too, the Slav army had a high percentage of women warriors, who were excellent archers. Vassily Potto, a Russian historian wrote (in *History of the Caucasian War*) about the kazachkah: *"Woman, the eternal toiler in peacetime, in moments of danger was the Cossacks full fighter, like her father, husband, son or brother."* Young Cossacks learned to ride a horse and fight. Cossack girls raised as a future wife, mother, homemaker, knew any job. It is known that in 1641, during the famous "Azov seats" in battles with the Turks in addition to the male soldiers, women Cossack riders also participated. They were great in archery and caused the Turks significant damage. They proved their mettle.

The Polish Slavs have also been raised on the feats of famous women warriors. **Emilia Plater,** a rich heiress gave up an aristocratic life to raise her own army of 350 partisan soldiers to fight in the November Uprising of 1830. She led her army successfully in the campaigns against the Russians. After successfully winning the campaign at Prastavoniai and Mejszagoła, she was awarded a lieutenancy in the Lithuanian 25th Infantry regiment. She commanded a unit until her death in 1831. She was widely celebrated not just in Poland but across Europe. She has been equated to Joan of Arc of France by the Poles.

Another modern example is that of **Maria Bochkareva** who served with the 25th Reserved Battalion of the Russian Army. When Tsar Nicholas II abdicated in March 1917, she convinced Alexander Kerensky, the interim Prime Minister who allowed her to form a women's battalion. It recruited girls from 13 to 25 and had about 2,000 members. They fought the German Offensive of June 1917. 250 women from this battalion survived the German Offensive after three months of fighting.

Over 800,000 Slav women served in WWII (Sakada, 2003), nearly 5% of the total military personnel (United States Military Academy 2015, pp. 235). Many received the highest Russian Award – the Hero of the Soviet Union. They served as medics, nurses, pilots, snipers, machine gunners, tank crews, partisans and auxiliaries.

Before this in WWI, 1914 in Serbia, **Milunka Savić** was awarded her first Karađorđe Star with Swords after the Battle of Kolubara. She received her second Karađorđe Star (with Swords) after the Battle of Crna Bend in 1916 when she captured 23 Bulgarian soldiers single-handed. She was the most decorated combatant in history.

Graves of Slavic warrior women have been found in Scandinavia. On the Danish Island of Langeland, between The Great Belt and the Bay of Kiel, in South Denmark, archaeologists also unearthed the grave of a Slavic warrior woman with her weapons and a 1,000-year-old Arabian coin. Other similar graves have also been uncovered in different parts of Europe.

Celts

According to Plutarch, female Celts were nothing like Roman or Greek women. They were active in negotiating treaties and wars, and they participated in assemblies and mediated quarrels.

The status of Celtic women can only be based on Roman writings, mythology, and history. Women played an important role even though it was a patriarchal society. It was a tribal society and the women were in a much better place in many ways like inheritance, than their European sisters and had many more rights and freedoms than the Greek or Roman women of the same time. They could own property, be a warrior, a priestess, a judge, a doctor, get divorced and remarry with no stigma attached.

A lot of information we have about the Celts of Britain is from Roman sources which is generally biased. After all, Rome was bent on conquering Britain and after many failures even when they dominated England there were constant uprisings. An unknown Roman soldier had this to say about the Celtic warrior women: *A Celtic woman is often the equal of any Roman man in hand-to-hand combat. She is as beautiful as she is strong. Her body is comely but fierce. The physiques of our Roman women pale in comparison.* Diodorus Siculus, a Greek writer says this: "*The women of the Gauls are not only like men in their great stature, but they are a match for them in courage as well.*"

In marriage, Celtic women were never considered property. They married if they wanted and who they wanted. Divorce and remarriage were a normal part of life. Trial marriages were also quite common. Polygamy and polyandry were accepted if it benefited the clan. The head of the household was whoever brought the most into the marriage. Arranged marriages were for political reasons and again with the woman's consent.

"The women of the Celtic tribes are bigger and stronger than our Roman women. This is most likely due to their natures as well as their peculiar fondness for all things martial and robust. The flaxen haired maidens of the north are trained in sports and war while our gentle ladies are content to do their womanly duties and thus are less powerful than most young girls from Gaul and the hinterlands." — Marcus Borealis

Celtic women could choose to be trained as warriors. There were even some who trained warriors themselves, like the legends about **Scathach and Aife,** two sisters, perhaps twins, who ran their own training camps. Christian scholars have tried to portray these women as less powerful than they in fact were. Celtic women could bear arms, train for battle, train others for battle, plan strategy, lead armies, and fight to the death alongside the men. The women could be proud of their prowess in battle. They also cut down deserters male or female. **Plutarch** says of them: *Here the women met them holding swords and axes in their hands. With hideous shrieks of rage they tried to drive back the hunted and the hunters, the fugitives as deserters, the pursuers as foes. With bare hands the women tore away the shields of the Romans or grasped their swords, enduring mutilating wounds.*

One of the most famous Celtic warrior-Queens was **Boudicca** who fought the Roman might for honour and to avenge the shame the Romans brought down on her and her daughters. Ammianus Marcellinus, a Roman soldier-historian has this to say about the Celtic women warriors: *A whole band* *of foreigners will be unable to cope with one [Gaul] in a fight, if he calls in his wife, stronger than he by far and with flashing eyes; least of all when she swells her neck and gnashes her teeth, and poising her huge white arms, begins to rain blows mingled with kicks, like shots discharged by the twisted cords of a catapult.*

Boudicca Celtic Warrior Queen fought Rome

Boudicca: was one the most iconic female warriors of the world whose name is known by all. She was the Iceni Queen who stood up to Rome and fought them in 60-61 AD. The Roman historian Dio Cassisus remembers it thus: *All this ruin was brought upon the Romans by a woman, the fact which in itself caused them the greatest shame.*

The image that accompanies her name is of a tall woman riding her chariot with long flowing hair as she charges the enemy with her horses snorting. It was a sight to frighten the Roman soldiers who only knew sedentary women.

But Boudicca was on a mission: she was firstly a woman wronged and her house shamed and then she was fighting for her country to either be a slave or to die. She chose death over dishonour.

Celtic women as mentioned earlier fought side by side with their men and died fighting if it so happened. And in this fight, it was about survival and honour. The other options were slavery or death. There were numerous other Celtic women warriors.

A 16th century Irish woman, also a warrior was not a queen but a pirate. **Grace O'Malley,** nicknamed **Gráinne Mhaol,** for her rebellious nature even when young, ruled over Umaill kingdom of Ireland after her father, chieftain O' Máill of the clan died. She also inherited a number of ships which she used for piracy. She even faced Queen Elizabeth I's ships when her son and brother were captured. But she agreed to fight only against England's enemies and so freed her family and she got back her confiscated goods from the Queen.

Teutonic and Scandinavian

The Germanic tribes dominated northern Europe for a long time. Theirs was an oral tradition and their women, like all olden cultures participated fully in all spheres of life in building their societies and the smooth functioning of them. There is much more to the Vikings than the Anglo-Saxon invasion of England and the Viking raids on Europe and America. They are generally called barbarians but they too, had sophisticated societies and women participating in them in all spheres, cultural, religious, military, social and economic. Women were not just wives and mothers but an integral part of the tribe in every way. They were excellent warriors too. And like all old cultures they had goddesses, who were very important and powerful. The Viking influence on German epic poems is clearly visible. Many elements are taken from Old Norse Literature like the tale of **Brunhild,** from the Norse Edda (epic poems) and *Voluspa* and *Helgi Hundingsbani* and in *Njal's Saga.*

This male-female equality was strongly visible in their marriage ceremonies. Both protagonists gave each other armour. To quote from Tacitus (*Agricola Germania Dialogus*, pp. 159): *Here is the gist of the bond between them, here in their eyes its mysterious sacrament, the divinity that the wife may not imagine herself exempt from thoughts of heroism, released from the chances of war, she is thus warned by the very rites with which her marriage begins that she comes to share hard work and peril; that her fate will be the same as his in peace and in panic, her risks the same.*

Germanic priestesses who followed the warriors were feared by the Roman. These were tall women with glaring eyes, wearing flowing white gowns often wielding a knife for sacrificial offerings. Captives might have their throats cut and be bled into giant cauldrons or have their intestines opened up and the entrails thrown to the ground for prophetic readings.

In Ari Thorgilsson's book *Íslendingabók* (the book of the Icelanders, 1120's) and his contribution to *Landnámabók* ('the book of the settlements'), among the men he mentions 13 women first settlers, some accompanied by brothers or sons, who claimed land in their own right. Among them was one named **Ásgerðr Asksdóttir**, who left Norway with her children when her husband was killed under the protection of her half-brother who claimed land with *her consent* (Jesch pp. 79-83).

The other widely used source is the late 12th and early 13th Century A.D. *Viking Lore: A Quick Introduction to Norse Eddas and Sagas.* These give information of Viking burial mounds, with their weapons. Many of these mounds are of women with their spears, swords, shields etc.

The Germanic tribes scattered over Europe assumed to be Scandinavian, from around 1000 BC. Around 600 to 300 BC waves of theses peoples came down en mass from Gotland and migrated to Germany pushing Westward and Eastwards. They thus came into conflict with the Slavic and Celtic peoples. They are mainly remembered during two periods of European history the Anglo-Saxon Invasion of England and the Viking raids on England. These tribes were regarded as barbaric but in fact they too had sophisticated societies where women had a dominant place. The place of women in general, in pre-Christian society was, in Northern Europe too, not only as homemakers and child-bearers but they also owned property, went on raids, fought in wars, traded goods and were of about the same social, economic and religious standing as their men. They were a highly aggressive people.

Women went to battle with the men and fought just as bravely and well. In some incidents it was a compelling and frightening sight. One such example was the Battle of Vosges (58 BC) which was the first time the Romans met yelling Teutonic women and it was a very unnerving experience. They also met them in the battle of Aquae Sextae (The Cimbrian War) where according to Plutarch, the Roman historian, when the Romans won, 300 of the captured women killed their children and themselves that day rather than be taken back to Rome enslaved.

German men held their women in high regard because they believed the women had the gift of prophecy combined with holiness. This set them apart and if they were captured or enslaved it boded ill for the clan. So it was rarely that their advice was disregarded or scorned. If the battle went badly, women fought and would rather kill themselves than face dishonour. They might also kill any male members of the tribe who attempted retreat. They could even kill their children and then commit suicide rather than submit to enslavement by another tribe or army as happened in the Cimbrian war.

Warrior women were a common occurrence in folklore as avengers, warriors, leaders. They are referred to as shield maidens in some places. In the battle between Rome and the Teutons, the Teutonic women generally fought alongside the men. They were fierce warriors using axes, and swords. They died with their men on the battlefield. The women not only attacked the Roman enemies but also the Ambrones of Jutland who tried to desert. Like the men they uttered hideous blood-curdling battle cries.

In 3 AD Emperor Aurelianus; (270-275 AD) paraded captured Gothic warrior women prisoners in his triumphal march in Rome. The puritanical Romans must have been really taken aback at this terrifying sight. Eastern historians also mentioned the presence of warrior women among their European enemies. Procopius (primary source for Emperor Justinian I's times) writes about an English princess who led the invasion of Jutland but this is not proven.

A number of women warriors appear in Saxo's 13th century AD *Gesta Danorum* (Chronicle of the Danes). But most of these women warriors are all from the upper class of their society. In Book 8 of his saga Saxo talks about individual warrior women like **Hede** who protected King Harald's right flank; **Visna** who carried the banner, **Vebjørg** who fought valiantly. Saxo also uses Icelandic sources for his women warriors from the Older Edda and the Sagas. Saxo Grammaticus, or "The Lettered", is the earliest chronicler of Denmark and one of the important historians of the Middle Ages: *The Danish History, Books I-IX Late 12th-Early 13th Century A.D. Viking Lore: A Quick Intro to Norse Eddas and Sagas* Icelandic writings known as the *Sagas and Eddas*. These give information of Viking burial mounds. In many olden ones, weapons have been found buried with the women – shields, spears, swords etc.

There were once women in Denmark who dressed themselves to look like men and spent almost every minute cultivating soldiers' skills; they did not want the sinews of their valour to lose tautness and be infected by self-indulgence. Loathing a dainty style of living, they would harden body and mind with toil and endurance, rejecting the fickle pliancy of girls and compelling their womanish spirits to act with a virile ruthlessness. They courted military celebrity so earnestly that you would have guessed they had unsexed themselves. Those especially who had forceful personalities or were tall and elegant embarked on this way of life. As if they were forgetful of their true selves they put toughness before allure, aimed conflicts instead of kisses, tasted blood, not lips, sought the clash of arms rather than the arm's embrace, fitted to weapons hands which should have been weaving, desired not the couch but the kill, and those they could have appeased with looks they attacked with lances. (Saxo, pp. 212)

Some other warrior women he mentions are: **Alvild, Lagertha** (who fought so well being braver than a man in the front rank with the King of Sweden, who was the bravest of men. The Danish king, Ragnar Lodbrok was so impressed by her courage that he married her), **Hetha, Randolin, Rusila, Sela, Stikla,** and **Vebiorg**. Some decided to challenge their kinsmen for the throne, while others merely liked to fight. Ultimately, they all end unmarried or dead as do all of us (Saxo Grammaticus pp. 83, 150, 210-212, 226-227, 238, 241-242, 246, 280-281).

The **Icelandic sagas** (*Egil's Saga*), demonstrated the importance of women's judgement of men's fighting abilities. At a feast Egil was to sit and drink with the daughter of his host. But when she came to the feast, she asked Egil to get up and move because she wanted a real man, a warrior, as her drinking partner. He recounted his prowess and she accepted him.

It was believed there would be no point in male heroics if there were no women to appreciate the deeds and prowess (*Egil's Saga*, 176 pp. 110-111).

Some women warriors mentioned are **Hervör,** who avenged the death of her father and uncles. Her son, **Heidhrekr,** avenged his grandfather and fathered the Royal Swedish dynasty (Kveldulf Gundarsson, pp. 132) & (*The Waking of Angantyr* pp. 101-105). Another warrior was **Freydis Eiriksdottir,** Lief Eiriksson's illegitimate sister who settled Greenland by frightening away the Skrælings – natives (*The Vinland Sagas* pp. 99-100). Eiriksson had discovered America (Vinland) and Freydis and her husband Thorvard decided to investigate if Vinland could be settled. They found a place with a lot of game and spent the winter there. In the Spring some Skrælings (Native Indians) came to trade but a bull broke out of its pen, the Natives got scared and rowed away. Three weeks later thy attacked and surrounded the Greenlanders who started to retreat. Freydis yelled for them to stop but when they didn't, she pregnant tried to run but couldn't. Soon she was surrounded. She took a sword, took one breast out and slapped the sword against it. The natives were terrified at this strange behaviour and ran away.

Warrior women are a common occurrence in folklore as avengers, warriors, leaders. They chose to live like warriors outside the traditional gender roles of the times and were easily accepted as part of Old Norse society. They are sometimes referred to as *'Shield maidens.'* They are not generally mentioned as warrior women otherwise. Other references can be found in *Njal's Saga, and the lives of Norse kings*.

Two other women that stand out are *the **Island Girl*** (Her exploits are recorded by Procopius, an Official at Emperor Justinian's court (535-552) and **Æthelflæd** (Anglo-Saxon), Lady of the Mercian's, daughter of King Alfred. She helped beat back the Danish invasion of England for a time after her father's death (from 901 AD in *The Exeter Book pp. 8-10* by Kathleen Howard). She built a chain of fortresses across Saxon England. She also had strongholds built or strengthened in places like at Bridgnorth, Tamworth, Stafford, Eddisbury, Warwick, Chirbury, Runcom as well as Hereford and Gloucester. In 916 she personally led a successful military expedition against the Welsh kingdom of Brycheiniog.

From the earliest recorded Germanic marriage ceremony through the Viking Age, women were able to bear arms in combat along with their male counterparts. Tacitus wrote of the Germanic wedding ceremony: that it was the man who brought the dower generally comprising of horse, shield, bridle, sword, spear and oxen; the woman also gave her husband armour.

It is also a familiar occurrence in Irish society. The most famous were **Scáthach and Aífe**, of Scottish-Celtic origin in the 5th or 6th centuries. Older sources claim warrior women were found in Northern Europe and Scandinavia around the time of Christ's birth. But Strabo and Plutarch (1st century BC) Dio Cassius (49 AD), Tacitus (100 AD) all talk about warrior women in Northern and Eastern Europe – not Scandinavia. In 1 AD Saxon men and women were regarded of equal value by the Romans. Tacitus says men gave the women oxen, horse with a bridle, shield, spear and sword when they got married. She returned them. It illustrates the warlike quality in their women. Saxon men and women shared all duties of physically protecting the family including fighting. Romans also comment on the strong physical build of both the sexes. Romans also reported that they regularly found dead women warriors along with the men. Saxon women fought as valiantly as their men to defend their land and homes.

Nubian

The first mention to this culture is in 3000 BCE during the time of Egypt's New Kingdom – 16th to 11th centuries. They are a very ancient ethnic group. Some Nubians still live on their ancestral land. The kingdom existed because of the Queen. She was the symbol; the king was the sign. Nubia had an exceptionally large number of warrior queens, more so than anywhere else. It is the only ancient culture that has an exhibit showing the queen *smithing her enemies*. Such exhibits have not been found in Egypt or any Western country. Nubian queens were warriors par excellence.

The first Nubian culture came into existence during the Bronze Age. It was conquered by Egypt under Tutankhamen, a strong king, and incorporated into Egypt. With the end of the 20th Dynasty, around 900 BC Egypt lost control and Nubia subjugated the Egyptian kingdom and wore the Double Cobra Crown of Egypt signifying the joining of the two kingdoms. The Kingdom of Kush was born.

Nubian women have always played a dominant role as goddesses, queens, warriors and were able to exert tremendous control. In Nubia the worship of Isis was paramount. Warrior Queens battled successfully. These queens were depicted as bearers of gods in Nubian art. In fact, even queens ruling with kings were regarded as very significant to Nubian history (Wenig, 1978 vol. II pp. 16 in Kneller T 1993). The queens were part of the queen-mother representation (Wenig pp. 70). They were called *gore* (ruler) and *kandake* (queen-mother) (Ibid, 1978, vol 1 pp. 98).

Nubia attacked Egypt under Roman rule and pillaged it. In 24 BC Rome retaliated and attacked Nubia ruled by queen, **Amanirenas.** She led her army of 30,000 warriors including her son Prince Akinidad armed with bows, arrows and swords and fiercely fought and defeated three Roman cohorts, defaced Augustus Caesar's statue, hacked off his head and took it back with them to Nubia and as a mark of final disrespect buried it under a public building (Keating, R 1963, pp. 71). The Romans never returned to Nubia. In the battle Amanirenas lost an eye but plucked out the arrowhead and continued fighting. She fought so well that the historian of the times commented *This Queen had courage above her sex* (Strabo in Diop). So the Europeans found a civilisation of warriors. They met with *fierce, unyielding resistance of a queen whose determined struggle symbolized the national pride of a people who, until then, had commanded others* (Diop, (1974, pp. 143).

Some other famous Nubian warrior queens were the following: **Shanakdakhete** was the earliest known queen (117-155 BCE). She ruled alone. She built up an empire and contributed a great deal towards the development of the Meroitic language and religion. Then there was **Amanitore** who is best remembered for her building projects including 200 pyramids. She also built water reservoirs and restored many temples that the Romans had destroyed. There was also **Amanishakheto** (10-1 BC) who was a warrior and a builder. And then there was **Amanikhatashan** who helped Rome against the Jews (70 CE) by sending the legendary Kushite archers whose deeds and accomplishments won the empire the title **The Land of the Bow for Kush.** And not only were the queens fierce fighters, so were the Kush women – fierce in war, unwilling to ever surrender.

Queen Amaniras of Nubia *Nehanda Charwe Nykasikana of the Shonas*

Warrior women from other African countries:

Besides these tribes, African women from many other tribes and areas were warriors like: **Dihya** 690 AD from modern day Algeria fought and defeated the Berbers; **Yennenga**, a 12th century princess of the Dagomba Kingdom in northern Ghana led her armies at the age of 14 against the Mali Empire. Her father refused to let her marry and wanted her to always be a warrior. She ran away, married, had a son and founded what is modern Burkina Faso.

In the 1400's the women warriors had to protect their people from Portuguese slavers. One among them was **Liinga** (in the Congo) who could behead a man with one slash of her sword. She was also proficient with bows and arrows and axe. Congo had standing women's armies.

The **Isadshi-Koseshi** women warriors of the Nupa tribe in Central Nigeria repeatedly repelled attacks by the Fula tribes hoping to capture cattle and slaves. But they were unprepared to meet the wrath of another female warrior **Amina** from the Hausa tribe. She defeated them and also the Northern Kano and Katsina cities and made them pay tribute.

Ana-Nzinga Mbande, queen of the Ndongand Matamba, was a great politician and diplomat and sealed the first treaties with the Portuguese and then The Dutch. She was also a great military tactician and led attacks on the Portuguese in 1644 and 1657 until they asked for a peace treaty.

Nandi of the Zulus was the mother of Shaka Zulu, a great chief. Being a single mother, she protected him from assassination attempts. When Shaka became ruler, he made his mother queen and formed a military settlement of both genders. Even the present-day Zulu warrior dances show both sexes have the exact moves. Zulu men and women were known as great fighters,

Kaipkire was chieftainess of the Herero tribe of modern Nambia. She led her army against the British colonisers in the 1700's. In 1884 they found themselves under German rule. They rebelled in 1904 and were put in concentration camps, used as slave labour and for medical experiments or driven into the desert to die. There are reports of Herero women attacking German soldiers as late as 1919.

Nehanda Nyakasikana, a priestess of the Shona in modern Zimbabwe preached against the British colonisers. She was one of the leaders of the revolt against the *British*

South Africa Company's colonisation of her country led by Cecil John Rhodes in 1889. They finally captured her, convicted her of having the Commissioner's head chopped off and ordered her hanged. It took them three attempts to do so. Her legacy was linked to the resistance especially by the guerrillas that started in 1972. She continued to be invoked in Zimbabwe's national movements (Mazama, 2009).

Taytu Betul was the wife of Menelik II, the Ethiopian Emperor. Italy had colonised neighbouring Eritrea and most of Somalia and were making incursions into Ethiopia. Betul convinced her husband to go to war. At the siege of Mek'ele she had the water supply to the fortress of Italians cut off. They surrendered 10 days later. At the battle of Adwa, she led a female contingent and Menelik II, a male one. The Italians were decisively beaten. She got her husband to move the capital to Addis Abbaba, and financed the first hotel in the country.

There were many other African warrior women. The African women warriors usually fought to the death to protect their kingdoms, communities and people.

Dahomey Amazons

Dahomey was a kingdom in West Africa that flourished between 1600 and 1900. It was settled by the Fon people who intermarried with the Aja and Gedevi people. The capital Abomey was established in the 17th century. It was founded by King **Houegbadja (1645-1685).** But soon he began raiding his neighbours and trading with others outside his kingdom

(Halcrow, 1982: Bay 1998). Thus, slave trade began and access to the coast was got through the conquest of Alande and Whydah in the 1770s which led to trade with the Portuguese, Dutch and British. So Europe got to know about Dahomey and the availability of slaves (Law, 1986; pp. 237-267).

It is at this period in the early 1700 under Queen **Hangbè** and her co ruler, her twin brother that the agojie or female warriors called the Daomey Amazons by the Europeans began. Queen Hangbè always had an entourage of female bodyguards. The first time they are mentioned is by the French slaver, Jean-Pierre Thibault who saw them at the port of Whydah (Ouidah) in 1725. The first reference to them historically was in 1729. These women were known to be fierce fighters but according to their descendants they were also very protective of children and never allowed them to be beaten or mistreated by anyone. And this long before there was any human rights charter.

By 1800 there were thousands of female warrior troops in Dahomey. In clashes, the defeated were sold as slaves. Most of these warriors had themselves been slaves at one time and got their place in the troop by their own merit. They trained strenuously from girlhood with swords, muskets, and climbed thorny barricades to toughen their bodies. They drank imported brandy and sang war songs. But all this came to a crashing end when France colonised them. Alpern, the American journalist said of them they *gave proof of very great bravery*. France did not get its hand very easily on Dahomey. For two years the women fought the French colonists. 2,000

Dahomey warriors died, only 50 survived. The last Dahomey warrior died in Benin in 1970. They are now called Benin Amazons and are often compared to the Spartans. Images of these women have been found, carrying rifles, brawling with men and clutching severed heads. Their statues are untended, overgrown. Their camp site is now owned by the Catholic Church.

This is the only modern women warriors documented. References to them, jottings of French officers, British traders and Italian missionaries have been found in the West Africa archives. But what is not recorded is their humanity. Colonisers have always dehumanised the colonised people in every case since history is written by the victors. And of course, they will always discredit the losers. For example we all know about Columbus' discoveries but very few know about his enslavement of the indigenous people of those lands. Britain recorded the colonisation of West African kingdoms in 1897 as *a punitive mission* but did not record the mass theft of priceless bronze artifacts from Africa as they also did not record all the gold, jewels and even the throne of Persia they removed from India and Persia and other countries they colonised.

All the wealth and power of Europe's colonising countries has been built upon the wealth they forcibly, surreptitiously and openly removed from the colonised countries much as Nazi Germany did with the arts and artifacts of conquered European, Asian and African countries during WWII. Britain,

France, Spain, Portugal, Netherlands and now USA became rich and powerful with the colonies' wealth.

France after seizing South Belize in 1894 immediately disbanded the female troop and never mentioned them or their unique qualities. Dahomey history, like that of other colonised people got thrown into the rubbish bin of history. A Benin business economist, Prof. Leonard Wantchekon, international affairs at Princeton University said: *The French made sure this history wasn't known.... They said we were backward, that they needed to 'civilize us,' but they destroyed opportunities for women that existed nowhere else in the world* at that time. All oral traditions met the same fate but at the same time they were passed down from generation to generation and so bits and pieces survived.

In 1793 a British administrator of the region, Archibald Dalziel wrote: *Whatever might have been the prowess of the Amazons among the ancients, this is a novelty in modern history.* Later a French official said about Dahomey women: *assuredly the only country in the world that offers the singular spectacle of an organization of women as soldiers.* The American journalist Stanley Alpern quoting French publishers Larousse said about the Dahomey women that they are: *the only historical (known) Amazons."*

Queen regent Hangbe – founder of the fearless female Dahomey warriors

Assacani

These were fierce warriors who inhabited North-Eastern Afghanistan and the Peshawar valley, from Swat and Buner valleys extending to the Indus River. They were excellent horse breeders and trainers. The word Assacani (Greek Assakani) means horsemen (Birdwood, 1915, pp. 113). These were very independent, rebellious highlanders who highly valued their freedom and resisted subjugation. Their descendants are the modern-day ethnic Pashtuns (Chattopadhyaya, 1950, pp. 48). They were part of the larger group of Kambojas inhabiting parts of Iran. The Assacani capital was at Massaga, a formidable fortress in the North of the Malakand Pass in Modern Pakistan. They were expert cavalry men and excellent horse breeders.

Queen Cleophis offers Alexander wine after signing the treaty

In 326 BC Alexander went to conquer Asia with an army larger than Julius Caesar's in the conquest of Gaul. During his campaign in the Indian subcontinent, he clashed with the Assacani who were defending their homeland. Alexander himself led the attack. To give battle to Alexander's mighty army the Assacani assembled their forces and asked for reinforcement from the Kamboj from Abhsara. The battle was long and very bloody. It lasted for nine days. But Massaga could not be breached. **Queen Cleophis** and the women fought alongside the men bravely and valiantly here and at other fortresses. Diodorus (in McCrindle 2020), the first to record this battle gave a vivid and graphic account of the battle and praised the valour and heroism of the Assacani people. Finally, Alexander asked for a ceasefire. The Assacani were to leave the fortress and the other tribespeople were to serve in Alexander's army. The Assacani vacated but when they were 80 stadia (approximately 5.5 km) away. Alexander treacherously unleashed his army on them. All were killed. It was carnage. Hanson described this event in detail. He said: *The women, taking up the arms of the fallen, fought side by side with their men. Accordingly, some who had supplied themselves with arms did their best to cover their husbands with their shields, while others, who were without arms, did much to impede the enemy by flinging themselves upon them and catching hold of their shields* (Hanson 2020, pp. 86). Plutarch (in Mccrindle 2020) says Alexander was an implacable enemy and because his army had suffered greatly, **he initiated the ceasefire and then broke it.** This act he says: *was a foul blot on his martial fame.* To this Quintus Curtius Rufus adds: Alexander *Not only slaughtered the entire population of Massaga but also did he reduce its buildings to rubble.* Cleophis and her granddaughter were captured. Their end is not known though there are many assumptions.

Alexander always destroyed anyone who stood up to him, even after signing peace treaties. This was not the only case. Everywhere in Asia if he met strong resistance, he made sure to destroy as much as he could of the people who stood up to him. This was a very ignoble, petty characteristic in him and not at all heroic.

Later accounts by writers like Arrian attempted to white wash this foul deed by showing the Assacani in a poor light, but evidence against his version is overwhelming in accounts much closer to Alexander's own time. Both Diodirus and Plutarch's versions discard the theories about a matrimonial alliance between Cleophis and Alexander. **Both say the**

ceasefire was initiated by Alexander due to his losses. Alexander's destruction of these people was a very ignoble, unheroic, dishonourable and petty act.

Alexander destroyed the Fortresses among them Massaga, Beira and Ora. The Assacani, both men and women, *preferred a glorious death to a life of dishonor.* (Dani, Vadim, Janos, Abramovich et al, pp. 76). The name of the *Aśvakan* or *Assakan* has been preserved in that of modern Afghān. Some believe Afghan base is derived from Asvakayana, an important clan of the Asvakas or horsemen who held this title from their handling of celebrated breeds of horses. The Scottish Geographical Magazine 1999, supporting this theory says: "*Their name (Afghan) means 'cavalier' being derived from the Sanskrit,* Asva, *or* Asvaka, *a horse, and shows that their country must have been noted in ancient times, as it is at the present day, for its superior breed of horses. Asvaka was an important tribe settled north to the Kabul River, which offered a gallant but ineffectual resistance to the arms of Alexander.*"

Note: And not just the Assacani, but many other Afghan women fought for their homeland even as late as the Afghan wars against British Imperialism. During the second Anglo-Afghan war, the Afghan woman **Malalai** carried the Afghani flag into battle after the soldiers bearing the flag were killed by the British.

Chinese

700 years before the Scythian women appeared on the scene, there were Chinese female warriors. One of them

whose history has been recovered from written inscriptions on bones was General Fu Hao (1200 BCE) who fought and defended the Shang dynasty (1300-1046 BC) in the Bronze Age (1600-046 BCE). She was the third wife of the Emperor Wu Ding, the 23rd ruler of the Shang dynasty, and also a successful military commander in her own right. She presided over sacrificial ceremonies in the Emperor's name. Wu Ding ruled for 59 years.

250 oracle bones with inscriptions on them were the earliest written Chinese records to be discovered here. The bones record a lot about her (Fu Hao). One bone records that she led 13,000 men on a campaign. They also document the sacrifices that were made on her behalf on her death. Then in 1976 a tomb, first assumed to that of a male ruler was discovered in Anyang, the site of the Shang capital. It was a very rich grave with a large number of weapons, precious stones, bronze objects and skeletons of 16 slaves. It was identified as Fu Hao's. It also seems from the records that she participated in almost all-important military campaigns at the height of Wu Ding's reign. She also led the army against Tu Fang and defeated him, and led her forces against three more attacks: the armed horsemen of Qiang Fang in the Northeast; Fang in the Northwest, the Yi Fang in the Southeast and Southwest defeating them all. She fell ill soon after and died.

But she was not the only female warrior of the times. The oracle bones give up a 100 female warrior names who were active in the Shang times and campaigns. Most were wives of powerful Fang kings, local lords and high-placed officials. In

2001 another **female warrior**'s tomb with a cache of weapons dating to the Zhou dynasty (1046-1071 BCE) was uncovered.

The female warriors were there fighting for their homeland since the time of the **Warring States (246-221 BCE) to the Ming dynasty (1368-1644 AD).** Chinese women led armies and fought in armies from their teenage years. After things settled down they returned to their homes and family duties as mothers, wives and daughters. They defended their borders from outside incursions, and barbarian attacks; they organised defence of besieged cities; they led peasant uprising but also put down peasant uprisings; they helped defend the ruling Dynasties and established new ones. They raised armies or inherited them. They also held official positions in the Chinese military and government. For example, a woman, **Qin Liangyu (1574-1684)** began her military career by following her husband the *pacification commissioner* of Shizhu, (modern Sichuan province) and became a general in the Ming Army. Her exploits were the first to be recorded alongside that of the men.

Some other women who won eternal fame were **Fan Lihua** who lived during the Tang Dynasty. She was very proficient in the martial arts and has been the heroine of many literary and artistic works and TV shows. She was a general from Western Liang but married a Tang officer and they fought alongside each other. Her story has passed into folklore.

Then there was **Mu Guiying** another legendary hero. She lived during China's Northern Song Dynasty (1127-1279) and was a prominent figure in the *Generals of the Yang family* legends. She was brave, loyal, insightful and resolute and a symbol of the steadfast woman. She too was a general who led the army in the battle known as the Heavenly-Gate Formation at 19 years of age. She fought many other battles too. She was also famed for her diplomacy and brought peace between the Song and their neighbours the Liao people. She is recognised as one of China's greatest female generals.

She Saihua, like Mu Guiying is another legendary heroine from ancient China's Northern Song Dynasty and like her, is prominent in the stories *Generals of the Yang Family*. She is also known as **She Taijun or The Dowager** as she was widowed very early. She was well known for her dragon-headed cane. She proved her prowess and loyalty many times over and the Emperor Taizong made her Commander-in-chief and awarded her the dragon-headed cane as a symbol of her absolute control of the male-dominated army.

Lin Hongu was a historical and legendary figure though her historical background is very sketchy. It is known, though, that she was born in modern day Anhui province in 1102 and that she married Han Shizhong. She fought beside her husband in the Hun invasion against Xiong Nu or Jin tribes in China. She was not only the brain but also commanded troops in battle. Using drums and flags as signals her 8,000 – strong army defeated the – 100,000 strong Hun Horde in 1129. Soon after, Lin Hongu and Han Shizhong quit their positions when a national hero **Yue Fei** was executed without any reason. She died in 1135 of an illness. She and her husband are particularly admired for their courage in standing up to both influential capitulationists within the court and the formidable foe in the North. **She was not only a warrior but also a good wife and mother.**

Lady Qi Wang (1530-1588) led the coastal defensive against Japanese pirates in 1561. However, she did not follow the general precepts. She was regarded as *rude, unreasonable and aggressive* but her courage and bravery got her a place.

And there was of course the legendary **Hua Mulan** and many, many named and unnamed others.

Most Chinese women began their military careers as mothers, wives or daughters of Chinese officials and they often fought besides their husbands or in place of male kinsmen. These women all possessed the Confucian qualities of bravery, loyalty and commitment to country and family.

Japanese Samurai women

Modern societies are strongly male-dominated. Among the strongest is that in Japan. But long ago before the male samurai archetype showed up, Japanese history was dominated by and replete with figures of powerful female samurais (warhistoryonline.com). They were not only trained in the martial arts and the use of weapons but also in mathematics, science and literature. They were the elite samurai class. They were known as the Onna-Bugeisha. This was the noblest class of feudal Japanese society, women who fought alongside men in warfare.

The Onna-Bugeisha women were trained to use the iconic weapon of the period, the Naginata or in female hands the Ko-Naginata, smaller than the males' ones, allowing for better balance in female hands. The other important weapon was the Kaiken-dagger, a double-edged blade up to 10 inches in length usually used in confined spaces for self-defense. It was also used for ritual suicide. A strange tradition of that time was that an Onna-Bugeisha had to have the dagger on her person at all times even if she moved in with her husband.

Besides this, all Onna-Bugeish also had to be trained when young in the knowledge of Tantōjutsu, (martial art) a system of fighting well known throughout Japan even today. The Onna-Bugeisha was expected to protect the family home in unsettled times and these warriors were ready to do so.

In the Sengoku period, between the 15th and 17th centuries things started to change. The shoguns faced many challenges – internal and external. They dealt with all of them including the Hun invasions. But the Onin War (1467-1477) posed a major challenge. It was a civil war between two rivals and brought a lot of death and destruction. The next century was one of bitter fighting. It was called the Sengoku period or the Warring States Period (1467-1568). This ended with the rise of the warlord Oda Nobunaga (1534-1582) who expanded his territory, defeating all who challenged him. Finally, he seized Heiank in 1568 and exiled the last shogun Ashikaga Yoshiaki in 1573.

He was followed by his two sons Hideyoshi and Ieyasu who also undermined the shoguns' power drastically. They are regarded as the unifiers of Japan that led to pre-modern Japan. However, the Tokugawa Shogunate based in Edo ruled from 1603 until January 1868 CE. Tokogawa unified Japan with a good combination of organisation, genius and, military skill. The clan presided over a country at peace for 250 years, until they were displaced by the Meiji restoration of 1868. Japan entered the modern age. The Shogunate era spanning almost 700 years was over.

From this time drastic changes to the female samurai's position began. Their husbands lost power and were forced to become bureaucrats. Their womenfolk also suffered severe restrictions. They were no longer allowed any freedoms. They were expected to marry, bear children, serve their husbands and devote their lives to their family only. They had quickly been relegated to a very subordinate position. From being able to influence alliances, exert influence on politics, as negotiators and even in the unwelcome positions as marriage pawns, the samurai women had played a vital and hazardous role even in Sengoku Japan. But again, with time, change came.

It was in the middle of the 17th century that there was a flourishing of female Samurais again. The Tokugawa Shogunate set to arming and training female samurais. Training with the naginata and in the arts of combat all over the empire proliferated and flourished. And for a short period, women turned into protectors, not just of their homes but of whole villages. Then in the 18th century war broke out between the Tokugawa shoguns and the Imperial court. A special female corps was created to be led by **Nanako Takeko.**

There were too many samurai female fighters to ignore them and theirs is another great untold story in Japanese history. They were found on the battlefields, in warships, on walls of castles defending them, in fact they were found everywhere when needed. And they came from all spheres of society from the noblest to the peasants. Some fought for religious beliefs, some for political beliefs, some just in defence of their country but whatever the reason, they fought as bravely and determinedly as the men and all were ready for the ultimate sacrifice in defense of their homeland as any of the male samurais.

Here are a few famous Onna-Bugeishas from history:

Empress Jingu was a legendary empress who ruled as regent after her husband's death in 200 AD. Events from her reign are recorded in the *Kojiki* and the *Nihon Shoki* (collectively known as the *Kiki*). After seeking revenge on her husband's murderers, she organised and led the conquest of Korea in 200 AD. She was the 15th Japanese imperial ruler until the Meiji period. She ruled until her son came of age. She was the last de facto ruler of the Yoyoi period which went on to 300 AD.

Tomoe Gozen: fought in the Genpai war in 1180-1185. Japan was fragmented between the Minamoto and Taira clans who set the stage for the Kamakura Shogunate of Minamoto. The Book Heike Monogatari recorded the formidable Tomoe Gozen's exploits in it. She was an excellent Samurai, beautiful, intelligent, Master of the katana, excellent horsewoman and a competent politician. She was equal to the greatest Samurai of the time. Her prowess as a general was legendary. The master of Minamoto always pointed to Tomoe as the first true general of Japan.

She fought in the Battle of Awazu in 1184, with her 300 samurais against 2000 warriors and was one of the last five to survive. She defeated them and beheaded Honda no-Moroshige, a famous warrior of the Musashi clan they were fighting. She was and is a cultural phenomenon, an inspiration and symbol of strength to all Onna Bugeishas.

Hagaku Gozen (1201): was another Onna-Bugeisha. She too was beautiful and a skilled commander who led her force of 3,000 men to defend the Torisakayama fort alongside her nephew, Jo Sukemori. This was part of the Kenin Uprising that tried to overthrow the ruling Kamakura Shogunate. But they were outnumbered by a force of 10,000 men. The fort was breached, Hagaku on horseback with her ko-naginata was wounded but her ferocity in battle impressed many of the enemy. Many warriors asked for permission to marry her.

Nanako Takeko: was highly skilled in the Ko-naginata, extremely intelligent and a master of martial arts. She was selected to command the new Onna-Bugeisha fighting force who were to join up with their male counterparts in the Battle of Aizu. Their army was called Joshitai or Women's army.

Nanako got shot in the chest in the battle but still managed to kill a number of male samurais in close combat. But before she died, she asked her sister **Nakano Yuko** to cut off her head so the enemy could not take it as a trophy. Her sister did so and buried it in the roots of a pine tree in the temple of Aizu Bangemachi where later a monument was erected in her honour.

Yamamoto Yaeko: was a gunner and nurse in the Boshin war and fought in the Battle of Azizu against the Meiji Restoration also. This battle marked the beginning of The Meiji Restoration and the end of the Onnna-Bugeisha and the Shogunate.

Mongol women

Mongol society was a patriarchal and patrilineal society but unlike most other such societies of the times, women were an integral and respected part of it. They rode to battle, fought in battles, helped in decision making. They generally held less rank than their fathers and husbands but there were many exceptions. Mongol children did not go to school but learned from their elders. Marriages were usually arranged but sometimes a woman was stolen from her clan like Genghis' father Yesuge stole his mother Hoelun, from another tribe. But this was not very common as it could lead to blood feuds. There were no aspersions cast on the women for these acts e.g. Genghis' wife Börte was stolen by an enemy tribe. He got her back and left the empire in her care when he went to battle. Mongol women rarely remarried when their husbands died. They could if they wanted to though.

Among the Mongols it was a tradition that women managed the affairs at home when the men went to war, hunt or herd. But during the 13th century, as war campaigns grew longer and further away, the women assumed the rule of the land in their husbands' absence especially from the time of Genghis Khan in 1227 and of his grandson, Kublai Khan from 1260. Genghis Khan always left the running of his huge empire to his beloved wife **Börte** who did an excellent job of it. She was a very strong and capable woman in a male dominated society.

Genghis Khan's son who inherited, Ogodei, was a drunk. He spent more and more time in drunken stupor and so his most capable wife, not the first wife, **Toregene** gradually took on more and more power. We know about her power in the Mongol yurt from an order to print Taoist texts, issued by her under the name Yeye Khatun or Great Empress. Her name was there but under Ogodei's seal. It was issued on April 10, 1240. This was proof of her power that was already established in the administration of the Empire.

Toregene assumed full power in 1241 as regent when Ogodei died. Soon she dismissed all her husband's ministers and replaced them with her own, the most important one being another woman, **Fatima,** a Tajik or Persian captive from a campaign. Fatima was allowed full access to Torogene anytime. She could also execute business and issue commands and prohibitions. According to the Persian chronicler Fatima *became the sharer of intimate confidences and the depository of hidden secrets."*

Torogene received dignitaries from all over the world at her capital of Karakorum or her nomadic camp – kings, princes, emirs, governors all came to her including Prince Yaroslav II Vsevdodovich of Vladimir, the highest-ranking guest to visit her, and Suzdal, who died suspiciously just after dining with Toregene Khatun. The Seljuk Sultan, representing the Caliph of Baghdad and the two Davids, both claimants to the Georgian throne also visited her.

There were two other female governor's divisions of Mongolia: Sorkhokhtani, the widow of Tolui, Genghis' youngest son ruled Northern China and Eastern Mongolia; and Ebuskun, the widow of Genghis' second son Chaghatai, ruled Central Asia or Turkestan

Only Batu Khan continued as the leader of the Golden Horde under male control.

Strangely enough many powerful Mongol women were not born Mongols but from captured tribes, married into the clan, except Fatima. Some were Christians some were Muslims but a person's rise to power lay not in race or religion but in their capabilities.

Never had women ruled over such a large empire nor did they do so later. Toregene handed over the Empire to her inept son Guyuk who made a mess of everything. Within 18 months he was dead under unknown circumstances. The Kingdom was taken over by his wife Oghul Ghamish, much like Toregene did. But her rule was contested by Sorkhokhtani, with the full support of her five capable sons. She organised the election of her son Monge to the office of the Great Khan in 1251.

Unlike Genghis Khan's weak sons, Sorkhokhtani's sons were strong, motivated and capable. In time each of them would be the Great Khan in turn: Mongke, Arik, Boke and Kublai. Her other son Hulegu conquered Baghdad and established the dynasty of the Persia Ilkhanate.

Sorkhokhtan was a woman who strongly influenced Mongol history and culture. She advised Genghis' son Ogodai when he was a khan. When her husband, Touli, Genghis' son died, she became head of the household. She insisted that her boys be educated and learn different languages. When Guyuk was the Khan, she kept the empire together by diplomacy. When her son Mongke was Khan, she opened truce, instituted intellectual exchanges throughout the empire, emphasised freedom of religion and advised against exploiting the conquered people.

A Persian chronicler wrote about her and her successes that had there been another like her, then surely women would be judged the superior sex.

The Mongol women were a strange sight to the civilizations that they helped conquer. They rode horses, shot arrows from their bows and commanded both men and women.

Unlike the Chinese women, the Mongol women rejected foot binding or wearing veils as among the Muslim women. But soon they lost power everywhere except in Mongolia.

When Kublai Khan ruled in China, he had to fight off his cousin Kaidu Khan from Central Asia. Kaidu's daughter fought beside him. Marco Polo says of her (Aiyaruk / Khutulan) that she was beautiful, a skilled archer and wrestler. She would marry on condition a man could defeat her in wrestling. None did. She stayed single. Puccini's Opera, Turandot was inspired by her.

Genghis' empire was destroyed by 1368 after lasting for one and a half centuries. The Mongols withdrew to their steppe heartland. However, the mongol women were not ready to let go. While the men squabbled over herds, the women kept the flame of the imperial spirit alive. And then in late 15th Century another conqueress arose determined to restore Genghis Khan's empire. Her name was **Manduhai**. Mongols called her the Wise Queen. She took to the battle field and one by one reconquered the steppe tribes and again united them into one nation. However, the Chinese by now had built the Great Wall to keep out all invaders. They also had artillery and gunpowder. The Mongols could not match this fire power. So passed away a great empire!

Persian women

Ancient Persia, ruled over the world 2000 years ago. Some of the toughest battles took place in regions where women played vital roles, while the men were out on faraway battlefields. These women fighting for their country and homes on the battlefield, left an important mark on history.

These ancient Persian women were fearsome fighters and made a name for themselves like the undauntable **Tomyris**. She did not tolerate any infringement on her land by anyone – king or commander. She was a very strong and forthright woman who was feared by her enemies.

Persian Warrior Queen

Another warrior was **Banu**. She and her husband Banak fought the Arab invaders for 23 years, killing thousands of them. They were both warriors in their own right and belonged to the revolutionary resistance in Persia at that time. They never lost a battle, but unfortunately, they were betrayed to the enemy. She was spared but her husband was condemned to be killed in a gruesome way: he was sewn up inside a cow hide and crushed to death, slowly.

Another famous female was **Sura,** a daughter of the last King of Parthia. She was her father's right-hand. Her father died suddenly in war and Sura set about to get revenge as she suspected foul play. She suspected them to belong to the fighting force. So she set about seeking them there. She was an excellent fighter and tactician and exhausted her enemies before delivering the coup de grâce. Consumed with seeking revenge and constant warring, she died on the battlefield without ever knowing who the culprits were who killed her father.

In the 2nd century BC, there was **Rhodogune,** (171-132 BC) daughter of the Parthian king Mithridates, and wife of Demetrius II Nicator, the Seleucid Emperor. When Demetrius was held hostage in the Parthian court after a disastrous campaign, Rhodogune vowed not to brush her hair or brush her teeth until she quashed the rebellion, riding at the head of her army. She defeated the rebels and was depicted on the seals of Persia with long dishevelled hair, due to her vow. This incident is also mentioned in the *Tractatus de mulieribus*, in greater detail. She is described with half braided and half unbraided hair.

These women were the stuff of legends even when they belonged to a patriarchal society. In 2004 the grave of a Persian woman warrior with her weapons was discovered.

Other European warrior women (France, Spain, Italy...)

Eastern Roman historians also mention **warrior women among their European enemies.** Procopius (primary source for Emperor Justinian I's times) writes about an English princess who led the invasion of Jutland but this is not proven. However, Johannes Skylitzes 12 AD, historical writer, writes women participated in the battle in Bulgaria with Prince Svjatoslav of Kiev (971) as mentioned earlier.

Other European women who also fought in the defense of their homeland were:

The Kazak women, (11 BCE to 4 CE): They had a special status in the hierarchy. Since ancient times, the Kazakh people used to pay tribute to the keepers of the domestic hearth. In Kazakhstan, there are many ancient legends about beautiful warriors who were also reliable partners for their men. A Kazakh folk proverb says that Kazakhstani women unite the people like salt, which gives taste to food. The clan to which a person belongs is determined by his or her ancestors. Their most esteemed ancestor is Genghis Khan. In war they fought alongside the men using sword and dagger. Many women of Kazakhstan were great warriors who demonstrated real courage and self-sacrifice no less than men.

Historically Kazak women did not experience any violation of their rights. Since ancient times, these women lived and worked on an equal basis with men. Equal status in society between Kazakhs allowed these women to contribute to the development of the culture and spirituality of these people.

Bracari (an ancient Celtic tribe living in Portugal) also fought alongside their men against the Romans, bravely and stoically, not saying a word amid the slaughter. Appian of Alexandria (a Greek historian during the time of Emperors Trajan, Hadrian and Antoninus Pius) wrote that the Bracari were a very warlike people. They fiercely resisted Roman rule. Their women fought defending their town, *"never turning, never showing their backs, or uttering a cry," preferring death to captivity.*

Iberians: The fighting in Iberia was incredibly fierce; women often took up the sword and fought alongside men, and many times talks of peace led to open betrayals. In 206 BCE - Iberian women assisted in the siege of Illiturgis against Scipio Africanus.

Some famous individual heroines

One famous Breton warrior was **Joanna of Flanders** (1295-1374) who took up arms in defense of her husband John of Montfort and the town of Hennebont in Brittany, in the war of the Breton Succession against the French House of Blois. Montfort was imprisoned and so Joanna raised her own army, took the disputed territory. The Chronicler Jean le Bel writes of her defense of the town: *the brave countess was armed and armored and rode on a large horse from street to street, rallying everyone and summoning them to join the defence. She had asked the women of the town, the nobles as well as* *the others, to bring stones to the walls and to throw these on the attackers, as well as pots filled with lime.* The highlight came when they were encircled by Charles' soldiers, she realised his army was too stretched out. With 300 of her men, she put his headquarters to the torch. This earned her the nickname Joanna the Fiery (*Jeanne La Flamme*). She is said to have gone mad in the end and was confined to Tickhill Castle in England. She is also believed to have influenced Joan of Arc.

Then there was **Joan of Arc,** one of the most famous female warriors. She was a Medieval, teenage, peasant girl who led the French into battle against the superior English forces. Her career lasted just one year but the mark she made on history is eternal. France was in desperate straits and Joan got visions to drive the English out of France. In 1429 she was able to convince the Dauphin of France, the future King Charles VII to give her an army to relieve the besieged city of Orleans, which he did in a few days. She went on to lead the French to many more victories and succeeded in having the Dauphin crowned king in Rheims. She was however unable to retake Paris and was captured in 1430 by the English. They tried her for heresy and burnt her at the stake three times in one day. Since then, she has been a French national symbol and has been canonised as a saint.

Another great warrior was **Matilda of Canossa** (1046-1115), in Tuscany. She was called the Great Countess and perhaps has the best record as a female military commander of the Middle-Ages. She was a major player in Tuscany for more than 40 years. She supported the Papacy under Pope Gregory VII, especially against Emperor Henry IV the Holy Roman Emperor in 1077 in many campaigns finally confronting him in her castle in Canossa and defeating him there.

Joan of Arc Warrior & Saint Matilda of Canossa, Tuscany

Isabella of Castile I was married to Ferdinand II of Aragon. They had an excellent partnership especially when it came to military matters. Ferdinand did most of the field commanding while Isabella was responsible for the military administration. From time to time, she participated on the field among her troops in full armour, often in the later stages of the battle to rally the troops. Sometimes she participated directly in the battle, successfully. She reorganised the government and reduced their debt drastically (See pp. 74 for more details).

Catherina Sforza, (1462-1509) is one of the most exceptional figures of the Italian Renaissance. She was the Countess of Forli and Lady of Imola. She governed wisely and well during the time of her son's regency (after her husband, Girolamo Riario's death). She was a fierce woman and participated fully in the Italian Renaissance Movement. She was a brave and bold woman and was involved in the papal politics of the time in the 15th century. She put up a great defence against the Venetian assault which earned her the Title of *"a La Tigre"* (The Tiger). 1499, the Pope Alexander VI sent his son Cesare Borgia to conquer her lands. She fought very well but was ultimately defeated and taken to Rome as a captive.

Sichelgaita Hauteville of Salerno, (1040-1090) was a Lombard princess and wife to Robert Guiscard, Duke of Hauteville and Calabria. She is best known for rallying the fleeing Norman soldiers at the battle of Dyrrachium in 1081. A Byzantine chronicler, Anna Comnena wrote that she confronted her fellow soldiers and urged then to fight. *"As they continued to run, she grasped a long spear and charged at full gallop against them. It brought them to their senses and they went back to fight."* Another chronicler says that she was wounded during the battle but the Normans still defeated the Byzantines. She was very much involved in her husband's military activities and participated much more than was previously known.

Jeane Laisne, (1456-?) When Charles the Bold of Burgundy led his soldiers against the town of Beauvis, the citizens of the town, including the women fought them in hand-to-hand combat. Among them was **Jeane Laisne,** a lady who grabbed a small axe and fought the Burgundian standard bearer. This rallied the defenders of the town and they fought them off. She was renamed **Jeanne Hachette** by the citizens of the town for her bravery.

Orderic Vitalis, an Anglo-Norman historian recorded a feud between **Isabel of Conches** the wife of Ralph of Tosny and **Helwise the Countess of Evreux** in 1090's. Vitalis writes: *Both the ladies who stirred up such bitter wars were persuasive, high-spirited, and beautiful; they dominated their husbands and oppressed their vassals, whom they terrorized in various ways. But they were very different in character. Helwise on the one hand was clever and persuasive, but cruel and grasping; whereas Isabel was generous, daring, and gay, and therefore lovable and estimable to those around her. In war she rode armed as a knight among the knights; and she showed no less courage among the knights in hauberks and sergeants-at-arms than did the maid* **Camilla, the pride of Italy**, *among the troops of Turnus. She deserved comparison with Lampeto and Marpesia, Hippolyta and Penthesilea and the other warlike Amazon queens.*

Modern general history that we have had access to over the post-Christian centuries have all been works by men and they were mostly interested in the heroic deeds of men. Women warriors unnerved them so when they did write about them, often it was also to denigrate them. All organised religions have consistently demeaned womanhood. They started being relegated to the background. Only in recent decades women are breaking free from bondage.

Some other recorded warrior women

Some female warriors recorded by Herodotus are:

- The **Amazons**, well known in history as excellent female warriors; e.g. Tomyris of the Massagetae who fought and defeated Cyrus the Great;
- The **Zaueces** people were from Ancient Libya. Herodotus describes them as always having their women drive their chariots to war
- The **Scythians** are recorded time and time again by many sources as great warriors. In 4th BCE there were: **Onomaris** who led her people to conquer and settle in new lands; **Cynanae,** a half-sister of Alexander the Great who fought and defeated an Illyrian champion in a hand-to-hand combat; **Artemisia II** of Caria led a fleet and played a role in the military-political affairs of the Aegean after the decline in the Athenian naval superiority. According to Heracleides of Cyme, Achaemenid kings had a **300 – woman entourage of concubines who served also as bodyguards**; **Mania** became satrap of Dardanus. The Greek writer, Polyaenus described her as going to battle riding a chariot. She was an excellent general and **never lost a battle.**

- Cleophis, queen of the **Assacani** (present day Swat in Pakistan) surrendered to Alexander the Great after a long, unsuccessful siege of her city and Alexander's desire for a ceasefire. Alexander killed all who surrendered and burnt the city. It showed his pettiness. The wives of the soldiers also fought and died beside their husbands against Alexander's army.
- From the 320s BCE, Chandragupta Maurya, started the custom of kings of ancient India **employing armed women as bodyguards**. These women rode war chariots, horses and elephants, and participated in battles. This custom continued till the end of the Gupta period (320 to 550 AD).
- In 324 BCE the **Achamenid** satrap Atropates of Media presented Alexander the Great with **100 horsewomen armed with war axes and light shields** after the decisive battle with the Persian King Darius.
- Another warrior queen was **Eurydice III of Macedon** (318 BCE) who fought Polyperchon and Olympias and defeated them. She was Alexander the Great's grandmother.
- Another warrior queen was **Cratesipolis of Corinth** (314 to 308 BCE) who commanded an army and forced cities to submit to her.
- In Japan **Empress Jingu** is supposed to have led an army of invasion into Korea in early 3 BCE.
- Around the same time in China, **Huang Guigu** led armies in her military campaigns in Northern China.

Also during this time **graves of women warriors were found** around the **Sea of Azov**.

- In **Sparta** the women very often assisted in the defence of the city against besieging forces, even leading the army and constructing defences as **Princess Arachidamia** did in the 3rd Century BCE.
- In 208 BCE During the siege of Petelia, in the 2nd Punic War women accompanied their husbands in sorties against Hannibal. Hannibal surprised the Romans and destroyed a large detachment of Roman soldiers.
- In 206 BCE **Iberian women** participated greatly in the siege of Illiturgis in Scipio Africanus' army against Hannibal.
- Between 206 and 202 BCE **Consort YU** accompanied Xiang Yu on all battles during the **Chu-Han Contention.**
- In 220 BCE **Vaccaei and Vetton women** (Spain) defended their city of Salmantica against Hannibal and his men. Hannibal was impressed by their valour and returned their city to them.
- In 220 CE **Cisalpine Gaul women** served as judges in their people's disputes with Hannibal.
- In 102 BC according to Plutarch in the battle at Aquae Sextiae, the Romans fought the **Teutonic Ambrones.** Plutarch describes it as *"the fight had been no less fierce with the women than with the men themselves... the women charged with swords and axes and fell upon their opponents uttering a hideous outcry. And the women not only attacked the Roman but any of their men who attempted to*

desert. The defeated 300 women killed their children and then all committed suicide rather than be Roman slaves (Plutarch, 2nd century AD, *Life of Marius).* These women fought with swords, axes, poles, lances and staves.

- Another female warrior queen was **Cleopatra II** who led a rebellion against Ptolemy VIII and Cleopatra III and drove them out of Egypt in 131 BCE (Gardiner, AH pp. 183).
- **Cleopatra VII Philopater** (69 to 30 BCE) was the last queen of the Ptolemaic Kingdom of Egypt and the last active ruler. Cleopatra actively influenced Roman politics at a crucial period and was especially known for her relationships with Julius Caesar and Mark Antony. She came to represent, as did no other woman of antiquity, the prototype of the romantic femme fatale. But according to Plutarch (in *Parallel Lives*) it was not the beauty of her face – many were more beautiful than her but as he explains: *Her actual beauty ... was not so remarkable that none could be compared with her, or that no one could see her without being struck by it, but the contact of her presence ... was irresistible. ... The character that attended all she said or did was something bewitching'*

Women then worked and distinguished themselves not only as warriors but in many other spheres of life, as rulers, judges, priestesses, healers, headed households, leaders in faith, land owners, in politics and medicine, like **Peseshet,** the first ancient Egyptian woman in recorded history to practise medicine. She may also have been the first female scientist. It took several millennia for another Egyptian woman, **Helena Sidarous,** to enter the medical field in 1930s.

Note: Possible Roman Descendants of **Cleopatra** Julia Domna married Emperor Septimus Severus, and became the mother of Emperors, **Geta** (ruled 209-211); and Caracalla (ruled 211-217). From the second Severan line, Julia Maesa was the grandmother of the two final Emperors of the dynasty, Elagabalus (ruled 218-222) and Alexander Severus (ruled 222-235).

Ancient History abounds in women warriors, warrior queens and women's armies. Some kings, like in Persia preferred to have women bodyguards (Stanley B Alpern). They were just as capable, brave, undaunted, devoted and patriotic if not even more so than men. This is just a small sample of their contribution to their societies. In pre and medieval and even quite modern times, women were relegated to the bedroom and kitchen, treated as incapable of being leaders and fighters. But in fact, the cliché is oh so true: that behind every great (and successful) man there is generally a woman.

Warrior women around the World

The women in ancient times who went to war from so many races and cultures signals the pervasive presences of women which were normal prior to the profound change that took place in cultures after the adoption of agriculture and then with the establishment of organised religion and their single-minded focus on male superiority.

Warrior women images from some countries

Muslin Arab warrior woman

Khawlah bint al-Azwar, Arab warrior woman

Japanese onna bugeish

Celtic woman warrior

Amazon warrior women

Chinese warrior woman

Europe

Greece

The status of women among the Greek city states differed. In Athens, the women had very few rights. It was about the worst. They were excluded from education and political life. But that was not the case throughout Greece. Spartan women had a lot of rights as did women of some other city states like Crete, Delphi, Gortyn, Thessaly, and Megara until the Archaic period when laws on gender and segregation worsened their condition. Still many women wielded power.

Plutarch says of **Spartan women** that they were strong and wealthy enough to refuse to bear too many children. He portrayed Spartan women as being heroic and proud.

According to the **law code of Gortyna, Crete**, women had the right to own, control and inherit property. A certain percentage of what she produced through her work belonged to her. In divorce a woman retained half her property.

There were at least 9 very well-known female poets during that time among them Corinne and Sappho. They were upper class women who had the leisure to write. None of them lived in Athens.

In the Hellenistic period, queens held real political power. Macedonian **Olympias,** Alexander's mother, ruled Greece; **Arsinoe II** co-ruled with her Egyptian husband, Ptolemy II, **Cleopatra VII** ruled in her own right. And others mentioned before.

Epipole of Carystus is one of the first women reported to have cross-dressed as a man to fight in a war. She was a daughter of Trachion, of Carystus in Euboea. In the disguise of a man she went with the Greek army against Troy, but when Palamedes discovered her sex, she was stoned to death by the Greek army.

Queen Gorgo – she was the wife of King Leonidas I, Cleomenes' half-brother, who fought and died in the Battle of Thermopylae (the famous battle with the Persian King Xerxes) Gorgo is one of the few female figures actually named by the Greek historian Herodotus, and was well-known for her political judgment and wisdom (Herodotus History). Once when asked why Spartan women were the only women in Greece that "ruled" their husbands, she replied: *because we are the only women to give birth to men* (Plutarch, Sayings of Spartan Women). In other words, only men that *were confident enough to accept women as equal were real men.*

Arachidamia was a Spartan queen most notable for her role in leading the Spartan women against Pyrrhus during his siege of Lacedaemon in the 3rd century BC. At the height of the siege, the Spartan council of elders wanted to send the Spartan women off to Crete for their safety. But Arachidamia refused. She entered the council, sword in hand, and contested this proposal, questioning whether the Spartan women were expected to survive the ruin of their own city. She then organised the women in building the trenches, supplying troops with weapons when theirs broke or were lost, and cared for the wounded on the battlefield, (Plutarch, *Parallel Lives: Life of Pyrrhus 27.2)*.

Women rulers were rare in Greek city states but some did have them like Gorgo of Sparta and Aspasia of Athens. Some won acclaim Sappho poetess of Lesbos, Arete of Cyrene philosopher, Agnodice of Athens, physician. Sparta gave a lot of freedom to the women and so, Aristotle claimed, the Spartan constitution should be rejected. But because women were such a harmonious part of society, Sparta became great, monopolized the sovereignty and was always considered the *City of Brave Men.*

While much of history has concentrated on the role of Spartan men, it cannot be ignored that the Spartan women were a vital part of the warrior society. They raised warriors, and were brave leaders in their communities. They encouraged the men to be brave in battle, while also knowing how to take care of themselves and hold their own. Life in the

Spartan state was very difficult and harsh. So it took a harsh and strong woman, to raise a fierce society.

Women of Troy and Anatolia (see above)
The Illyrians (See Above)
The Amazons (See above)
Scytho-Sarmatian (see above)
Slavs (see above)
Celts (see above)
Teutonic and Scandinavian (see above)

Warrior Women of Asia

Asian women have received a very bad press as to their social status in the Western world. A lot of these preconceived notions are far from the truth. Like all societies around the world there are always cases but in general Asian women had a very high status in society pre-colonialism, their position was quite different to that of post-colonial Asia. Colonialism along with its other negative outcomes demeaned female roles in society very strongly and negatively.

The war field, since medieval times, written history, has been dominated by the exploits of men. Nevertheless, women have also fought very bravely and competently, leading armies, planning strategy successfully in the face of extraordinary challenges. Certain women throughout the world have left an indelible mark on history.

Asian women like their counterparts in Europe in ancient times have fought in battle, ruled countries, led armies, planned strategies and were trained in battle. They were lawgivers, poets, philosophers, could wrestle against men and even defeat them, trained in martial arts in most parts of Asia from the Middle-East to Mongolia, China and Japan.

Women warriors

Khutulun the Great Mongol warrior

Mongol female warriors

Scythian warriors

North Asia
China (see above)
Japan (see above)
Mongolia (see above)
Persia (see above)

Korea: Though many women participated in the Korean War of 1950, about 120,000 of them from health care to volunteers on the battle field to service in the Army Corps, Air Force and Navy reserves, in the Korean War memorial Wall all statue figures are males. No females are to be seen. Yet in the past Korean women did play an important role, even that of warriors in their history. There is the story of the **Wonhwa female warriors.** One legend is about 300 of them. There were two groups in the Kingdom of Silla, well known for their beauty and their martial skills especially on the battlefield. This very fierce force of female warriors was assembled by King Jinheung of Silla. The two female leaders were jealous of each other. One, **Junejeong**, invited the other **Nammo** got her drunk and then murdered her and dumped her body in the North stream. Next morning her subordinate after a long search found the body. Junejeong was put on trial, found guilty and executed. After that the female warriors were disbanded and the male warriors, the Hwarang were born.

This story shows the existence of female warriors in Korea, lost to us now.

Legendary Princess Urduja

Vietnamese Warrior Sisters Trungtrac & Trung Nhi

West Asia including Yemen

In pre-Islamic Arabia women served as warriors, administrators, ambassadors and in all other capacities. Some of them are the following:

Zenobia, Queen of Palmyra (240-274) whose husband was Septimius Odaenathus, King of Palmyra (Syria) rode to battle and fought beside her husband against the Goths, the Persians (Meltzer) and later alone, after Odaenathus' death against the Romans. She seized Roman territories and expanded her kingdom. Her capital was in Palmyra from where she sent out armies to conquer and extend her empire. Her empire included Anatolia, Lebanon, Roman Judea and Southern Egypt. In 269 she conquered Egypt and had the Roman Prefect beheaded. She was as brave and daring as her husband in combat (Meltzer pp. 36). Rome responded by the Roman Emperor Aurelian, an excellent general, leading the attack against her. Zenobia took to the battlefield but left the overall command to an experienced general. It was a bitter fight but Zenobia's army lost in the end. There are conflicting reports of her death. Some say she surrendered, (which seems unlikely) some that she was dragged to Rome and forced to participate in a humiliating victory parade, some that she starved herself to death on the voyage to Rome in defiance. Whatever the truth, she was a great woman, a tolerant ruler and gladly embraced different ethnic peoples into her empire allowing them to practice their own customs and traditions. Her court was a centre of learning and philosophy.

Captive Queen Zenobia fought Rome

Mavia Arab warrior-queen, led a devastating rebellion against Rome in the 4th century AD

Queen Mavia: was a warrior queen of the Tanukhida, a confederation of semi-nomadic Arabs of South Syria in the 2nd half of the 4th century (Bowersock et al 1999, pp. 569; Shahid, *Byzantium and the Arabs*, pp. 141). She led her troops in rebellion against the Romans during the reign of Emperor

Valens, riding at the head of her army. The Romans thought it was funny and when the commander of Palestine asked for reinforcements, he was removed from his post for needing help in fighting a woman. Mavia rode into Phoenicia and Palestine. After she reached the frontiers of Egypt, she defeated the Roman army repeatedly (*Sue M. Sefscik, "Zenobia", Women's History*). The Roman Commander of Palestine was reinstated. Finally, the Romans made a truce with her on condition that she helped them when they needed it (Jensen, 1996, pp. 73-75). The Romans asked for her help soon after when the Goths attacked them. She sent a force of cavalry to their aid.

Mavia was considered the second most powerful queen after Zenobia (Bowersock et al). Much of what is known about her is from the writings of Rufinus, recovered from the lost works of Gelasius of Caeserea. Some later authors have transformed her into a Roman or Christian but it is patently obvious that she was a pagan Arab.

Queen Sammuramat of Assyria (811-792 BCE) was well-known for her tactical military skills, nerve and cunning. Once her husband, the royal advisor, Menos sent for her in the middle of a battle. When she arrived to the battlefield, she took over the strategy and won the battle by outflanking King Ninus' army. He was so impressed that he kidnapped her. Her husband committed suicide. Sammuramat asked Ninus to allow her to rule the kingdom for a day. He granted her wish. She immediately had herself crowned and then executed

Ninus. She went on to rule for 42 years and expanded the kingdom with her military conquests.

Khawlah bint al-Azwar was the sister of a leading Muslim commander during the early Islamic conquest in 7th CE. She took up arms on a number of occasions leading troops of women into battle including in 636 against the Byzantine army in the Battle of Yarmuk. She has been described as one of the greatest female soldiers in the world. She fought in the battles in Syria, Jordan and Palestine and was a close companion of the Muslim Prophet Muhammad. She has been compared to the great Muslim soldier Khalid bin Walid.

Some other famous warrior women of this area were **Tumāḍir** bint ʿAmr ibn al-Ḥārith ibn al-Sharīd al-Sulamīyah, better known as the **poetess Al Khaansa.** She was a poet and a warrior who participated in the Battle of Qadisiyyah in 16 AH with her four sons who all died on the battlefield. She was a contemporary of the Prophet Mohammed. Another renowned warrior was **Sharifa Fatima** (her real name was Fatima bint al-Hassan), a female Zaydi Sayyid chieftain in 15th century Yemen (Mernissi, 1993, 2006 pp. 20). She was the granddaughter of Zaydi imam Al-Nasir Muhhammad Salah-al-Din. She conquered Sa'dah and Najran according to Al Zirikli (pp. 130). She fought her relative Al–Mansur an-Nasir who wanted the power for himself. She conquered San'aa.

Still another female warrior was **Ghaliyya al-Wahhabiyya,** who in the early 19th century led a military resistance movement in Saudi Arabia to defend Mecca against foreign takeover by the Ottoman Empire during the Ottoman-Wahabi War for which she was given the title of Amira. She was from the Hanbali Bedouin tribe of Ta'if and the wife of Prince Hamad Ben Abduallah ben-Umhay, the governor of Tarba. She successfully defended Mecca with her boldness and strategy. She has been described in the chronicles in the following way: *Never had the resistance of the Arab tribes from the vicinity of Mecca been so strong as was that of the Arabs of Tarba.... They had at their head a woman who bore the name of Ghaliyya."* This was at the Battle of Turaba in 1814. The Ottomans were repulsed and incapable of admitting that they were defeated by a woman. So they spread the rumour that she was a witch.

Some Yemeni warrior queens were **Sayyida Hurra, Queen Arwa of Yemen, Queen Asma:** *The Little Queen of Sheba*, **Al-Hurra and the Fatimid princess Sitt Al-Mulk.**

Queen Asma was married to Ali Al-Sulaihi who ruled Yemen and established the Sulayhid Dynasty ruling from Haraz in Yemen in 1047 with the support of Hamadi, Himayari and other Yemeni tribes. Ali united many Yemeni tribes under his rule. He made Asma co-ruler in actual fact and had her publically proclaimed through the Friday Khutbah (Friday Sermon). She is said to have attended council meetings with an unveiled face, along with her husband. She was strong, generous and outspoken and also a poet, much respected by her husband who left her in charge of the kingdom from time to time and who highly valued her opinion.

She was taken prisoner by the tribal chief prince of Zubayd a province in Yemen when her husband Ali was killed on pilgrimage in Mecca. She stayed a prisoner until she managed to send a message to her son Ahmad Al-Mukkaram in Sana'a who rescued her. After her death in 1074, Queen Arwa took over ruling of the kingdom.

Queen Arwa (11th-12th century) was unique in that she held political as well as spiritual authority simultaneously. She was Queen consort, regent and then queen in her own right until her death in 1138. When it was possible for a contested succession, she safeguarded the Caliphate and kept all the competitive and powerful tribal leaders in check. She was very popular with the people. She was much influenced by her mother-in-law, Queen Asma-bint Shihab of Egypt.

Arwa consolidated Sulayhid rule during her tenure. The Fatimid Caliph Al Mutansir-bilah granted her the title of Hujja, the highest rank in Yemeni religious hierarchy and was the first woman to get this title. Like Asma she attended council meetings but always with her face covered. She was said to be very beautiful, and much younger than Arwa.

Both women were intelligent courageous very independent, pious, having great integrity and beautiful. Literature flourished under them. They were both wise rulers.

Some other Arab queens who distinguished themselves were:

Another very famous Eastern **Queen was Balqees**, the **Queen of Sheba** who is referred to in the Torah, Bible and

Quran. She was supposed to have travelled from her kingdom of Ethiopia with a caravan of precious gifts for king Solomon of Israel to *"to prove him with hard questions"*. Solomon answered to her satisfaction. After exchanging gifts, she returned to her land (*Encyclopaedia Judaica, vol. 18 pp. 755-763*). But others have claimed she was a Syrian. Recent archaeological finds place her as the Queen of Sheba in the Yemeni town of Marib with a temple there known as *Mahram Bilqis*. After 3,000 years there are still remnants of the civilisation of the kingdom of Sheba in Yemen. There is a temple dedicated to her, a throne, the Almaqah courtyard, and annexes. There was also the Great Dam of Marib in the Sabaean Capital, part of which was destroyed in the airstrikes against Yemen in recent history (*Queens of Arabia Yemen* by Noor Almohsin).

Central Asia

It stretches from the Caspian Sea in the West to China and Mongolia in the East and from there to Afghanistan and Iran in the South to Russia in the North. It consists of the former Soviet Republics of Kazakhstan, Kyrgyzstan, Tajikistan, Turkmenistan, Uzbekistan, Azerbaijan, Georgia, Mongolia, Afghanistan and others.

Medieval Mongolian women were very outspoken. They had martial training and participated in regular campaigns against the Turks and Europeans. Their influence extended way beyond North-east Asia.

It was inhabited by the predominantly Iranian speaking people: Bactrians, Sogdians, Chorasmians and the semi-nomadic Scythians and Dahae language-speakers. Central Asia also became the homeland for the Kazakhs, Uzbeks, Tatars, Turkmen, Kyrgyz, and Uyghurs; Turkic languages mostly replacing the Iranian language, except in Tajikistan where Tajik is spoken. There is a vast variety of cultures in Central Asia and too many warrior women to encompass in one book. Here we will look at some of the most well-known warriors from the different cultures.

Khutulun was the daughter of Kaidu Khan, brother of Kublai Khan and a royal descendent of Genghis Khan. She is known in history as one of the most powerful military commanders and influential rulers. Khutulun was born at the height of civil war in the vast Mongol empire. She was known as a legendary soldier. Her father ruled the khanate while Kublai Khan ruled from China. She was the best warrior among her father's warriors, rode with his army and was never bested by anyone in a wrestling match. When a Mongol prince asked for her hand in marriage, she challenged him to a wrestling match and defeated him. Many others tried and failed. She never married.

Saikal, another Central Asian woman from modern Kyrgyzstan, comes from the Kyrgyz oral *Epic on Manas,* much like the Greek epics of Penelope (wife of Ulysses) or Clytemnestra (wife of Agamemnon) or Medea, wife of Jason and daughter of Aetes of Colchi. She was famous for courage in battle and prowess in combat wounding her suitor Manas whom she later married.

There was also **Gulayim,** the Amazon of the steppe. She was the daughter of Allayar, a tribal chieftain who ruled near the Southeast part of the Aral Sea. They lived in a fortress in Sarkop but when Sarkop was invaded and Allayar killed, Gulayim gathered a group of 40 women and defended the fortress. She has been and still is honoured as a warrior.

Another warrior of Kyrgyzstan, was **Kurmanjan Datka,** also called the *Tsaritsa of Alai'* and *Queen.* She was born in 1811 into the Mungush clan but fled to China at the age of 18 because she did not want to marry the man chosen for her. There she lived with her father. In 1832, she married Datka Alymbek, a feudal lord in the Kokand Khanate. When he was assassinated in 1862, Kurmanjan was recognised as the Dakta of the region by all the other khans of the Alai region.

Her son Abdylda-Bek commanded the army of Pulat Khan when he rebelled against the Russians. He was defeated and fled to Afghanistan and died there in 1877. Kurmanjan realised her people could not fight the might of the Russians and surrendered.

Her grandsons were charged with smuggling and her favourite one was executed by the Russians. The others were banished to Siberia. She withdrew from public life and died in 1907. She is well known and her exploits preserved in Chagatai, Turkic, Farsi, and Kyrgyz manuscripts for being a powerful woman who held her own in a male-dominated world.

Nodira was another powerful stateswoman and a poet of renown. Her name was Mohlaroyim, but she wrote under the pen name of Nodira. She was the regent for her son during his minority in the Uzbek Khanate of Kokand in 1822. She kept the kingdom together but the expansionist policies of her 15-year-old son Madali led to war with Nasrullah, from the Emirate of Bukhar. He invaded Kokand and killed Madali. He wanted to marry Nodira but as she refused, he had her hanged.

She became a hero under the Soviets and had her portrait on the first postage stamp of Uzbekistan.

South Asia

Banu Goshasp: An epic from the 11th-12th century called Banu Goshasp-Nama comprising 900 verses was composed by an unknown poet. He talks about a woman warrior, Banu Goshasp, Rustam's daughter in Persian literature. There is a manuscript of the poem at the Bibliothèque Nationale in Paris (Cat. Bibliothèque Nationale, pp. 18, no. 1194). Goshasp also appeared in other Persian epics. The *Banu Goshasp Nama* is one of the oldest Persian epics about a warrior woman. It tells the story of Banu Goshasp's exploits and journey through Turan and India along with her brother Faramaraz. In one episode they meet with a man and she battles him. But before the end she realises it is their father Rustam who has followed them to dissuade them from these exploits. Luckily everything is resolved happily.

She has many suitors but will not accept anyone without a battle. She battles many and they lose and are killed. Finally, she battles Giv and he wins. Reluctantly she agrees to the marriage but on the wedding night she overpowers him and ties him down. Her father comes and rescues Giv. Later they have a son Bijan or Bēžan/Bižan who becomes another famous Persian hero. Banu Goshasp's exploits are also celebrated in the Farāmarz-nāma, (pp. 32-78) Borzu-nāma, and Bahman-nāma and are collectively featured in the cycle of stories called the Sistani Cycle. All stories here revolve around heroes of the Sistan region. The poem itself is called *Banugoshaspnameh*.

Persian warrior woman *Rani Jhansi*

Gordāfarīd (Persian) is another heroine in the "*Shāhnāmeh of Ferdowsi*" (pp. 214) "*The Book of Kings*" or "*The Epic of Kings.*" It is an enormous poetic opus written by the Persian poet around 1000 AD. Gordafarid (Khaleghi-Motlagh, pp. 138) was a champion warrior who fought against

Sohrab (another Iranian hero who was the commander of the Turanian army). She was the daughter of Gaždaham the castellan of Dež-e Sapid, the Persian fortress on the frontier with Turān. She plays a martial role in the tragic episode of Rostam and Sohrāb (*Šāh-nāma*, II, pp. 130-37). After Sohrāb's attack on Dež-e Sapid and the defeat and capture of the Persian hero, Hojir, Gordāfarid is very angry that he allowed himself to be taken. She puts on her armour and challenges the Turanian heroes to single combat saying: *Where are your heroes, your warriors, your tried and tested chieftains?"* In this way she buys time for the defenders as the Turanian main force was on its way to Persia. But she, too could not stand against Sohrab and is defeated by Sohrāb, who only realises that his adversary is a female when he removes her helmet. He promptly falls in love with her. Gordāfarid, who does not see herself as Sohrāb's equal in battle, deceives him by false promises. She takes him up to the gate of the fortress, which she enters, and the gate closes behind her. The most haunting part of this episode is her conversation with Sohrāb (vv. 213-21, 236-48) and her foreboding of Sohrāb's downfall. Gordāfarid, was a symbol of courage for Persian women.

Queen Vishpala's (7000 BCE) deeds and fame come down in the Righveda, an ancient Hindu religious book. She was probably a real person but it is difficult to prove after 9,000 years. She fought on the side of the Ashvin twin – horsemen gods but lost her leg in the war. She continued to fight with an artificial limb.

In **Kerala,** in India women trained as intensely as the men in the martial art of Kalari Payattu. Using these women and even young girls can kill or paralyse with one blow. The Nizams (rulers) of Hyderabad had female guards. The kings of Kandy in Sri Lanka had all female archers to protect him.

The Indian queen **Rani Lakshmibai** of Jhansi (1828-1858) had practised the arts of war since childhood. She became an accomplished military leader and even led armies on the battlefield against the British colonial forces in India and resisted them to the bitter end in India's First war of Independence in 1857. She has often been called *the Indian Joan of Arc*. She was an excellent warrior and claimed a lot of lives on the battlefield. Rani Lakshmibai soon became a symbol of India's resistance against foreign oppression and led the first direct confrontations with the occupiers of her land.

Nayakuralu Nagamma is said to be one of the most powerful women of medieval India and the world. She is credited with being the first feminist. In the 12th century war epic, she rose to be the world's first Minister for King Nalagamaraju, of Palnadu. She proved herself as an excellent stateswoman and well trained in warfare.

Rani Abbakka Chowta, Queen of Ullal is regarded as the first female freedom fighter of India and **_the only_** *woman in history to confront, fight and repeatedly defeat the Portuguese.* She defended the region for 4 decades from 1525 to 1579. This was after the Portuguese found a sea route to India in 1498 (Vasco da Gama). She led her army successfully against the Portuguese in their 6 attacks during her reign. In the last attack, her husband betrayed her to the Portuguese, who were then able to imprison her. In prison she began a revolt which led to her death while trying to break free. It embodies a fight to the death.

Her army and navy consisted of soldiers and sailors from all religions and castes of Indian society from the Mogaveeras, to Billava archers, to Mappilah oarsmen. She was very intelligent and tenacious and has come down in folklore in the Dakshin Kannada region where there is an annual celebration (Veera Rani Abbakka Utsava) held in her memory until today.

Bibi Dalair Kaur was a 17th century Sikh woman warrior who fought against the Mughal Governor, Wajir Khan of Sirhind. His army broke through the walls of Sirhind. Bibi Dalair collected 100 women warriors and put up a stiff fight. Wajir taunted the women telling the men: *"Cowards, are you afraid of women? They are gifts for you, capture them and do what you want with the rewards of your hunt."* To this Bibi Dalair responded: *"We are the hunters, not the hunted. Come forward and find out for yourself!"* It was a very uneven fight and she and many of her warrior women were killed. However, she is still considered to be a martyr among the Sikhs and a source of inspiration to feminists.

Onake Obavva was a resident of Chitradurga, a city in Karnataka. She was married to Kahale Mudda Hanuma, a soldier whose duty it was to guard the gate of the fort. In the 18th century, the ruler of Mysore attacked this fort and his soldiers saw an opening and seeing it was unguarded (as Onake's husband had gone to get some water), he slipped in.

Onake armed with only a pestle killed the first soldier and relocated his body. In this way she killed all of them but was found slain, later that day. Onake has become a symbol for female pride in Kannada (a classical Dravidian language spoken in Karnataka).

Rani Veeramangai Velu Nachiyar was the Queen of the Shivagangai kingdom — now Madurai, Tamil Nadu — from 1769 to 1790. She is celebrated by the Tamilians as Veeramangai, (brave woman) because she was the first woman to successfully lead a revolt against the British colonisers. She was well-educated, (spoke French, English, and Urdu) and very well-trained in weaponry, martial arts, and archery. In 1772 the British invaded Shivagangai and killed her husband and young daughter. So in 1780 she struck back by carrying out the first recorded suicide bombing. Velu Nachiyar found out where the British ammunition was stored, then she and her adopted daughter Udaival doused themselves in oil, set themselves alight and walked into the ammunition storage. The women formed an army in her honour and fought and defeated the British taking back Shivagangai and reinstalling Velu as Queen.

On her death, the British East India Company took over her kingdom – as was usual for them.

South East Asia

Warrior queens and princesses were not uncommon in this part of the world before the Spanish conquest. It is said that a **blind princess** resided on an island near Luzon (Philippines) and no one was allowed to come near her without passing thorough her formidable bodyguards. The only man who succeeded, still could not touch her because even though blind, she was a trained fighter.

Princess Urduja was another warrior princess of the Philippines who ruled over a vast area in the 14th century. She refused to marry anyone but a warrior equal to her in prowess or better. She never married.

Gabriela Silang in the 18th century also in the Philippines led the longest revolt against the Spanish.

Teresa Magbanua (1871-1947) along with others fought in the Filipino revolution. A Filipino of Spanish descent said: *The present-day cultural machismo was introduced by the Spanish; old Filipino culture gave great respect to women* (Alpern pp. 2).

In the early centuries of the 1st millennium, Vietnamese women warriors commanded armed forces. There were the sister **Trung Trac** and **Trung Nhi** in the 1st century CE and **Triệu Thị Trinh** in the 3rd century CE who led uprisings against the Chinese rule in Vietnam. Triệu Thị Trinh, dressed in bright yellow with two swords and riding a war elephant, liberated her land but lost the battle to the Chinese. She committed suicide. There are extant records of Vietnamese women riding war elephants.

In Siam the king was guarded by a contingent of **400 women warriors with spears**. They were said to be better than the male soldiers in drills and were crack spear throwers.

It is similarly reported of Javanese princedom that they too, employed women bodyguard for the kings.

East Asia

Early **Japanese** history is filled with mighty deeds of female warrior queens leading their armies against enemy stronghold that lie in Yamato and Korea (Ratti, O / Adele Westbrook, pp. 114). The history tome *The Heike Monogatari* records a Japanese general **Tomeo Gozen**, the beautiful, female samurai who predated Takeo by about 700 years served the warrior warlord, shogun Minamoto-no **Yoshinaka,** who gave her the title Gozen out of respect for her abilities. She fought alongside male samurais in the Genpei war (1180-1185) and was an unusual sight. She played a **major role** in the capture of Kyoto city. It is said of her that she was a famous rider of untamed horses and *the equal of a thousand* in her ability to deal with the enemy even with *demon and gods* (Paul Varley, *Warriors of Japan as Portrayed in the War Tales*). Yoshinaka's high esteem of her overcame the prejudices against a female samurai. When Yoshinaka died in the Battle of Awazu, Tomeo surrendered her sword and went into retirement.

Another known female samurai (Onna Bugeisha in Japanese history) was **Nakano Takeko.** She was educated in literary and martial arts before she distinguished herself in The Boshin War, a Civil war in Japan, which lasted from 1868 to 1869. In the Battle of Azizu, (1968) the female warriors' contributions were not recognised but nevertheless she led her peers and won that battle. Later her unit was called **Jōshitai** (Women's Army). Her weapon of choice was the Japanese pole arm. She was shot in her chest while leading a charge against the Imperial Japanese army. She asked her sister to cut off her head and bury it to avoid defilement by the enemy. It was done. There is a monument in her honour there now.

China has its share of formidable female warriors. Chinese martial arts made famous by the Bruce Lee films, was developed by two women – **Yan Yongchun** and the **Venerable Wumei** – founders of the Yongchun (Wing Chun) martial arts system. Military families trained their daughters to follow in the same tradition and even served as generals in the army.

There is the 4th-5th century poem of **Hua Mulan** (The Ballad of Mulan) and her deeds but there is no other written record of her. According to the story, Mulan's elderly father was called up to serve in the Army (Sui Dynasty) but he was too sick to go. So Mulan dressed as a man went instead. On the battlefield she showed exceptional courage and the emperor offered her a post in the government. She declined and went to live in her village. When her warrior friends visited her, they found out that she was a woman.

Lin Siniang (1629-1644) was born towards the end of the Ming dynasty to a poor military family. Her father trained her in the martial arts from a young age. By the age of six, she was deadly with a sword. Her family died when she was young and she had a hard time surviving and went into prostitution. She kept up her training on her own. The King, Zhu Changshu of the state of Qingzhou saw her and fell in love with her looks and martial skills and made her his concubine. She taught her skills to the other concubines. A few years later, he was attacked by rebels and captured. Siniang organised the concubines into an army and went to rescue him. They fought very well but were greatly outnumbered. She refused to surrender and died on the battlefield. Her courage encouraged Changshu's army to fight harder. They defeated the rebels and rescued the King. She was then buried with great honour.

Xun Guan: in 316 AD, at the age of 13, Xun Guan found herself besieged in the city of Yuan where her father Xun Song was the commander during the Jin Dynasty. The city was besieged by the formidable Du Zeng and his army of 2,000 men. He pretended to surrender to Xun Song but in fact blockaded them. This was the turbulent time of the Three Kingdoms where there was a lot of jockeying for power. Xun Song asked for volunteers and only his daughter was ready to breach the walls, which she did successfully, brought help to the city and freed it. Guan was a very unusual girl and won the trust of men by her prowess and martial expertise at a time when few women were allowed to train in weaponry. She defied the attitudes of the times showing strategic acumen, prowess in battle and great courage. A short entry is found in the *Book of Jin Chapter 96* entitled exemplary women. It was put together 3 centuries later, during the Tang dynasty.

Ng Mui was said to be one of the legendary Five Elders (survivors of the Shaolin Temple destruction by the Qing dynasty. She founded the Wing Chun, Kung Fu Wu Mei Pai, Dragon Style (along with Wú Méi), White Crane, and Five-Pattern Hung Kuen styles of martial art in the 1700's. She was a Buddhist and trained in the Shaolin Temple. She fled to the White Crane temple and there taught **Yim Wing Chun** how to defend herself without needing a lot of physical strength. Many people today are experts in this martial art like Jackie Chan and Yip Man thanks to her.

Princess Pingyang (590's to 623) was the third daughter of an influential Sui dynasty military commander, Li Yuan who later became Emperor Gaozu of the Tang dynasty. The Sui Emperor Yang, was ineffectual and harsh. She helped her father to seize the throne by bringing 70,000 men to her army. Her husband joined her as did many other people. The peasants saw her as a liberator as she distributed food to them during the famine. Emperor Yang of the Sui surrendered and her father became emperor. She led the men to battle and fought bravely and on her death was honoured with a grand military funeral.

Wú Méi in 1647 she survived the Shaolin Monastery attacks and went on to become an all-rounder in martial art and fought against the Qing attacker in 1674. Later she took refuge in the White Crane Temple in the Hunan province of China. Later in life she founded the martial art styles like the Five Pattern, Hung Kuen and the Dragon Style (along with Ng Mui) ... She is now a respected member of the legendary *Five Elders* – survivors of the Shaolin temple arson attack and that of the Qing Dynasty.

Sān Máo (Chen Ping) 1943-1991 was a traveller and a writer who visited many places when it was very difficult to do so. She wrote a lot about her travels in foreign countries. Disillusioned, she committed suicide in 1991.

Wú Yí (1938 to-present) She was China's chief trade negotiator and was named to Forbes as the Most Powerful woman in the World, three times. She was also the vice premier of China. She worked her way up the ladder to Health Minister during the SAARS outbreak, getting a spot in the Time Magazine. She retired from Chinese politics in 2008 and is remembered as the Iron Lady of China and the Goddess of Transparency for her exemplary public service record.

Ching Shih was born Shi Yang aka Zheng Yi Sao, and Shi Xianggu in 1775. She was a Chinese pirate and was active in the South China Seas from 1801–1810. She married a notorious pirate named Cheng Yi who died 6 years later. Zheng Yi Sao was an honorific given her by the people of Guangdong. She began to amass power. Soon she became well-known and very successful, in fact the most successful pirate ever, easily beating names like Blackbeard, Henry Morgan and Sir Francis Drake. At the height of her power, she commanded over 800 large ships, 1,000 smaller vessels and had about 70,000 men and women pirates in her employ. Through political manoeuvring she entered into conflict with the Portuguese, English and Chinese authorities but managed to get out of them all successfully. At the height of her power, she ruled the South China Sea with her Red Flag Fleet.

Wang Zhenyi (1768-1797). She fought against the patriarchal customs of 18th century China by educating herself in astronomy, mathematics, geography, medicine and poetry. She studied the works of other scientists. She also conducted her own researches and published her works. She is mostly remembered for her poetry. She advocated that within society all, both men and women have the same reason for studying (Peterson, Notable women of China)

Soong Ch'ing-ling (1893-1981) was the daughter of a missionary and businessman, Charlie Soong. She received an international education at the Shanghai McTyeire School and then Wesley College in the USA. She was the third wife of Sun Yat-Sen who was Premier of the Kuomintang and President of the Republic of China, and through him rose to power. She was often referred to as Madame Sun Yat-Sen. She broke away and joined the Communist party. She held many positions after the establishment of The People's Republic of China. She was the first female President of the People's Republic of China: from 1968 to 1972 she served jointly with Dong Biwu as head of state. On 16 May 1981, two weeks before her death, she was admitted to the Communist Party and was named Honorary President of the People's Republic of China. She is the only person ever to hold this title.

Empress Dowager Cixi (1835-1908) of the Manchu Yehe Nara Clan, was a Chinese noblewoman, concubine and later regent who effectively controlled the Chinese government in the late Qing dynasty for 47 years, from 1861 until her death in 1908. She is often blamed for the collapse of the Qing

Dynasty. Like Empress Wu, she started as a concubine of the emperor but soon cemented her power especially after her son became the emperor. She was the most powerful woman since Empress Wu of 7th century China. She ruled China from behind the scenes as the young Emperor Tongzhi's mother and regent and then for her nephew Guangxu for 47 years until her death in 1908. She always surrounded herself with good advisors who contributed to the reign. She was the last Empress Dowager of the ethnic Manchu Qing dynasty and the very last Empress Dowager of China.

Cixi was conservative and opposed foreign influences that were destroying the very fabric of the Chinese people. During that time, she supported fiscal and institutional reforms that might have turned China into a Constitutional Monarchy. But that was not to be. She instituted technological and military reforms in China, overhauled a corrupt bureaucracy and supported the push to free China from the European powers that had forced unpopular and harsh policies on China. She supported the Boxer Rebellion of 1899-1901. She is often blamed for being a devious despot who contributed to China's slide into corruption, anarchy and finally revolution but there is no evidence of that. What is a fact is that what began as trade with England soon degenerated into attempted European colonisation of China and the Opium wars. The aftermath of the second Opium war and the Taiping Rebellion led to chaos and great suffering for the Chinese. Cixi appointed General Zeng Guofang who crushed the revolt and in 1881 she turned her attention to dealing with the much more dangerous and insidious foreign influence and interference that was the result from the *learn from foreigners programme of the West.* This was beggaring the country and destroying its nationhood. In 1898 Cixi's nephew felt China needed political and cultural reform and initiated the Hundred Days' Reform of turning back to the West. Cixi put a stop to that by a coup putting Guangxu under house arrest. Chinese resentment towards the West for their mistreatment of the Chinese led to the Boxer Rebellion. Cixi supported it. The Rebellion failed as many European powers were involved. Later from 1902 to 1908 Cixi softened towards the West and encouraged the modernisation of China along Western lines.

The Last Chinese Empress Cixi

Soong Mei-ling (1898-2003), was also known as Madame Chiang Kai-shek. She was a Chinese political figure who was First Lady of the Republic of China, the wife of Generalissimo and President Chang Kai Shek. She was also the sister-in-law to Sun Yat-Sen or Soong Ching Ling. She remained loyal to the Nationalist Kuomintang party and represented them all through her life even on her tour in the USA.

Chinese women faced great obstacles from its 5,000 years of Patriarchy. Yet some women were able to overcome all these obstacles and become rulers, warriors, pirates, scientists, and spies. They have left behind a legacy that contradicts the idea that only Chinese men had power.

Africa

The women of Ancient Africa had a lot of freedom and power, much more so than European women of the same time. Society was mostly matriarchal. Women's bearing of children was regarded as making them much closer to nature which was important in such predominantly agricultural societies. Women played very important roles in every aspect of production as well as healers seers, mediums and religious leaders. African societies were very much spiritually oriented and so women had a pivotal place as the head of the household, owned lands and shared equal political power. They were strong, ferocious, physically strong women, able to hold their own in every sphere of life. There were many women warriors. Kings were chosen through the female line. A new king would be the son of the King's sister. This was to ensure the purity of the line. Some of the most famous queens were **Makeda**, Queen of Sheba, Queen **Nefertit**i, Queen **Cleopatra** of Egypt, Queen **Nandi** of the Zulu Kingdom, Queen **Aminatu**, Queen **Ranavalona** the First of Madagascar who was condemned by the Europeans as a tyrant or mad as she worked towards keeping Madagascar free from European colonisation and also trying to extend her borders.

Cleopatra VII of Egypt　　*Ranavalona I of Madagscar*

Where society was patriarchal, again the leading men referred to their women as their top advisers. European colonialism changed and destroyed their lifestyle, livelihood and enslaved them when and where possible. They have not recovered from that period yet. Now instead of colonialism, they (old colonisers) incite wars and rebellions so violent that death is a daily occurrence.

Today's African women suffer and have lost their lofty position due to the oppression and suppression that the colonisers brought with them and due to the spread of Christianity that places women in a secondary class. Western women during that time had no power but were solely dependent on their fathers or husbands. This idea of women as the weaker vessel in every way, including morally was transferred to Africa. *"Patriarchal Christianity, and its masculine fundamentalism, have brought to Africa the monogamous nuclear family unit, whose sole purpose was to pass on private property in the form of inheritance from one generation of males to the next. Under Colonial Christianity, the modern nuclear family is founded on the somewhat concealed domestic slavery of the wife"* (Chengu, 2015).

Warrior Women of Africa

Aminatu, commonly called **Amina** was a great Hausa warrior who became queen of Zazzau, apparently known as Zaria. She inherited the throne after the death of her uncle. She ruled for 34 years. She went on her first military expedition 3 months after coming to the throne. She expanded the kingdom into one of the greatest domains in Nigeria. She also fought to grant the Hausa traders a safe passage through her kingdom.

Candace Empress of Ethiopia (332 BCE) When Alexander the Great was attempting to conquer Egypt, he had to first invade Ethiopia in 332 BC. But his army could not do so as Ethiopia was then ruled by one of the greatest and most dreaded generals of that time – Empress – Candace. She led an army mounted on elephants to confront him. So he decided to pull back rather than be defeated by a woman. She is known even now as one of the strongest female military tacticians with great military skills of all times.

Candace Amanirenas another empress defeated the Roman governor Patronius of Egypt and sacked the city of Cyrene in 30 BC.

There were a number of Ethiopian queens and military leaders named Candace. These were just two of them.

Asbyte (died 219 BC): was a Libyan princess who was in the Carthaginian army before the second Punic War (Silus Italicus in poem Punia according to Walter Duvall Penrose Jr. 2016). She is rooted on a real tradition of warriors of North Africa according to several ancient chroniclers. Even Herodotus spoke about the Ausean and Machlye tribes of Libya, which hosted martial tournaments for young girls and hated those who lost or died. Then there were the **Zaueces**, whose war chariots were driven by women. Diodorus went further claiming that the Amazonians lived in Libya before immigrating to the Black Sea. Herodtus and Pliny believe that Abyste is a reference to the Asbytheans, known as great charioteers.

In 937 AD, **Judith, Queen of Falash** attacked the sacred capital of Ethiopia, Axum and killed all its inhabitants including the descendants of Solomon and the Queen of Sheba

Ethiopia under **Makeda, Queen of Sheba (960 BC)** was considered to be the second most powerful and famous kingdom after Egypt at that time, in spite of being much smaller in size. She had remarkable achievements as recorded in the Glory-of-Kings or the Kebar Nagast (14th century epic written by Is'haq Neburä -Id of Axum). She was regarded as the epitome of beauty and this piqued King Solomon's curiosity. The revered position of this small kingdom made Solomon want to open commercial relations with them. He invited her to Israel and the rest is public knowledge and often quoted. She was very clever, wise and intelligent but not a warrior. She had children with Solomon.

Throughout the 10th and 11th centuries the **Hausa states** (Nigeria) were ruled successfully by **Habe** warrior queens: **Kufuru, Gino, Yakumo, Yakunya, Walzana, Daura, Gamata, Shata, Batatume, Sandamata, Yanbamu, Gizirgizir, Innagari, Jamata, Hamata, Zama** and **Shawata**. Then centuries later by **Amina**, (1536-1573), daughter of Queen Turunku of Songhai (mid Nigeria) ruled the Hausa state and led 20,000 men into battle and extended her empire to the Atlantic and founded many cities.

Mbande Nzinga represented her brother the king of Angola as his advisor to the Portuguese and became queen after his death in 1624. She appointed women including her sisters **Kifunji** and **Mukumbu** to government offices. When the Portuguese broke the Peace treaty, she led her army of mostly women against them inflicting terrible casualties, and on the way conquering the neighbouring kingdoms in an attempt to build a federation. She accepted a truce with the Portuguese and agreed to a Peace treaty in 1635. She ruled till she was 81 and saw Angola become an independent nation in 1975. A street in Luanda is named in her honour.

Nzinga warrior queen of Angola

Llinga, a warrior queen of Congo fought the Portuguese in 1640, armed with her axe, bow and arrows leading her army of women warriors. The **Monomotapa confederacy** had a standing army of women warriors.

Kaipkire, a warrior leader of the Herero tribe in Southwest Africa led her people against the British slave traders in the 18th century. Extant records show **Herero women** fighting Germans in 1919.

Nandi the Zulu warrior mother of Shaka Zulu fought the slave traders and taught her son to be a warrior. When he became king, he had an all-female regiment that usually fought in the front line in battles.

In the early 1800's **Mantatisi,** warrior queen of the Tlokwas, fought to preserve her tribal lands in the wars between the Matinawe and the Shaka Zulus. She succeeded but her son lost them to Mahweshwe when he succeeded her to the throne.

Madam Yoko ruled over the 14 tribes of the Kpa Mende Confederacy in Sierra Leonne. It was the largest tribal group in the 19th century. She led this army whenever needed. Sierra Leonne had at least 19% of the tribes which were led by women. Now only 9% have female rulers.

She-Dong-Hong-Beh was a Dahomey leader of Amazons under King Gezo of Present-day Benin. In 1851 she led an army of 6,000 women armed with spears, bows and swords against the European-supported Egba fortress who were supplied with cannons. Only 1,200 Dahomey survived the encounter. Then in 1892 the King led his army of 12,000 including 2,000 Amazon women against the French colonists over trading rights. The Dahomey had rifles but the French has machine guns and cannons. In the ensuing bitter hand-to-hand fight, the French were forced to retreat. Finally, the French defeated the Dahomey after fierce fighting. The Amazons burned the field, villages and cities. But they were finally defeated and Dahomey became a French colony.

Menen Leben Amede, Empress of Ethiopia commanded her own army and was regent for her son. She was wounded and captured in the civil war in 1847 but was ransomed by her son and ruled till 1853.

Mukaya the Luba leader in Central Africa, whose land stretched along the rainforest from Zaire to Northern Zambia led her warriors against enemy tribes and factions. She fought alongside her brother but when he was killed she took over full control of the army and the empire.

Nehanda (1862-1898) was a priestess (spirit medium) of the Zimbabwe nation of Zezuru Shona people. When the British invaded Zimbabwe, she became the military leader and led her army into battle against them. She fought successfully for a time but was ultimately defeated, captured and executed. Her legacy of resistance especially guerrilla warfare is still commemorated in the nationalist movement.

Taytu Betul (1850-1918), Empress of Ethiopia led her armies to battle and negotiated treaties. During her 14-year rule, she established the modern capital of Addis Ababa. She retired from public life after the death of her husband.

Yaa Asantewa, Ashanti Kingdom of Ghana was the African queen who fought the British colonists fearlessly until her exile. Her speeches inspired the men and chiefs to rise up against the British and demand they release their king, King Prempeh. Yaa Asantewa and her soldiers managed to keep the British out of the fort for a long time but were finally defeated captured and exiled.

Queen Nefertiti is most famous for bringing to an end the war between Upper and Lower Egypt by marrying Ramses II (Akhenaten) Pharaoh of Lower Egypt. She was the daughter of Amenhotep II pharaoh of Upper Egypt. She played a very active role in reshaping Egypt.

Al-Kāhina bint Djarāwa al-Zanāt: Berber Queen, a religious and military leader of the people led the indigenous rebellion against Arab expansion in Numidia (Present day Algeria) in the 7th century. She led the Berbers as their war leader from 680 and was considered the most powerful monarch of North Africa. She met the Arab army at Meskiana and defeated them and they took refuge in Libya for 4-5 years.

Dihya (in Berber: Daya Ult Yenfaq Tajrawt, Dihya, or Damya): was a Berber queen and religious leader who led the Berber resistance against the Arab expansion into Northwest Africa, then known as Nuidia, now Algeria. She was born in early 7th century and died at the end of the century in Algeria. She successfully defeated Hasan and his Umayyad army that he fled to take shelter in Cyrenaica (Libya, today) for 4-5 years. Dihya realised that the Umayyad army was too strong and would return reinforced, so she started a scorched earth policy. But this had little impact on the mountainous areas and the desert tribes. However, she lost the crucial support of the sedentary oasis-dwellers.

One great African warrior queen of the ancient world was **Majaji-Modjadji**, who led the Lobedu (Lovedu) tribe. She was the hereditary queen of the Balobedu tribe and also their Rain Queen. This tribe was a part of the Kushite Empire in Nubia along the Nile Valley in what is now Northern Sudan and Southern Egypt and fought with them against Roman aggression for centuries. The empire ended in 350 AD when the Kushite stronghold of Meroe fell to repeated Roman attacks. Majaji led her warriors into battle carrying her shield and spear. It is believed she died on the walls of Meroe.

Egyptian warrior queens descended from the royal house of Kush included **Ahotep I**, **Cleopatra VII**, and **Arsinoe I** and **II**. They were all warrior queens and ruled through the Roman times and wars.

Ahotep I was the daughter of Queen Tetisheri, and Seqenenre Taa II, the mother of Ahmose I, Queen Ahmose Neferti and other children. Seqenenre Taa II died fighting the Hyksos and was succeeded by Kamose who died fighting them too. Ahotep took over for her son, rallied the army and kept her son's inheritance intact until he came of age. Later in his reign during his absences, she fought the rebelling dissenters and maintained peace till his return from wars.

Cleopatra VII Philopator (69 to 30 BC): was the last active Pharaoh of Ptolemaic Egypt. She was a descendant of its founder Ptolemy I Soter, a Macedonianian Greek general and commander of Alexander the Great's army. She is known in history for her great intelligence, statecraft, political astuteness, her beauty, culture her charm, unpredictability and courage. She saved Egypt from civil war at a very dangerous time but lost in the end. One of her biographers Eleanor Goltz Huzar described her as *"imperious, determined, courageous, ambitious, intensely alive"* person. Many have said she was Caesar's counterpart in intelligence and education.

Yet history to a great extent remembers her for her two attempts to save her empire – her affair with Julius Caesar and then Mark Anthony and her marriage to him. For these two affairs she has been labelled an evil harlot, a femme fatal by many. Yet there are female rulers who have done much worse and males that have done much, much worse, who have not been painted in the same way. Her real guilt lay in her desire to safeguard her country's independence at all cost. She fought at Actium and when she realised the battle was lost, committed suicide rather than be paraded in chains down the streets of Rome. She had great enemies to contend with and she did so bravely, without flinching.

Shajar al-Durr, Sultana (1257 CE): she was a slave girl who was elected to be the queen by a group of military men in a medieval Islamic country. She must have been a very capable person. She married the Ayubbid Sultan Al Salih-Ayubb who originally bought her along with other Mamelukes of Turkic origin. These people always remained faithful to him and after his death they established a Mameluk state in Egypt.

Al Salih's final years were spent in military campaigns against the Crusaders. Meantime Shajjar al-Durr exercised a lot of influence over the army and eventually ran the kingdom when Al Salih fell ill. Then when he died amidst the crisis of Louis IX of France invading Egypt, she kept the death a secret until she had the army's support. She put Al-Salih's son Turanshah in power. But Turanshah was very incompetent and he was murdered by his father's Mamelukes. Then they convened and elected Sahjjar al-Durr as queen of Egypt. The Abbasid Caliph, theoretically the overlord of all Muslim territories, objected and threatened to send one of his own men to take over. So a co-regent was chosen, Ezz-al-Dinn Aybak whom Shajjar was forced to marry. However, she kept the reigns of power in her hands. When she learnt that he planned to marry someone else, she had him murdered. Three days later, in retaliation his other widow murdered Shajjar al Durr using wooden clogs.

Suhayr al-Qalamawi, (1911-1997), Academic and Journalist was a trail blazer belonging to later times. She was the sole woman in a class of 14 other men at the school of literature in Fuad University of Egypt in 1929. It was an awkward situation but Suhayr al-Qalamawi wasn't upset or intimidated at all. She consistently topped the classes every year. She was one of the first female university graduates. She completed her Master's and was the first woman to get a PhD degree on *One Thousand and One Nights*. This would come under criticism 50 years later as being 'immoral.'

In 1956 she became professor of Modern Arabic Literature and then Head of the Department in Egypt's leading University for 9 years. The Dean of the School of Literature was Taha Hussein and he helped Suhayr to find work as a writer with the University magazine from which she worked her way up to be an editor. This launched her into a career of writing and journalism.

In 1967 she joined the Egyptian Parliament and helped establish the first Cairo Book Fair, an institution till today. She saw to the establishment of libraries and projects that offered affordable books to the general public. There were also numerous translations of international classics for the locals. She also introduced modern Egyptian Literature as a university discipline. Though she did not fight with arms, she fought for education.

Native American Warrior Women

Recently an excavation in Guatemala unearthed the long-sought remains of the famous **Mayan** warrior queen **K'abel** who belonged to the ancient Mayan civilisation of Waka who ruled from 672 to 692, K'abel belonged to the Snake dynasty and one of her titles was Lady Snake-Lord. She was more than just a symbolic figure-head. She commanded armies and went to war. It is very probable that she outranked her husband.

The past can serve to legitimize the present. For decades, anthropologists and archaeologists assumed that only men hunted in hunter-gatherer societies, while women gathered berries and had babies. It was a convenient assumption that reinforced modern gender norms. But when scientists look harder, they find a material record that often tells a different story. Men weren't the only ones hunting in ancient Peru, for example. Women were taking down big game with the best of them. (Marin Pilloud, anthropologist, University of Nevada, Reno).

Sioux warrior woman   *Cherokee Warrior Woman
                             by Talmadge Davis*

Native Indian culture treated the women and men as equals. Ackerman In *a Necessary Balance* (2003, pp. 21), studied the balance of power and the responsibilities expected of the men and women within each of the 11 tribes of the Plateau Indians, presently in the Coleville Indian Reservation in North-central Washington State. The Indians are seen from the perspective of a traditional past, through the phases of farming and their forced removal to Reservations when the colonists came, to the present times.

Of the prehistoric 27 burial sites of warriors uncovered here, 11 are of women warriors, which goes to show that like the men, the women also participated in every aspect of life including hunting and war.

And not just in **Peru** but throughout history Native American women warriors have abounded. They won prestige due to their abilities and significant contributions to their culture. They were not recorded like the men because it did not sit well with their European annihilators who belonged to an exclusively masculine society by the time they came into contact with these women and their histories.

These ancient warrior women led armies, hunted big game, fought on horseback, cut down moving prey the same as men did. They were chosen not because of gender but because of ability. Both history and archaeology are replete with their histories. Their role should not and cannot be downplayed. They were used to being around death in that they skinned the hunt, cut them prepared them. They too saw the violence in nature and were familiar with it. They were partners rather than superior and inferior.

Some famous female warriors are: Lozen, Fallen Leaf, Running Eagle, Colestah and Buffalo Calf Road, Dahetese, Woman in Chief Pine Leaf,

Lozen was a Chihenne Chiricahua **Apache** medicine woman, a skilled warrior and strategist and an excellent fighter on the battlefield. Her incredible skills, her eventful and tragic life got her the nickname *Apache Joan of Arc*. She was the sister of Victorio, a prominent Apache chief and later she became the ally of the famous Geronimo. Her brother said about her: *Lozen is my right hand.* (She is) *strong as a man, braver than most, and cunning in strategy. Lozen is a shield to her people. (Farrer, C. R, 1996)*

From childhood she demonstrated prolific abilities way beyond her years and was always more interested in the art of war than anything else. So she became a medicine woman and a warrior. As an adult, she fought alongside her brother as his right-hand in the fights to stop American encroachment on their lands.

Her abilities on the battlefield and her gift for strategy became legendary. She usually seemed to know the enemy's attack plan and so her people always consulted her. She consulted the highest Apache god, Ussen before battle and this is one of the reasons her people called her *Apache Joan of Arc*.

The Chiricahua Apache endured unimaginable hardships due to the US military incursions on their lands and they had to move from place to place for basic survival. During these times, too, Lozen did all she could to protect her community.

In 1877, her people fled the San Carlos Reservation, termed *Hell's Forty Acres* for the horrific conditions endured there. Between 1877 and 1880, almost half her people were butchered by the US and Mexican armies who had occupied the surrounding lands.

After this she joined up with Geronimo, another famous Apache leader and fought the US army until he surrendered to them in 1885. Lozen and others were imprisoned in an army arsenal in Alabama, where she died of tuberculosis in 1887. **Her story is not found in any history book.**

Lozen fought alongside Victorio, Geronimo

Cheyenne Warrior: Buffalo Calf Road woman

Buffalo Calf Road Woman: was a Northern **Cheyenne** woman warrior, famous for saving her brother, **Chief Comes in Sight** who was shot during the **Battle of the Rosebud** in 1876. She rode into the battlefield and rescued him. This motivated the rest of the warriors to regroup and fight on and win the battle. Later that year she fought alongside her husband, (itself an act of courage as he would be in the midst of the fight and so would she now), Black Coyote, in the famous **Battle of the Bighorn,** the last Apache campaign. In Cheyenne folklore, she is credited with striking the blow that knocked Lt. Colonel George Armstrong Custer off his horse which led to his death.

After this battle, she was captured along with her husband and two children and other Northern Cheyennes and sent to the Southern Cheyenne Reservation in Indian Territory (Present day Oklahoma).

Moving Robe Woman (Tashenamani): also participated in the 1876 Battle of Grassy Plain in modern day Montana against Lt. Col George Armstrong Custer who was defeated. Moving Robe had led the counter attack.

Daheteste was a Choconen **Apache** warrior who participated in many raids with her first husband Ahnandia. Being a wife and mother did not in any way compromise her military skills. Later in life, she joined Geronimo and Lozen.

She was a brave and skilled warrior, fluent in English and often served as a messenger and translated for the Apache. She played an important role in the final surrender of the Apache in 1886.

Woman in Chief Pine Leaf: was a warrior of the **Crow** people. In Crow she is Woman Chief Biawacheeitchish. She is probably the same person as Pine Leaf. When she was 10, a Crow party raided her tribe the Gros Ventres and then a Crow warrior adopted her.

From an early age she exhibited an interest in warrior activities. She became a proficient horsewoman, excellent markswoman and in fighting. She was recognized as a warrior in a raid by the Blackfoot on a fort sheltering the Crow and some white families. She is said to have played a major role in beating back the raid. Then she gathered a group of her own warriors and attacked the Blackfoot settlements. As a reward she was named Biawacheeitchish and given a seat in the Council of Chiefs. She rose to be third among the Council's 160 lodges.

Running Eagle: was a warrior woman of the **Piegan tribe of the Blackfoot Nation,** born in in Alberta Canada. When she was young, she was named Brown Weasel Woman. She was well known for her brave deeds. While hunting with her father, when young, they were attacked by the Assiniboine and her father's horse was shot from under him. She rode home with him safe and sound.

Later, her husband was killed by some Crow warriors. She decided to avenge him and became a Blackfoot warrior.

The Sun-Spirit was said to have told her; she would have great power in war if she restrained from intimate relations with any other man. She did so and was very successful for a long time, until she slept with a man from her party.

It is alleged that soon after she lost her power and then her life. Running Eagle was killed in 1878 by the Flathead Tribe while stealing a horse before a battle.

Colestah was born around 1800 in the Yakama Native American tribe. She was a medicine woman, a psychic and a woman warrior. She was a wife of Chief Kamiakin and fought by his side with a stone war club in the Battle of the Four Lakes in 1858 against Colonel George Wright. She dressed formally for this battle *"in her finest" buckskin dress, with her hair braided tightly* (Kurt R. Nelson, historian of criminal justice) and when her husband was seriously wounded, she carried him back to the family camp nursing him back to health using her medicinal knowledge and skill. She fell sick and died in 1865.

Nonhelema: a Shawnee chieftainess and sister to Cornstalk promoted an alliance with the Americans on the frontier in Ohio. She was called Grenadier Squaw to the settlers because of her height.

These are only a very few. There are many more very interesting women warriors around the world.

Comparison of Asian and European women in the same historical Timeline

One is generally under the impression that women of the Asia and Africa are oppressed while those of Europe are free.

In many cases, the amount and type of freedom available to women everywhere depended on individual cultures. In Medieval Europe, women often led fettered lives with hardly any freedom or opportunities. Some noble women were the exception and had the opportunity to practice martial arts. It was not the rule though. It was considered the male domain. Fewer women still, marched into battle on an equal footing with the men. In Asia and Africa more women were trained in martial arts and led armies into battle and generally ruled the roost. The woman's position as the mother and bringer of life was sacrosanct. Earth the mother was all important.

The role of women will be considered during the following periods:

Ancient times to 47 CE

In ancient times both Asian and European women participated in war. There were leaders who were women and women were also found in the rank and file. Many armies were solely constituted of women warriors. Roman armies (all male always) fought Germanic tribal armies of men and women, Tartars, Uzbeks, Tajiks and people from Central Asia – all had male and female warriors riding side-by-side. Then the Romans faced the Celtic warriors of the Iceni led by Queen Boudicca. In eastern Asia the Romans faced among others the might and courage of Queen Zenobia. There were the Volscians (an Italic race) who fought to the death against the Trojans. The Slavic women have their place as great warriors too and Slavic female warrior graves have been uncovered with their weapons as far as in Scandinavia. And we should not forget the mighty Amazon warriors. In China and Vietnam and Japan and the Arab lands especially Syria and Yemen, there were also many women warriors and leaders like the Trang sisters of Vietnam. These were just a few names. There were many more as you have read by now in this book.

Medieval times (476 to 1450 CE)

Medieval history also has many women warriors but their position has started becoming weaker due to the practices instituted by organized religions. Strong women were assumed to be under the power of malign, dark and evil forces. Still there were some in Europe like Joan of Arc who led the French army successfully and was then burned as a witch and a heretic by the Church. There was also Jeanne Hachette who fought against the foreign oppression of Charles of Burgundy. In China there was Liang Hongyu the mighty drummer and the Lady of the Nation's peace led an all-female corps that fought the Khitan invaders. Slavic and Mongol women also commonly served as soldiers and fought side by side with men.

The *kinalakihan*, were an army of women warriors in the Philippines. They were of the Shri-Visayan Empire and appeared quite muscular and manly. India too, had its share of women warriors.

There were women warriors in the Middle-East, Arabia, China, Japan, Mongolia, Persia, Syria, Yemen, and many other places in Asia.

Africa had its own share of women warriors like the Moorish women's army in Valencia in 1099 and many women from different tribes and states as well as **in Libya,** Egypt, South Africa and other places in Africa

Modern Times

In 19th century Europe women had to disguise themselves as men to fight at Waterloo, American Civil war and so on. Asian women fought openly in armies as the Chinese women serving in the Taiping rebellion or the Filipino women's resistance to the Spanish. One of them, General Gabriela Slang led a fierce attack in the province of Ilocos. Other women in this fight were Theresa Magbanua (General Isay) and General Agueda Kahabangan of Laguna and Batangas. In the American Civil war, it is believed that about 400 and 750 women had enlisted to fight. Many died. They participated in the following clashes: *Antietam, Fredericksburg, Gettysburg, Shiloh, and Vicksburg, and others. Dressed as men, women took on a range of military roles in the Civil War.*

Women in Communist Europe and Asia fought side-by-side openly in the frontlines. In North Korea, women served in the Special Forces as agents. In Vietnam, Viet Cong women were combat soldiers. In contrast the American women serving in Vietnam were not given any combat positions. In China women served as combatants and generals in the Communist and Nationalist Armies.

In Aceh, Indonesia, in the Muslim separatist movement, girls and women were recruited as fighters. In Sri Lanka, Tamil women joined the Tamil Tigers, some became suicide bombers, as did some men.

So in the so-called sexist Asian countries women have been given the same opportunities as the men and in most places even surpassed that given to European women.

In Africa women fought in the armies and were often even more loyal than the men till the 19th century. They were very well trained and as late as the end of colonisation of Africa, the colonisers faced and from time to time and suffered defeat at the hands of the African women warriors like the French in a battle with the Dahomey. In India, Libya, Morocco too, the colonists faced women warriors often to their discomfort.

To sum up, world history is replete with the actions of brave, strong influential and dynamic women. Over the past many centuries, we have lived in a greatly male-dominated world where brave exploits of women were not a popular topic. So they were ignored, cast aside while it was all about the greatness and glory of men. In modern times, when a woman manages to wrest power in a male-dominated world, whispering campaigns begin against her. She automatically becomes unfeminine. I believe it is because of the fragility of most manly egos. We have been raised on a diet of male superiority even though it is not really so and has never been so. Some women have been immortalized in the films and books like Cleopatra, Boudicca, Joan of Arc but they are the rare exceptions. Most are unsung heroines belonging to forgotten history. The time has now come for their stories to come to the fore. It is up to us to bring their names and deeds to the attention of the world. In our modern world the task ahead of the women in a strongly male-dominated world is not going to be easy – as it has never really been easy from the time of the establishment of patriarchy. Women are mentally and spiritually much stronger but they have also exhibited great physical strength too through the ages. They have fought with swords, spears, axes guns, bows and arrows, the same weapons as men. They have also been suicide bombers. These women warriors in history have left an indelible mark on the canvas of time.

Women Then and Now

History has recorded the great deeds mostly of men and very occasionally of some women. You get the impression that women were basically homebodies, not warriors. But this is incorrect. Besides great warriors like Boudicca, Joan of Arc, Esther there were many, many others, from Asia to Africa to Europe and Native Americans. Most of their stories are relatively unknown. We have read here about the deeds of many of them and they are just a short list. There is not enough space to encompass them all nor write in detail about their achievements.

Social life began in quite a different way to what we see today. Women were the being from which all came. Mother worship was predominant. The Cult of the mother, beginning from Mother Earth was practised throughout the world. She was the beginning of all life. All statues and forms of the earliest worship honoured her and was dedicated to her. After all she is the one that brings life to the earth whether it is the land, the sea or the woman. They all create.

From the Mother and Matriarch slowly society changed and so did their position. With agriculture, patriarchy began asserting itself. Female worship started giving way to male dominance. There was no longer equality between the sexes. Society started becoming more violent, aggressive. Male ego started asserting itself. Monogamy but only for women, started. Men were allowed as many concubines, prostitutes, slave girls as they could afford. It was accepted that men couldn't help it. Women's fate was sealed (for a long time) with the Abrahamic religions beginning in the Middle-East, especially in Judea and Moses. Men needed to compete to feel strong. They wanted to pass on what they accumulated to their direct progeny. Matriarchal society did not. For them children were children.

So with time from warrior queens, tribal leaders, priestesses they were slowly disempowered, reduced to a voiceless, inferior position in many societies. Religion played a great part in this disempowerment. Moses in the 10th commandment of the Tabernacle, Exodus 19-20 and also in the Bible, Exodus 20: 2-17 states: *You shall not covet your neighbor's house; you shall not covet your neighbor's wife, nor his male servant, nor his female servant, nor his ox, nor his donkey, nor anything that is your neighbor's.* So women became reduced to the level of an ox, donkey, slave and servant. In other words, just a possession. This continued and even worsened in the Middle Ages. Things started improving after the World Wars when there was a dearth of working age men and women stepped in. Now it is improving but there is still a long way to go. In most countries including many

Western ones there is no equality. In Asia, Africa the situation is even worse and women do not have much of a voice even today and no equality.

According to the Wikipedia, **Enheduanna** (2286-2251 BC) was the first poet-priestess in the world. She was the priestess of the moon goddess Inanna in the Sumerian city-state of Ur in the reign of her father, Sargon of Akkad. She was likely appointed by her father as the leader of the religious cult in Ur in an attempt to cement ties between her father King Sargon and the local Sumerian religion. Works like the *Exaltation of Inanna* and *Sumerian Temple Hymns* are attributed to her. Her memory disappeared after the fall of the First Babylonian Empire. It was discovered in 1927 by Sir Leonard Wooley when he excavated ancient Ur. She is the first known female author in the world and has attracted a lot of attention including from feminists.

In more historic times Athens where democracy began, gave women no voice. The only poetess from Athens was **Aelia Eudocia**, though other Greek states did produce warriors and poetesses like Sappho, (Lesbos 570 BCE), Corinna (Boeotia, 500 BCE), Erinna contemporary to Sappho, Telesilla (Argos) Antye of Tegea (Arcadia, Peloponnesus) and many others.

The Romans did not allow women any direct power but they wielded great influence behind the scenes, making and getting rid of unwanted contestants for power. Also unlike in Greece, Roman women could attend banquets with their spouses.

The Celts, Slavs, Norse, German, Scandinavians allowed women much more equality and freedom whether in war or peace. They were equals.

In Asia women in India, Mongolia, China. Japan, Vietnam, and the Middle-East fought and led armies. They were not voiceless or helpless.

In Africa, women were excellent warriors and leaders, well-known from the North to the South.

The Amazons and Scytho-Samaratians are well known for their female dominated societies.

All these women lived and fought on equal terms in a world of men and women. Many women led armies against all male Roman cohorts and even defeated them.

But all this was in more ancient times. With the advent of monotheism, women's place in society took a sharp downward turn. In Judea Moses announced the Ten Commandments. These Commandments are also mandatory for us, as Christians, not just the Jews. The 10th was/is the most discriminatory. It says: *"You shall not covet your neighbour's house; you shall not covet your neighbour's wife, nor his male servant, nor his female servant, nor his ox, nor his donkey, nor anything that is your neighbour's."* Exodus 20:17. Also in Exodus, 34:28, Deuteronomy 4:13, Deuteronomy 10:4. So women belong to the same level as the domestic animal, servant and slaves! How much more can the mother, the bearer of children, be demeaned? How did this happen?

In Judea women started being segregated from men, their moon cycle and childbirth became a time for them to be unclean, untouchable and so on. Then with the advent of Jesus things became better for women. Mary Magdalene and a few other women played a big part at the beginning in spreading the Word and helping in arranging meetings of the Christians. Mary played perhaps the biggest part at least on par with the other apostles. She is the one who brought word of the risen Christ to all. Women's high position continued in the early church. In Gnostic Christianity of the 1st and 2nd centuries women were also appointed as bishops.

However, by the 4th and 5th centuries change began with the systematic degradation of women by the church fathers and Christian writers like Tertullian, Saint Augustine, Saint Jerome and many others denigrating women, calling them weak, hysterical, unable to resist temptation. More and more rules to control women and their dress-code, mannerisms, behaviour began to be initiated. Their hair was to be covered at all times as it was the devil's work; men stood between women and God, women were responsible for the Fall from Grace and so on. Some Church leaders, saints, and Church reformers through the ages, who did a lot against women were the following from ancient to modern times, From pre Middle ages to the Fall of the Roman Empire, to the Spanish Inquisition (burning of witches, torturing heretics, killing and dispossessing all non-Catholics) and even now: St Clement of Alexandria (150-215 CE), Tertullian, *father of Latin Christianity* (160-225 CE), St Augustine, Bishop of Hippo (354-430), St Albertus Magnus, Dominican theologian,

Thomas Aquinas, 13th Century Doctor of the Church, Martin Luther, Reformer (1483-1546), John Calvin, Reformer (1509-1564)), John Dod, Puritan guidebook (pub. 1603), Joseph Smith, founder LDS movement (1805-1844), Heber C. Kimball, early LDS apostle (1801-1868), Official statement of Southern Baptist Convention, (SBC) Summer 1998, Pat Robertson, (SBC leader 1930–) James Fowler (1999, *Mark Driscoll, founder, Mars Hill nondenominational mega-church franchise.(1970–).* These are only a few names. The list of women haters is long and found in every walk of male life from Church to politics, societal everywhere. They were all misogynists, fearful of female power supported by the Judeo-Christian tradition of blaming women for all wrongs in society, usually fomented by the males. It is found in the Book of Genesis and continues right down through the ages into the New Testament – all of which, we must always keep in mind, were written by men for men.

But we should not forget how many women contributed to Christianity, beginning from Mary Magdalena, the women martyrs like Perpetua of Carthage thrown by the Romans into the Arena for her unwavering faith, to the saints and mystics like Catherine of Siena, Joan of arc. Hildegard von Bingen, Teresa of Avila, St. Catherine of Genoa, St. Clare of Assisi, Thérèse of Lisieux, Julian of Norwich, St. Bridget of Sweden, St. Beatrice of Silva, St. Angela of Foligno, Mechthild of Magdeburg, Hadewijch to name only some.

In the Middle-Ages women had a very, very hard time. Throughout history women had always been medicine women, very familiar with what plants work for what. Now suddenly the men knew more. Herbal and natural medicine was out. Any who practised it were witches. And yet now in the 21st century more and more people are turning towards natural medicines. In the Middle-Ages women were not only forbidden from practising it and passing the knowledge and wisdom down but were also forbidden to study medicine anywhere or practise it. Men had decided to take over with no previous knowledge of herbs or care. Doctors, apothecaries, alchemists, barbers (all men) all began competing and denigrating herbal medicine as quackery. Instead, they went in for leeches, bloodletting, balancing humours etc., for large sums of money. Soon women were forbidden to study medicine at universities – only men could and only men could practise medicine. If women practised medicine, they were burned as witches beginning from the 1600s. Women were now further denigrated as being unstable – hysterical, lunatics, easily controlled by the moon cycle and madness until the 1900s. Only then did some realise that women contributed at least 50% to the child's DNA – male or female!

In the 1500s the renaissance came with the beginning of modern history. But in art, it was the painting of nude women – as sexual and sensual creatures, their role still stayed defined as child bearers, homemakers and for the first time openly as sex symbols and nothing more. This last persists till today in and is part of huge business chains around the world especially in Europe and America. Women were not welcome to participate in public debate, not allowed to vote, own businesses or properties, but were pawns in marriage deals.

On getting married all their properties were transferred to the husbands. They had very few rights – could not complain about sexual abuse, or file for divorce. Marriage was a trap without escape. Men could be as promiscuous as they desired; women HAD to be virgins – chaste. Breaking the rules, marrying without permission of the families led to chastisement, social exile or worse. Their lot was extremely hard.

After WWI and WWII, the situation for women changed quite drastically. There was a shortage of working age men as a great many had died in the wars. Women stepped into the vacuum but for much less pay, longer hours and harder work. Children also started being employed under very harsh conditions for a pittance

Then the Feminist Movements began to bring redress to women. Finally, there was some light at the end of the tunnel. It was a hard fight but finally women's liberation had begun.

Today there are very few countries where women have equality (Iceland, Norway, Finland, Sweden, are the exceptions). In most countries around the world Europe, Asia, Africa and mostly USA, women are NOT equal no matter what we say, read or write. Women are still expected to work much longer hours at home and at the office. They are still paid less than the men, they cannot generally rise to the highest positions in the company with the same salaries as men, rape has become too common and the woman, girl or child is always guilty, child pornography is rampant, sex abuse of children boys or girls is too; sex trafficking is at its highest since the beginning of time. Women, girls, children are no longer safe in any place. Often not even at home. **So how are we equal???** We are still struggling for equality!!

Modern history has not dealt with women fairly nor recorded their achievements correctly. Without women there would have been no civilisation. Women not only bear children but they are the first and primary teachers and role models. Olden society was aware of the importance of women and paid due homage. The first societies were matriarchal where men were equally welcome contributors. But olden cultures were aware that if there were no women, there would be no life nor civilisation so worship of the mother goddess was all important. The earth that feeds us has always been regarded as a female entity – not a male one. Modern man, I think, fears the influence of women beginning from organised religion and the male priests. Olden religions all honoured womankind but the modern religions taught that women were weak, unworthy, impure and not fit for any high position. They were to be disposed, hobbled, relegated to lower, second-class citizens. Men were the final arbitrators, the final judges, the rulers and women's roles were to serve them and put their needs, wants desires, as their reasons to live. We forget without Mary there would have been no Jesus and Joseph has never been regarded as an important part of the Jesus story. Yet Christianity, Judaism and Islam today have reduced women to minor supporting role. In spite of how far women's suffragette has come, women are still not regarded as equal to men. When women become leaders of a state, in some parts of the world, all sorts of whispers are spread to bring them down as happened with Margaret Thatcher. Men are **never** judged as harshly as women. They are allowed to be immoral and corrupt and cruel and still their sins are forgiven. History is replete with stories of these men. If any woman were to do the same thing, the judgement passed on them would make all woman-kind cringe. Yet women are generally better at what they do than men and they are much better at multitasking. Yes, there are many very bad women in the world, immoral, cruel but they are not in the same sort of power position as men with similar tendencies.

There is more rape and sex traffic and women in bondage today than ever before in the history of the world. And worst of all, often in rape cases, we are told: *women like it, women want it* simply to sweep the male guilt under the rugs. In the past couple of years men would again be the decision maker of what should happen with women's bodies and childbearing. If this is not stupid and crass, I do not know what is! I say to men first bear the children, go through childbirth, spend sleepless nights, be used when you don't desire it – if you can really do that, then sit with women and discuss what is the best way about it. Till then do not assume to pass judgement on matters that are none of your concern. In our so-called democratic world of equality, let men then judge about how men should deal with their needs and women with theirs. And young boys too, are no longer safe. Paedophilia is rampant.

In ancient times women were treated much better. They were equal to men, able to participate in evert aspect of life. At the very start, women were held in very high esteem and position. They represented Mother Earth. They were the life givers and on them depended the continuance of humanity, of life – as it still does today. Even gay couple need a surrogate woman to bear their child. Women were mothers, warriors, hunters, commanders of armies into battle, priestesses, oracles equal to men, in everything. In some societies the inheritance of the throne, power, property passed through the female line, not the male line. Women not only kept the hearth fire burning, ministered to all the needs of the family but participated in the running of the clan, tribe or whatever. They could choose their partners and leave them as they wished. They could not be raped or forced. That was taboo. In our modern, democratic, advanced world it is a very common occurrence. Women could not be traded, bought and sold like horseflesh. Now sex trafficking is a very lucrative business, popular among many men, worldwide. The change in concept towards women began in the Middle Ages (Allen, 2006, pp. 6). They went from warriors and queens to sex objects and pin-up girls. Now it is at its lowest point.

On the positive side women have won the lost freedoms and rights over the past two centuries. Some of those rights and freedoms are: the right to vote; the right to marry by choice, right to join the workforce, right to equal education (though some colleges especially in the state refuse to consider female applications); in many countries women now have the right to join the Forces; in 1993 the United Nations adopted *The Declaration of the Elimination of Violence Against Women*. This has not really worked as female sex trafficking, rape and abuse is at an all-time high. But they have the right to choose their job opportunities, right to change their sexual orientation and many other rights. That is good but I believe we still have a long way to go to achieve parity.

Warrior women had lost the freedom to choose to be a warrior, now it is back again, to a degree. Many countries allow women to join the forces. True, they often have a hard time, unlike before but still they can be soldiers, navy women, pilots, Special Forces or whatever.

Following are the countries where women can join the Forces:

Africa: Algeria, Eritrea, Libya, South Africa, The Gambia

Asia & Oceania: Australia, Bangladesh, India, Indonesia, Iraq, Israel, Japan, Kazakhstan, Nepal, New Zealand, Pakistan, Philippines, Saudi Arabia, Singapore, Sri Lanka, (Taiwan) Thailand, UAE, People's Republic of China

Europe: Bulgaria, Denmark, Finland, France, Germany, Ireland, Italy, Norway, Poland, Russia, Serbia, Sweden, Turkey, Ukraine, United Kingdom

North America: Canada, United States

South America: Argentina, Bolivia, Brazil, Colombia

https://en.wikipedia.org/wiki/Women_in_the_military_by_country)

The time has come for us to re-evaluate history through the ages and see where humanity took a wrong turn.

In conclusion, women in pre-monotheistic world helped shape culture through social, economic, and religious influences. Some women travelled throughout the world, from Russia to North America, trading, settling, and defending what was theirs. They had a social standing that, if not equal to their male counterparts, exceeded men's especially as they grew older and more respected.

I think that the women in the ancient world proved that although the members of each gender had definite advantages / disadvantages that the other did not, women could and can accomplish anything they set their minds to. Even in a male dominated society, these early women were able to live, love, and fight as they wished. Today's women should be able to do the same. We are two halves of a whole and the time has come to acknowledge that a whole cannot be lopsided or larger and smaller. Two halves are even. We await such a time again: to be a healthy whole, working, living, loving in tandem.

Conclusion

This book is an attempt to look back and apply knowledge of the past to forge forward to a better and more equal future. It is time to learn from all our past successes and mistakes and try and make a better world especially at a time when the world seems to be going totally mad. Corruption is rife. Murder is always, everyday around the corner. Even schools and holy places are no longer safe sanctuaries. If you can grease a palm, you can get away with anything, you can break any law judicial, moral or whatever else. Justice can be bought by the corrupt. The innocent sometimes suffers for this. The weak are exploited without pity or compunction. And unfortunately, most women fall into this category. Law that is supposed to be equally applied to all is not. Women have a different set of laws – depending on their financial value and their contacts; the average woman is at her weakest here. All men except those who belong to a different race from the country where the acts are perpetrated have different laws applied to them. They are only guilty, if they have no contacts or money or power. It is repeated time and time again. It is a man's world where abusing women and children and the weak has become a lucrative pastime. Women and children, once again need to feel safe. Women need to become partners in life as they used to be and as the marriage vows profess but do not follow through.

Feminist theologians are concerned about areas of theological discourse that relate to gender and power inequality: as in regards to LGBT, ecology, church response to abuse and trauma, colonisation and post-colonial works, class inequality, gender inequality, racism and so on from a feminine perspective. It is more than time to counter the practices and beliefs of women's inferiority. There has been too much discrimination between the genders already, since we became "civilised and advanced".

Men and women can live and work as equals and in harmony as many ancient societies have shown us here. What is required is mutual trust and respect, one is not better than the other, they are equals to make a success of things. If a man cannot do so, he should retire and sit by the hearth, not dictate what should or should not be done to women's bodies (abortion).

The Suffragette Movement, Women's Liberation Movement, The Feminist Sex Wars, Black Feminism, Riot Grrrls (rape, racism and body image. Riot Grrrls also addressed their sexuality in frank terms that attempted to reclaim negative cultural stereotypes as ownership over one's body). These are only some of the movements today.

Some might say the disappearance of the Goddess occurred naturally with the march of modern civilization. But, as many historians and theologians have pointed out, in Riot Grrrls it is likely no coincidence that the patriarchal cultures that conquered earlier indigenous populations are fundamentally intertwined with the downfall of the Goddess, and the reframing of this revered form of worship as cultic, lewd, and primitive.

There lies before us a rich history of Goddess worship altogether separate from the patriarchal religions, customs, and laws most of us were raised on. Goddess worship is evident from the beginning of civilisation, from antiquity. They played prominent parts in prehistoric culture and throughout the development of agriculture, the beginning of urban life. Archaeological evidence suggests that God was considered a female for the first 200,000 years of human life on earth, even if male-dominated religions sought to displace the matriarchal order. Ultimately, by making ourselves independent of male culture, we can better understand our heritage, and, as Stone writes, cultivate *a contemporary consciousness of the once-widespread veneration of the female deity as the Wise Creatress of the Universe and all life and civilization.*

Yet there are still pockets of civilisation today that thrive against all odds that follow the matriarchal pattern. There they still continue to be an excellent source of religious experience in our contemporary world.

Besides the religious aspect, in the matriarchal world there were no genocides or massacres of innocents. Women generally value life much more than men, it seems. For women, killing is not a pastime but something that is only undertaken when there is no other option. In our male-dominated world massacres, genocides, school killings have become a common, everyday occurrence.

With the passing of goddess worship also passed the influence and freedom of women and the safety of children male and female. Today neither women nor children are safe from male exploitation. It is time for us to now reclaim our heritage. We can be partners rather than opponents – the male and female to work in harness amicably and together with neither being superior or inferior – both equal partners in the game of life.

BIBLIOGRAPHY

Web

https://en.wikipedia.org/wiki/Paleolithic#cite_note-Merlinstone-84
Goddess Worship: Goddess Worship in the Ancient near East | Encyclopedia.com
https://jfpenn.com/ancient-goddesses/
https://www.encyclopedia.com/environment/encyclopedias-almanacs-transcripts-and-maps/goddess-worship-overview
https://www.vice.com/en/article/paw8bv/god-is-a-woman-history-goddess-worship-ariana-grande
https://www.vice.com/en/article/paw8bv/god-is-a-woman-history-goddess-worship-ariana-grande
Matriarchy - Wikipedia
https://www.worldatlas.com/articles/matriarchal-societies-around-the-world.html
https://www.nytimes.com/1986/04/28/style/patriarchy-is-it-invention-or-inevitable.html
Women and religion - Wikipedia
Women and religion - Wikipedia
Women in Judaism - Wikipedia
https://womenpriests.org/articles-books/tetlow1-the-status-of-women-in-greek-roman-and-jewish-society/#:~:text=T.
https://en.wikipedia.org/wiki/Women_in_ancient_Rome
https://en.wikipedia.org/wiki/Women_in_Judaism
Women in Classical Greek Religion | Oxford Research Encyclopedia of Religion
https://griekse-les.nl/women-and-their-role-in-ancient-greece-and-rome
9 Female Warriors Who Made Their Mark on History (mentalfloss.com) (Kristy Puchko)

https://www.magellantv.com/articles/goddesses-of-the-ancient-world-legends-of-powerful-religious-deities

https://bookery.ca/ancient-goddess-religion-the-celts-goddess-herstory-demise/

https://en.wikipedia.org/wiki/Western_Roman_Empire

Women in Christianity - Wikipedia

Women In Ancient Christianity | From Jesus to Christ - The First Christians | FRONTLINE | PBS

women and the beginning of Islam - Search (bing.com)

Women in Islam - Wikipedia

Women in Islam | Facts about the Muslims & the Religion of Islam
Women in the Catholic Church: A Brief History - Good Faith Media

https://en.wikipedia.org/wiki/Protestantism_in_the_United_Kingdom

https://www.bing.com/search?q=role+of+women+n+religion+in+modern+times

https://sophia.smith.edu/blog/buddhistthought15/2015/02/15/women-in-buddhism

The 4 main branches of Christianity (with explanation) psychology - 2022 (warbletoncouncil.org)

https://universe.byu.edu/2021/01/25/the-changing-expanding-role-of-women-in

https://www.beliefnet.com/faiths/islam/the-role-of-women-
https://egyptianstreets.com/2015/06/09/meet-the-nine-muslim-women-who-have-ruled-nations/http://www.slavorum.org/women-warriors-in-slavic-and-scytho-sarmatian-culture/*Ancient Slavic Woman Warrior Buried In Viking Graveyard With Her Brutal Weapon Of Warcraft* / Ancient Origins (ancient-origins.net)

Women Warriors- Slavic Tradition - Slavic Chronicles |
Eastern European Slavic Warriors – Miniatures, models, paints & hobby tools (classicminiatures.com.au)

https://www.sheathenry.com/roles-of-pre-christian-germanic-women/
https://weaponsandwarfare.com/2018/12/02/viking-women-warriors/
https://medium.com/legendary-women/ancient-celtic-women-
https://thecelticlifekaren.weebly.com/famous-celts.html
https://metal-gaia.com/2012/04/26/ancient-celtic-women
"The Suppressed Histories"; Female Liberators. Retrieved1 May2006 web
https://www.worldhistory.org/Shogun/
Onna-bugeisha - The Female Samurai Warriors (warhistoryonline.com)
http://www.colorq.org/Articles/article.aspx?d=2002&x=asianwarriors
https://www.arabamerica.com/queens-of-yemen
https://wikizero.com/en//Ghaliyya_Al_Bogammiah
https://www.worldhistory.org/Wu_Zetian/
https://amazingwomeninhistory.com/lin-siniang-ming-dynasty-warrior
The Story of Ching Shih, the 18th Century Prostitute Turned Pirate Lord (allthatsinteresting.com)
https://www.rferl.org/a/qishloq-ovozi-who-was-kurmanjan-datka/26770979.html
https://en.wikipedia.org/wiki/Kurmanjan_Datka
https://www.bbc.com/news/av/magazine-38393984/100-women-2016-saikal-kyrgyzstan-s-original-nomad-warrior-womanTen Medieval Warrior Women - Medievalists.net
Ten Medieval Warrior Women - Medievalists.net
https://en.wikipedia.org/wiki/Epic_of_Manas
https://en.wikipedia.org/wiki/Khutulun
http://www.akdn.org/press-release/aga-khan-music-initiative-premieres-qyrq-qyz-forty-girls-pioneering-multimedia
http://badassoftheweek.com/index.cgi?id=822456431891

5 Women Warriors We Should Know About | #IndianWomenInHistory (feminisminindia.com)

Chinese women in history - soldiers, pirates, scholars, sages and rulers

5 Most Powerful African Queens from History (answersafrica.com)

https://culturewhiz.org/articles/women-ancient-african-civilizations

warhistoryonline.com).

https://www.digmandarin.com/8-influential-women-in-chinese-history-to-remember-this-women-day.html

Apache Warrior Women | Gouyen, Lozen, Dahteste (newmexiconomad.com)

https://militaryhistorynow.com/2013/05/15/women-warriors-meet-seven-of-historys-most-amazing-female-commanders/

https://en.wikipedia.org/wiki/Matilda_Joslyn_Gage

History of Women's Suffrage.

Notable & important Native American warrior women of the 19th century - The Vintage News

11 Of the Fiercest and Bravest Women Warriors and Female Fighters Throughout History

Queens & Women Warriors of Africa (geni.com)

https://theculturetrip.com/africa/benin/articles/meet-the-dahomey-amazons-the-all-female-warriors-of-west-africa

https://culturewhiz.org/articles/women-ancient-african-civilizations

Appian's Roman History: Empire and Civil War on JSTOR

https://www.worldhistory.org/Alfred_the_Great/

Alfred the Great - World History Encyclopedia

https://www.ancient-origins.net/history-famous-people/khutulun-001084

https://greekreporter.com/2022/03/08/warrior-women-gamers-ancient...

https://sculptingpaintingandgaming.com/2018/10/women-warriors-in...

https://en.wikipedia.org/wiki/Women_in_ancient_warfare

https://www.ancient.origins.net/news-history-archaeology/ancient-ivory-tablets-reveal-high-status-illyrian-women

5 Myths About the Amazons – Ancient Female Warriors - Ancient Pages

https://weaponsandwarfare.com/2018/12/02/viking-women-warriors/

https://www.definitelygreece.com/females-in-greek-mythology/

https://metal-gaia.com/2016/06/15/ancient-spartan-women/

https://www.livescience.com/who-were-amazon-warriors.html

https://www.thoughtco.com/female-warriors-4685556 (7 female warriors and Queens you should know)

Warrior Women of the World of Ancient Macedon - World History Encyclopedia

https://www.thoughtco.com/notable-women-of-medieval-europe-352968813 Notable Women of Medieval Europe

https://www.bing.com/search?form=NINENH&mkt=enau&PC=NBWS&qs=n&sk=&q=Ancient+womens+warrirs+of+Asia

www.thoughtco.com/legendary-warrior-women-of-asia-195819

Warriors: Asian women in Asian society - ColorQ Articles Etc

www.colorq.org/Articles/article.aspx?d=2002&x=asianwarr...

List of women warriors in folklore - Wikipedia

Wikipedia:

https://www.bing.com/search?form=NINENH&mkt=en-au&PC=NBWS&qs=n&sk=&q=Ancient+womens+warrirs+of+Asia Enheduanna - Wikipedia

By authors

Abramsky, Samuel S. David Sperling; Aaron Rothkoff; Haïm Z'ew Hirschberg; Bathja Bayer (2007): *SOLOMON*", *Encyclopaedia Judaica*, vol. 18. (2nd ed.), Thomson Gale, Macmillan Reference USA

Ackerman, Lillian A, 2003: A Necessary Balance: Gender and Power among Indians of the Columbia Plateau, University of Oklahoma Press,

Ailes, Mary Elizabeth, "Camp Followers, Sutlers, and Soldiers' Wives: Women in Early Modern Armies (c. 1450–c. 1650)", A Companion to Women's Military History (Brill, 2012)

Allen, Prudence (2006a): The Early Humanist Reformation, 1250-1500, Part 2. The Concept of Woman Wm. B. Eerdmans-Lightning Source

Almohsin, Noor 2018: Queens of Arabia Yemen, Web

Al-Zirikli, Khairaddin (2002), *"Al-Sharifa Fatima", Al-a'lam* (in Arabic), vol.5 (15th ed.), Beirut: Dar al-'Ilm li al-Malayyin

Aristotle's *Politics* (Second Edition) Published March 29th 2013 by University of Chicago Press.

Bachofen, Johann Jakob, (Trans. Ralph Manheim) 1992: *Myth, Religion, and Mother Right*, Princeton University Press

An English translation (2003) of Bachofen's Mutterrecht (Mother right) (1861): a study of the religious and juridical aspects of gynecocracy in the ancient world, Edwin Mellen Press, Lewiston, N.Y.

Banerjee, Roopleena (2015). "Matriarchy' and Contemporary Khasi Society", *Proceedings of the Indian History Congress* **76**: 918–930

Banu Goshap-Nama at Bibliothèque National, Paris (Cat. Bibliothèque Nationale, no. 1194

Baring, Ann & Jules Cashford (1993): *The Myth of the Goddess: Evolution of an Image*, Penguin Books Limited

Bay, Edna (1998). *Wives of the Leopard: Gender, Politics, and Culture in the Kingdom of Dahomey.* University of Virginia Press

Bess, Savitri, L (2000): The enduring presence of the divine feminine in Hinduism. In The Path of the Mother, Ballantine Wellspring,

Beau Elle (2018): *The History of Patriarchy*, Published in Inside of Elle Beau

Bennett, Judith (2011): *History Matters: Patriarchy and the Challenge of Feminism.* Philadelphia, United States: University of Pennsylvania Press,

Birdwood, G C M 1832-1917 & Brown, F, H (1915): *SVA, P.L. Warner, London*

Bhardwaj, Surinder Mohan (1973): *Hindu Places of Pilgrimage in India,* Berkeley, Calif.

Blondel, David, (1647): Familier esclaircissement de la question si une femme a este assise au siege papal de Rome entre Leon IV et Benoit III; Amsterdam: Blaeu, 1647

Blythe, James: *Women in the Military: Scholastic Arguments and Medieval Images of Female Warriors,*" History of Political Thought, Vol. 22:2 (2001)

Bouchard, Constance B. (1981). "Consanguinity and Noble Marriages in the Tenth and Eleventh Centuries, Speculum, **56** (2)

Bowersock, Glen Warren; Brown, Peter; Brown, Peter Robert Lamont; Grabar, Oleg (1999):*Late Antiquity: A Guide to the Postclassical World,* Harvard University Press

Browne, Sylvia (2004): Mother God: The Feminine Principle to Our Creator, Hay House Inc.

Bury, John Bagnell (2005): *History of the Later Roman Empire Vols. I & II,* London: Macmillan & Co., Ltd

Chattopadhyaya, Dr, S (1949): *The Achaemenids in India,* The Indian Historical Quarterly, originally published by Michigan University

Chengu, Garikai *(2015): Women of Ancient Africa,* Countercurrents.org,

CNN Karimi, Faith (January 30, 2019). *"She grew up in a community where women rule and men are banned"*

Coffen, Richard (2007): *Wake Up Your Bible Study: Getting the Most from Your Time with God.* Hagerstown, United States: Autumn House Publishing,

Condren, Mary (1989): The Serpent and the Goddess: Women, Religion, and Power in Celtic Ireland, Harper San Francisco

Conger, Cristen: Top 5 Feminist Movements

Cornell, T.J (1995). The Beginnings of Rome: Italy and Rome from the Bronze Age to the Punic Wars (c. 1000-264 BC). Routledge

Cornwall, Andrea (2001): Making a Difference? Gender and Participatory Development: Discussion Paper; Pub. Institute of Development Studies

Cunliffe, Barry (1997): *The Ancient Celts,* Oxford and New York: Oxford University Press.

Dani, Ahmad Hasan; Masson, Vadim Mikhaĭlovich; Harmatta, János; Litvinovskiĭ, Boris Abramovich; Bosworth, Clifford Edmund: *History of Civilizations of Central Asia* (PDF). UNESCO, 1999

Davidson, Hilda Ellis (2002 [1998]): *Roles of the Northern Goddess,* Routledge

de Pizan, Christine (2003): *The Treasure of the City of Ladies, or The Book of the Three Virtues,* Translated by Sarah Lawson, Penguin Classics.

Davis, Philip G.1998: *Goddess Unmasked,* N.Y, Spence *Publishing,*

D'Emilio, John& Estelle B. Freedman (2012) 3rd ed: *Intimate Matters*

Del Giorgio, J.F. (2006), *The Oldest Europeans,* Published by A. J. Place, *A History of Sexuality in America*, University of Chicago

Devereux, Paul (2000): The Illustrated Encyclopedia of Ancient Earth Mysteries Cassell 1st pub 1668

DeVries, Kelly "*The Use of Gunpowder Weaponry by and Against Joan of Arc During the Hundred Years War*", War and Society, Vol.14 (1996)

DeVries, Kelly (2002): "*Teenagers at War During the Middle Ages*", *The Premodern Teenager: Youth in Society, 1150-1650*, Toronto,

Diner, Helen, Edited and translated by John Philip Lundin, (1965): *Mothers and Amazons: The First Feminine History of Culture.* New York, NY: Julian Press

Diodorus, Siculus: The Historical Library of Diodorus the Sicilian: In Fifteen Books. to Which Are Added the Fragments of Diodorus, and Those Published by H. Valesius, I. Rhodomannus, and F. Ursinus: Nabu Press 2012

- *Diodorus, Siculus*: *Bibliotheca historical,* Stutgardiae: In aedibus B.G. Teubneri, 1964

Diogenes Laertius, (1972 Trans. R.D. Hicks): *Lives of the Eminent Philosopher*, Cambridge. Harvard University Press, 1972 (First published 1925)

- Diogenes Laertius (2011): *Lives of the Eminent Philosophers*, Tran. Robert Drew Hicks, Witch Books.

Diop, Cheikh Anta & Mercer Cook (2012): *The African Origin of Civilization: Myth or Reality,* Chicago Review Press,

Duffy, Eamon (1997): *Saints and Sinners: A History of the Popes* (Third ed.), New Haven: Yale University Press.

Dworkin, Andrea (2021): *The Rape Atrocity and the Boy Next Door*, (essay)

Eads, Val "Sichelgaita of Salerno (2005): Amazon or Trophy Wife? Journal of Medieval Military History, Vol.3

Egil's Saga (1976, Trans. Hermann Palsson and Paul Edwards) London: Penguin Group

Ehrman, Bart D (2006): *Peter, Paul and Mary Magdelene: The Followers of Jesus in History and Legend*, Oxford University Press

Eller, Cynthia (2011): *Gentlemen and Amazons: The Myth of Matriarchal Prehistory, 1861–1900*, Berkeley, CA: University of California Press

Ellis, P. B. (1994): *The Druids*. Grand Rapids, Michigan: William B. Eerdmans Publishing Company.

Engels, Friedrich (1984): *Der Ursprung der Familie, des Privateigenthums und des Staates. Im Anschluss an Lewis H. Morgans Forschungen* (in German), Berlin: Dietz.

Epstein, Barbara (1991): Political Protest and Cultural Revolution: Nonviolent Direct Action in the 1970s and 1980s, Berkeley, CA: University of California Press

Erler, Mary C.; Kowaleski, Maryanne (2003): *Gendering the Master Narrative: Women and Power in the Middle Ages*, Cornell University Press.

Fairchild, Mary (2019): The Great Schism of 1054 and the Split of Christianity

Farāmarz-nāma (ed. R. Tafti) printed: Bombay, 1324/1906

Ferdowsī Tūsī, Hakīm Abū l-Qāsim: *Shahnama*, written in 1000 AD

- Ferdowsī Tūsī, Hakīm Abū l-Qāsim: Šāh-nāma, II, ed. Khaleghi

- Farrer, Claire, R (1996): Thunder Rides a Black Horse: Mescalero Apache and the Mythic Present, 2d Long Grove, IL: Waveland Press, Inc.
- Fischer, Henry George (2000): Egyptian Woman of the Old Kingdom and of the Heracleopolitan Period, Second Edition, revised and augmented, New York 2000
- Forsythe, Gary (2005): A critical history of early Rome: from prehistory to the first Punic War. Berkeley: University of California Press
- French, Marilyn (2008): *'The History of Women' (Vol I)*, Published by The Feminist Press at CUNY
- Gage, Matilda, Joselyn (1893, 2002) (intro Saly Roesh): Woman, Church, and State, Humanity Books
- Gage, M. J; Stanton E-Cade; Anthony Susan B (2011): History of Woman Suffrage (6 vol) Nabu Press

Gardeła Leszek (2013): *"'Warrior-women' in Viking Age Scandinavia? A preliminary archaeological study,*" Analecta Archaeologica Ressoviensia: Funerary Archaeology (Archeologia Funeralna), Volume 8, Rzeszów

Gardiner, Adams, Henry (1857): *A Cyclopaedia of Female Biography: Consisting of Sketches of All Women*, Groombridge

Gethin, Rupert (1998): *The Foundations of Buddhism*, Oxford: Oxford University Press,

Gibbon, Edward (1776-1789): *History of the Decline and Fall of the Roman Empire* in six-volumes Strahan & Cadell, London

Gimbutas, Marija (1991): The Civilization of the Goddess: The World of Old Europe, Harper, San Francisco

- Gimbutas, Marija, (1999) *The Living Goddesses*; edited and supplemented by Miriam Robbins Dexter., London: Univ. of California Press

Graves, Robert (1955): *The Greek Myths, Volume 1*, Edition, 2 Penguin Books

Greif, Avner (2011), [2005]: *Family Structure, Institutions, and Growth: The Origin and Implications of Western Corporatism* (PDF), Stanford University.

Gundarsson, Kveldulf: (1993) *Teutonic Religion*, St. Paul: Llewellyn Publications,

Halcrow, Elizabeth M. *(1982) Canes and Chains: A Study of Sugar and Slavery*. Oxford: Heinemann Educational Publishing.

Halkias, Georgios (2013): (Emmanuel Steven, ed.): *A Companion to Buddhist Philosophy*, UK: John Wiley & Sons Inc.

Harari, Yuval Noah (in manda Penn's article, 2019) 2011 (in Hebrew): *Sapiens: A Brief History of Humankind*, Harper

Harvey, Susan Ashbrok & David G Hunter eds. (2008): *The Oxford Handbook of Early Christian Studies*, Oxford University Press, (*Which Early Christianity?* By Karen L King

Hay, David J (2010): The Military Leadership of Matilda of Canossa, 1046-1115, Manchester University Press,

Herbert, Kathleen **(1997):** in *Exeter Books - Peace-Weavers and Shield Maidens: Women in Early English Society* Anglo-Saxon Books, Norfolk

Herodotus of Halicarnassus (440 BC): *The Histories* (Trans. Tom Holland Penguin 2014)

Hesiod's *Theogony*, Ed. Nelson S.A.; Caldwell, R.S. (2009): *Theogony, Works and Days*, Newburyport. MA, 2009

Homer: (800 BC: pub. 1997) *Odyssey* (trans, by Fagles, R), Penguin Classics (1st printed in Greek 1488

- Homer (750 BC): *The Iliad: Book VI,* (Trans. A. S. Kline 2009)

Howard, Zinn, (1980, 2009): A People's History of the United States, Harper & Row; HarperCollins

Hubbs, Joanna (1982 in James' Preston's) Mother worship, University of North Carolina Press

Hultkrantz, Åke (1983): The Goddess in North America in The Book of the goddess, past and present: an introduction to her religion ed. Carl Olson, New York: Crossroads,

Hultkrantz, Åke (1981) Trans. Monica Setterwall): The Religions of the American Indians, University of California Press

Icks, Martijn (2011): The Crimes of Elagabalus: The Life and Legacy of Rome's Decadent Boy Emperor, London: I.B. Tauris & Co. Ltd

Ishtar, Zohl del (1994) Daughters of the Pacific; Pub. Spinifex Press (Gabriela Ngirmang, quoted)

James Harrod, Research Director: Center for Research on: the Origins of Art and Religion, Cultural Evolution Department

Jensen, Ann 1996, God's Self-confident Daughters: Early Christianity and the Liberation of Women, Westminster John Knox Press

Jones, David E (2000): Women Warriors: A History, Brassey's,

Josephus (late 1st century): The Works of Josephus, Complete and Unabridged New Updated Edition, Transl. Whiston, William; Peabody, A. M. 1987, M.A. Hendrickson Publishers, Inc.

Jung, C. G. (1963): Memories, dreams, reflections, Crown Publishing Group/Random House.

Kazantzakis, Nikos trans. Theodora Vasils (1988): In the palaces of Knossos, Ohio University Press

Keating H.R.F (1963): Death of a Fat God, Crime Club; Collins, London

Khaleghi-Motlagh, Djalal (1989): Encyclopaedia Iranica Online, on Ferdowsī's Šāh-nāma

- Khaleghi-Motlagh Djalal ed. (2002): Gordāfarid, Encyclopedia Iranica Vol. XI, Fasc.

- King, Karen L (2003): The Gospel of Mary of Magdala: Jesus and the First Woman Apostle, Polebridge Press,
- King, Karen (1998): Women in Ancient Christianity: The New Discoveries, Frontline
- King, Karen L (2009) The Secret Revelation of John, Harvard University Press

Kneller, Tara, L (1993): *Neither Goddesses Nor Doormats: The Role of Women in Nubia* http://historicaltextarchive.com

Kottak, Conrad (2003): *Cultural Anthropology* (10th edition), pub. McGrawHil (ref. to Sutee)

Kramarae, Cheris & Spender, Dale (2004*): Routledge International Encyclopedia of Women: Global Women's Issues and Knowledge,* Routledge

Kuhn, Anthony (2016): The Place in China Where the Women Lead in Parallels: NPR many stories, one world

Kunz, Keneva, (2005): *The Sagas of the Icelanders*, London: Penguin,

Laërtius, Diogenes: (ed. R.D. Hicks,) 1972: *Lives of Eminent Philosophers I, 33.* Loeb Classical Library,

Lampridius, Aelius (400 AD) (trans. E. H. Warmington): *The Scriptores historiae Augustae. LCL 139–140, 263*, Cambridge: Harvard University Press; London: Heinemann.

Lassen, Inger (2011): *Living with Patriarchy,* Philadelphia, United States: John Benjamins Publishing,

Law, Robin (1986: "Dahomey and the Slave Trade: Reflections on the Historiography of the Rise of Dahomey," The Journal of African History. **27** (2): 237–267.

Leach, Edmund (1996): Virgin Birth, Cambridge, U.K., The Henry Myers Lecture.

Lerner, Gerda, (1986): The Creation of Patriarchy, Oxford University Press

Lev, Elizabeth, (2012): The Tigress of Forli: Renaissance, Italy's Most Courageous and Notorious Countess, Caterina Riario Sforza de' Medici, pub. Mariner Books

Levin, Eve (1995): Sex and Society in the World of the Orthodox Slavs, 900-1700, Cornell University Press.

Livy, Tacitus (510BC) trans, Vaklerie M Warrior 2006: *Ab Urbe Condita*, (The History of Rome Books 1 to 5), Hackett Publishing Company, Inc.

Mackenzie, G. Muir (1877): Travels in the Slavonic provinces of Turkey-in-Europe. London, Daldy, Isbister and Co.

Maier, Christoph T. (2004): "The Roles of Women in the Crusade Movement: A Survey," Journal of Medieval History, Vol. 30, no. 1

Magnusson, Magnus. 1987 (1960): "Introduction", Njal's Saga, Penguin Classics, Dover Publications

- Magnusson, Magnus; Palsson, Hermann, (1973): The Vinland Sagas, London: Penguin,

Malherbe, Abraham (ed.) 1977: *The Cynic Epistles*, Missoula, Montana: Scholars Press,

Mann, Susan (November 2000). "Presidential Address: Myths of Asian Womanhood", The Journal of Asian Studies. **59** (4): 835–862

Marshack, Alexander (1972): *The Roots of Civilization*, Weidenfeld and Nicolson, New York,

Mayor, Adrienne: *The Amazons: Lives and Legends of Warrior Women Across the Ancient World*" Princeton University Press, 2014, Foreign Affairs Magazine, (2015)

Mazama, Ama (2009), *Nehanda Encyclopedia of African Religion*, SAGE Publications, Inc.

McCall, Daniel F (in Preston, James J., ed.) *Mother Worship: Theme and Variations* (1982) Chapel Hill, N.C.,

MCCrindle, JW (2020): The Invasion of India by Alexander, Hansebook

McCoppin, Rachel S (2015): *The Lessons of Nature in Mythology*, McFarland.

McDougall, Sara (2013) eds (In Judith Bennett; Ruth Mazo Karras): *"Women and Gender in Canon Law Oxford Handbook of Women and Gender in Medieval Europe*, Oxford: Oxford University Press.

McLaughlin, Megan (1990): *"The Woman Warrior: Gender, Warfare, and Society in Medieval Europe."* Women's Studies, Vol. 17 Dept. of History, University of Illinois

Mellaart, Jams (1967): Çatal Hüyük: A Neolithic Town in Anatolia, McGraw-Hill Collection New York

- Mellaart, James (1965): *Earliest Civilizations of the Near East*, Thames and Hudson London

Meltzer, Milton (1998): *Ten Queens, Portraits of Women of Power*, pub. by Dutton Juvenile

Mernissi, Fatima (1993): *The Forgotten Queens of Islam*, pub. University of Minnesota Press (first published 1990)

Middleton, Chris (1981): "Peasants, patriarchy and the feudal mode of production in England: 2 Feudal lords and the subordination of peasant women", Sociological Review. **29** (1): 137–154.

Mikaberidze, Alexander (2011). Conflict and Conquest in the Islamic World: A Historical Encyclopaedia, pp. 836.

Mitterauer, Michael (2010): *Why Europe? The Medieval Origins of Its Special Path* (Trans Gerald Chapple), University of Chicago Press.

Mohr, T & Tsedroen, J, eds. (2010): Dignity and Discipline: Reviving Full Ordination for Buddhist Nuns, Wisdom Publication

NBC : *"In Kenya's Umoja Village, a sisterhood preserves the past, prepares the future"*, NBC News. Retrieved May 11, 2021

Neumann, Erich (1954) *The Origins and History of Consciousness*, Princeton, N.J., Princeton University Press

- Neumann E (2015): The Great Mother: An Analysis of the Archetype (Trans)) Ralph Manheim, Foreword by Martin Liebscher

Noble, Thomas, F.X. (2013): *Why Pope Joan?* Catholic Historical Review, 99(2): 299, doi: 10.1353/cat.2013.0078, S2CID 159548215.

Olson, Carl, ed. (1983): The Book of the Goddess, Past and Present: An Introduction to Her Religion, New York,

- Olson, Carl, (2002): *The Book of the Goddess, Past and Present: An Introduction to Her Religion*: Waveland Press, Prospect Heights, Ill. (Bleeker CJ; Mackenzie-Brown, C)

Osborne, R Hornblower, S; Cornell, T & 5 more (2009): *The Routledge History of the Ancient World (8 books)*

Origen (185-254 quoted in): 1 Corinthians 11:5: Did Paul Allow Women to Prophesy in Church

Palmer, Martin; Jay Ramsay, & Man-Ho Kwok (2009): Kuan Yin Chronicles: The Myths and Prophecies of the Chinese Goddess of Compassion, Hampton Roads Publishing.

Patai, Raphael (1967, 1968): *The Hebrew Goddess*, Ktav Pub. House, New York,

- Patai, Raphael (1990). The Hebrew Goddess (3rd ed.), Detroit: Wayne State University Press

Penrose, Walter Duvall Jr. (2016). Postcolonial Amazons: Female Masculinity and Courage in Ancient Greek and Sanskrit Literature, Oxford University Press.

Pester, Patrick (2021): Did the Amazon female warriors from Greek mythology really exist? Live Science

Plato: Protagoras, Published 2009 by Oxford University Press, USA (first published: 390)

Plutarch: Lacaenarum Apophthegmata II, 240c ff. Cited by A. Oepke, "Gyne," in Gerhard Kittel: Theological Dictionary of the New Testament (Grand Rapids: Eerdmans, 1964-74), I, 777

- Plutarch 2nd century AD: *Life of Marius*, (trans. Bernadotte Perrin) 1920, Cambridge MA Harvard University Press
- Plutarch (1917): *Parallel Lives*. (Trans Bernadotte Perrin), Loeb Classical Library
- Plutarch: *Parallel Lives: Life of Pyrrhus* (Trans Bernadotte Perrin) 1920 Loeb Classical Library
- Plutarch (Talbert Richard, 2005): Plutarch on Sparta, Penguin Books, London,
- Plutarch (trans. Frank Cole Babbitt 1931): *Bravery of Women, Moralia III*, Loeb classical Library

Pope Joan: Discussed in Hotchkiss, V. R. (2012): The Female Pope and the Sin of Male Disguise", in Clothes Make the Man: Female Cross Dressing in Medieval Europe, London: Routledge

Potto, Vasily Aleksandrovich (2011): The Caucasian War in Different Essays, Episodes, Legends, and Biographies (1885–91), British Library, Historical Print Editions

Preston, James J., ed. (1982): Mother Worship: Theme and Variations, Chapel Hill, N.C

Procopius of Caesarea: De Bello Gothico, Volumes I–IV (the Gothic War of 535-552) 1919 Loeb Classical Library

- Procopius (trans Dewing, H B, 1914): *History of the Wars: Book VI (continued) and Book VII*, William Heinemann Limited, London
- Procopius: *The Gothic War of 535-552 De Bello Gothico I-IV; Vol III, Books 5, 6.15* (Trans. H. B. Dewing 1916) Loeb Classical Library 107, Cambridge, MA: Harvard University Press,

Quintus, Smyrnaeus, Alan James (2007): *The Trojan epic: Posthomerica*, Johns Hopkins new translations from antiquity, Baltimore and London: Johns Hopkins University Press,

Raine Eisler, (1987): The Chalice and the Blade: Our History, Our Future, Harper Collins

Rathnayake, Zinar: *"Khasis: India's indigenous matrilineal society"*, vol 1-2, no.4, www.bbc.com, Retrieved May 17, 2021.

Ratti, Oscar /Adele Westbrook, (2016) Secrets of the Samurai: The Martial Arts of Feudal Japan, Tuttle Publishing

Rohrecker, Georg (2003): *Die Kelten Österreichs*, Pichler Verlag, Wien (English: The Celts of Austria)

Rogers, Lynn, 2004: *Goddesses of the Ancient World: Legends of Powerful Religious Deities* in Edgar Cacyce: *The Eternal Feminine*, We Publish Books

- Rogers, Lynn, (2016): *Edgar Cayce and the Eternal Feminine* Inkling Press
- Rogers, Lynn, (2004): *Edgar Cayce and the Eternal Feminine*, We Publish Books.

Rohrlich, Ruby (1977): *"Women in transition: Crete and Sumer"*, In Renate Bridenthal; Claudia

Koontz (eds.): *Becoming Visible: Women in European History*. Boston, MA: Houghton Mifflin.

Ruether, Rosemary Radford, (2005): *Goddesses and the Divine Feminine: A Western Religious History*, University of California, Berkeley

Rufus, Quintius Curtius (1935): Alexander the Great, Bolchazy-Carducci Publishers, U.S

Rustici, Craig M. (2006): The Afterlife of Pope Joan: Deploying the Popess Legend in Early Modern England, University of Michigan Press.

Sakaida, Henry (2003): Heroines of the Soviet Union 1941-1945, Osprey

Salgado, Nirmala (2013): Buddhist Nuns and Gendered Practice: In Search of the Female Renunciant, Oxford: Oxford University Press

Salmonson, Jessica Amanda, (1991): *The Encyclopedia of Amazons*, Paragon House.

Saxo Grammaticus: *The History of the Danes, Books I-IX*. (Trans)Peter Fisher & Hilda Ellis Davidson, 1979, Boydell & Brewer

Savitri L. Bess: (2006): *The Path of The Mother*, New Age Books

Schaus, Margaret C., ed. (2006): *Women and gender in medieval Europe: an encyclopedia*, Routledge

Shahnameh of Ferdowsi, Mage Publishers published 1997

Scottish Geographical Magazine, 1999, Royal Scottish Geographical Society

Sefscik Sue M.: *"Zenobia"* Women's History, Retrieved 2008-04-01.

Shahîd, Irfan (1984), Rome and the Arabs: A Prolegomenon to the Study of Byzantium and the Arabs, Dumbarton Oaks

Skylitzes, John (Ioannes Scylitzes 11th century): *A Synopsis of Byzantine History, 811–1057 Trans. John Wortley*, (2010) Cambridge University Press

Stanford, Peter *(1999): The She-Pope: a quest for the truth behind the mystery of Pope Joan*, Arrow

Stanton, Elizabeth-Cady et al (Susan B Anthony, Matilda Gage, & Ida Husted Harper), 1898: *History of Women's Suffrage*, Rochester, New York

Stone, Merlin (1976): *When God Was a Woman*, New York, Dial Press, *1976*, republished (1978), Harcourt Brace

- Stone, Merlin (2012): *When God Was a Woman*, Knopf Doubleday Publishing Group Strauss, Jovanovich; Barry; Bryce, (2019): Ten Caesars: *Roman Emperors from Augustus to Constantine*, Simon & Schuster; Susan Abernethy, 2013: *The Siege of Beauvais in 1472*, on the net medievalist media

Sturluson, Snorri (1990): *Heimskringla: Or, the Lives of the Norse Kings*, Dover Publications

Symmachus, Quintus Aurelius (Trnsl. J.F. Matthews)," *The Letters of Symmachus*" in *Latin Literature of the Fourth Century* (edited by J.W. Binns), London: Routledge and Kegan Paul, 1974, discusses them. J.F. Matthews, (1990) *Western Aristocracies and Imperial Court, AD 364-425.* Oxford: Clarendon Press,

Tacitus, Cornelius Oxford Translation (2013): *Agricola Germania Dialogus, 159 (The Germany and Agricola of Tacitus)* online at www.gutenberg

- Tacitus, Cornelius Trans & pub 1914, 1980): *Aricola Germania Dialogus*, Harvard University Press, Cambridge

Tedlock, Barbara, 2005: *The Woman in the Shaman's Body: Reclaiming the Feminine in Religion and Medicine*, New York: Bantam.

Tertullian, Quintus Septimius Florens(155-230): m (Apology) Church Fathers: On the Veiling of Virgins pub 197&*Assessing Tertullian on the Status of Women in the Third Century Church vol 97, (2016)*Open Access- Online http//: www.pharosjot.com

"The Waking of Angantyr" in The Elder Edda, trans. Paul B. Taylor and W.H. Auden (1969, reprint 1973) Faber and Faber, London

Thomson, George (1965): The Prehistoric Aegean, N.Y.: Citadel Press,

Thurston, Herbert (1908): "Deaconesses" In Herbermann, Charles (ed.), Catholic Encyclopedia, New York: Robert Appleton Company

Turner, Victor, and Edith Turner (10 978): Image and Pilgrimage in Christian Culture, New York,

The United States Military Academy (2015): West point History of World War II, Vol 1, Simon and Schuster

Valerie Eads, (2006) "Means, Motive, Opportunity: Medieval Women and the Recourse to Arms" -Paper presented at The Twentieth Barnard Medieval & Renaissance Conference,

"War and Peace in the Middle Ages & Renaissance," December 2, 2006

Varley, Paul H (1994): Warriors of Japan as Portrayed in the War Tales Pub. University of Hawaii Press

Verbruggen, J. F. (2006): "Women in Medieval Armies," Journal of Medieval Military History, Vol. 4, pub online by Cambridge University Press (2012)

Wagner Sally Roesch *(2001): 'Sisters in Spirit: Haudenosaunee (Iroquois) Influence on Early American Feminists,'* Published by Native Voices

Wagner, Peter (2001): Modernity, Capitalism and Critique, Paper *Thesis Eleven 66 (1):1-31*

Weatherford, Jack (2004): Genghis Khan and the Making of the Modern World, Crown and Three Rivers Press

Wenig, Steffened. (1978): *Africa in Antiquity, The Catalogue*, illustrated, Brooklyn Museum

Willis, Janice's (1985): Nuns and Benefactresses: The Role of Women in the Development of Buddhism, In Women, Religion, and Social Change, (ed. Yvonne Haddad & Ellison B Findly).

Wax, Emily: (2005): A Place Where Women Rule, in The Washington Post, July 9, 2005, p.1 (online), as accessed October 13, 2013.

Wooloch, N (1994): Women and the American Experience, McGraw-Hill; original: Uni. of Michigan

Xinhua News Agency-CEIS (2021): Mosuo People Maintain Rare Matriarchal Society 2 ProQuest. Web. 18 Apr. 2021.

Yonge C.D, (2019): The Roman History of Ammianus Marcellinus during the Reign of Emperor Constantinius Julian Jovianus Valentinian and Valens, Pub. Alpha Editions

Zinn, Howard (1980): A People's History of the United States, Harper & Row; HarperCollins

Zohl de Ishtar (1994): Daughters of the Pacific, Spinifex Press

www.ingramcontent.com/pod-product-compliance
Lightning Source LLC
LaVergne TN
LVHW021955060526
838201LV00048B/1579